A Compendium of Italian Economists at Oxbridge

Mauro Baranzini • Amalia Mirante

A Compendium of Italian Economists at Oxbridge

Contributions to the Evolution of Economic Thinking

palgrave
macmillan

Mauro Baranzini
University of Lugano
Switzerland, and Lincei Academy
Rome, Italy

Amalia Mirante
SUPSI
University of Lugano
Switzerland

ISBN 978-3-319-32218-6 ISBN 978-3-319-32219-3 (eBook)
DOI 10.1007/978-3-319-32219-3

Library of Congress Control Number: 2016950016

Printed on acid-free paper

This Palgrave Macmillan imprint is published by Springer Nature
The registered company is Springer International Publishing AG Switzerland

Preface

On 25–26 September 2013, the *Accademia Nazionale dei Lincei*, at its splendid headquarters in Rome, organized a conference titled '*Gli economisti italiani, protagonisti, paradigmi, politiche*'. The organizing committee included Alberto Quadrio Curzio (then President of the class of Moral Sciences of the Academy), Lilia Costabile, Giorgio Lunghini, Alessandro Roncaglia and Roberto Scazzieri. The meeting was organized jointly with the *Archivio Storico degli Economisti* and the *Società Italiana degli Economisti*. The authors of this volume were invited to report on 'The Anglo-Italian Economics School at Oxford and Cambridge'. In this volume, we provide a much revised, enlarged and updated version of the paper presented at the Lincei Academy. The choice of the authors by the organizing committee was no casual choice, since both authors were educated outside Italy—more precisely in Switzerland where, at present, they both teach and undertake research. Additionally, the first author, from 1971 to 1984, was first a D.Phil. Student, and then a lecturer and acting director of economic studies, at The Queen's College, Oxford. Also, since the early 1990s, he has been closely associated with the University of Cambridge, where he spends long research periods. In Oxford, from 1971 to 1975, he was supervised by David Soskice, John Flemming and Jim Mirrlees. From 1975 to 1984, the first author took up the teaching of economics at The Queen's College; Nicholas Dimsdale (previously Fellow and Praelector in economics), took up the duties of financial bursar of the College. In this way, authors who do not directly belong to the Italian academic world have undertaken this assessment of the Anglo-Italian school of economics at Oxbridge. While this volume mentions numerous scholars belonging to the Oxbridge-Italian school of economics, particular attention has been paid to the research programmes of the economists with whom the first author has worked for decades, in Oxford, Cambridge and elsewhere. Gratitude is due to all of them for their inspiring scientific and personal friendship.

Lugano, Switzerland
February 2016

Mauro Leo Baranzini
Amalia Mirante

Contents

1

Introduction

1.1 The Historical and Factual Background

In the years following the end of the Second World War, the teaching of and research into economics in Italy were slowly catching up after more than two decades of dictatorship and war that had led to a progressive isolation and brain drain, especially to Great Britain and North America.[1] It could be argued that the feeling of isolation experienced by the Italian scientific community is illustrated by the fact that J. M. Keynes wrote four prefaces to his *General Theory*: for the English edition (13 December 1935), the German (7 September 1936), the Japanese (4 December 1936) and the French (20 February 1939). However, either he was not asked, or was not asked in time, to write a preface for the Italian translation that appeared in 1947, eleven years after the English edition, since he died on 21 April 1946.

In Italy, it was generally felt that new ideas and impulses could only arrive from abroad.[2] But from where? Continental countries had been

[1] On this point, see the contributions in Garofalo and Graziani (2004), as well as the recent work of Ferrulli (2012).

[2] Pasinetti (2007, 28) maintains that, in the late 1930s in the United Kingdom and United States, the young generation of economists especially was convinced that Keynes's theory was an

M. Baranzini, A. Mirante, *A Compendium of Italian Economists at Oxbridge*, DOI 10.1007/978-3-319-32219-3_1

losing influence between 1930 and 1950; English was quickly becoming 'the' language in which to present economics. One should remember that the majority of the allied forces who liberated Europe were from English-speaking countries. Looking at the scant figures that are available, we may say that a first wave of young Italian economists (say, between 1950 and 1975) mainly chose to pursue their studies in the United Kingdom. The second and third waves chose more evenly between North America and the UK. So, where in the United Kingdom did these young economists choose to study? The statistics that we have gathered are clear. The Oxbridge Colleges had been, and still were, a strong magnet. First, there was Cambridge: most, if not all, of Keynes's pupils were there; additionally, Sraffa, Stone, Goodwin, Meade, Champernowne, Dobb and many others were there, too. Then came Oxford, especially because Harrod and Hicks had been there for a long time, and because from the mid-1960s onwards Seton, Bacharach, Soskice, Glyn, Eltis, Dempster, Dixit, Dimsdale, Enos and Flemming were there, followed shortly thereafter by Mirrlees and a little later on by Sen and many others. A considerable number of young Italian economists chose to attent the London School of Economics and other London colleges, but Oxbridge still prevailed.

1.2 The Structure of this Volume

It is not an easy task to summarize the almost five decades of scientific contributions made by three generations of Italian economists who studied at Oxbridge in the second half of the twentieth century—more precisely, from 1950 to about 1990–95. Due to their numbers—about 100 students attended Oxford and at least 200 went to Cambridge, most probably more—it is not easy to trace them all. Some Italian students enrolled with the aid of official grants, of which there is a record;

'exceptional, extraordinary work'. In a footnote, Pasinetti adds, 'The Italian case was characterized by the same pattern, but with a ten-year delay, as it was compounded by another event. It coincided with the opening up of the post-war generation of Italian economists, after many years of exclusion from the outside world, to the cultural developments that had taken place elsewhere. As already mentioned, Caffè was a precursor. Other early Keynesians were Ferdinando di Fenizio and Vittorio Marrama.' (Pasinetti 2007, 28).

many others came with the support of grants, foundations, or personal resources in regard to which no official records exist. Because not all of them read for Oxbridge First or higher degrees in economics, they do not appear in official records. A number of them stayed for up to several years; they most certainly worked hard. However, either they departed without leaving any official trace in the university or college records, or such trace is difficult to find. Finally, the lines of research that were taken up and expanded by these students are too numerous and heterogeneous for them to be presented in this volume.

We are unable to mention in our book all the Italian research students or research associates who were at Oxbridge universities between 1950 and, say, 1990–95. We therefore extend our apologies to the numerous economists who have contributed significantly to their areas of study and who will be disappointed at not receiving mention. Instead, we shall concentrate on ten major lines of research and mention only a limited number of the 300 or so economists of Italian origin who were at Oxbridge during those 40–45 years. We estimate that around 150 of these economists earned First or higher Oxbridge degrees.

It is not our intention to undertake the systematic consideration of a number of research lines—such as labour and public economics, economic policy, industrial economics, and applied and quantitative economics, as well as related fields such as sociology or demography. Rather, we shall discuss a number of scholars whose scientific contribution has been significant by applying alternative criteria—such as seniority, *alma mater*, College affiliation, or the period of study spent in Oxford or Cambridge.

A number of Italian economists have held official posts in Oxbridge—either teaching or researching, or sometimes both; with and without tenure; at Faculty, sub-Faculty, College, Department or Institute level. At the same time, a number of Oxbridge college fellows, lecturers, readers or professors have taken up official appointments in Italian universities. We shall report on a number of these instances; it would be a daunting task to mention them all.

While this volume mentions numerous scholars belonging to the Oxbridge School, emphasis is placed on the research programmes of the many economists with whom the first author of this essay has come in contact in Oxbridge and elsewhere since the late 1960s.

1.3 The Circulation of Ideas and Cross-Fertilization

The fact that between 200 and 300 Italian economists, or even more, spent various periods of study, research or specialization in Oxbridge is not by itself a warranty for a significant circulation of ideas and cross-fertilization among schools (or streams) of economic thought. For instance, Swiss banks require that their future managers spend at least six months working in major UK or US banks, in order to 'learn' the job. Nevertheless, this does not necessarily entail a rich circulation of ideas. Much more is required in a scientific playing field. Italian research students or scholars of economics admitted to Oxford or Cambridge between 1950 and 1990–95 made positive and critical contributions to the advance of the research programmes carried out in their host academic institution; contributed actively to the development of new research programmes, or even of new schools of thought; were pivotal in the launching of new scientific journals, dictionaries and so on; were at the forefront of scientific controversies; and came to occupy strategic positions within their host institutions, such as teaching at the highest grade, heading a department, or chairing a faculty.

The ensuing chapters will prove that most, if not all, of these requisites were largely satisfied in the case of the Oxbridge-Italian school of economics of the second half of the twentieth century. It is unsurprising that this accomplishment led to a counter-flow of scholars, 'bred' in Oxbridge, who came to spend long periods in Italian universities or research centres, thereby reinforcing the process of the circulation of ideas and cross-fertilization. It is precisely the aim of the present work to expound what we think is an astonishing, and probably exceptional, occurrence in the academia of economics.

Bibliography

Ferrulli, S. (2012). *Economisti italiani a Cambridge (1960–1980). Processi formativi, aggiornamenti teorici e nuovi orientamenti di politica economica*. Ph. D. thesis, Rome Tre.

Garofalo, G., & Graziani, A. (Eds.). (2004). *La formazione degli economisti in Italia*. Bologna: Il Mulino.

Pasinetti, L. L. (2007). *Keynes and the Cambridge Keynesians: A 'revolution in economics' to be accomplished*. Cambridge: Cambridge University Press.

2

The Oxonian-Italian School of Economics, 1950 to About 1990

2.1 Who's Who

As Carlo Casarosa (2004) points out, the stream of Italian economists going to Oxford, broadly from 1950 to 1980 and beyond, was not as extensive as was the case for Cambridge. The details of recipients of the Stringher and Mortara awards and grants from the Bank of Italy between 1950 and 1975 confirm this; even so, an important number of young scholars went to Oxbridge with other grants or by other means. Other grants, such as those of the British Council, the Leverhulme Trust, British or Italian foundations including those of the University of Oxford and its colleges, the Florey European fellowships of The Queen's College and so on, did encourage Italian-speaking economists to spend two or more years in Oxford. The ratio is, however, one:three; during the period 1950–75, 12 scholars went to Oxford with a Stringher or Mortara grant, while 34 went to Cambridge. By taking into account the period 1931–85, Simona Ferrulli (2012, 40) maintains that the Bank of Italy allocated 48 grants to economists who went to Cambridge, 16 to Oxford and 24 to the London School of Economics (LSE). Why so few to Oxford? There are several reasons for this trend. First, at least until the late 1960s, Oxford

M. Baranzini, A. Mirante, *A Compendium of Italian Economists at Oxbridge*, DOI 10.1007/978-3-319-32219-3_2

ranked only two major economists (Roy Harrod and John Hicks), while Cambridge was the 'bastion' of the direct heirs of John M. Keynes (Joan Robinson, Nicky Kaldor, Richard Kahn, Maurice Dobb and Piero Sraffa). Additionally, Richard Stone, James Meade, David Champernowne and Richard Goodwin were also important Cambridge scholars. Second, until the early 1970s Oxford had dispersed its economists in the colleges, where they were occupied mainly with undergraduate teaching in the course on Politics, Philosophy and Economics (PPE). The exceptions were Nuffield College, Linacre, St Antony's and the secretive All Souls. Cambridge, since the construction of the sub-Faculty headquarters in Sidgwick Avenue in 1960–61 and the subsequent addition of the Department of Applied Economics, has attracted most (but not all) economists. Finally, graduate and Ph.D. teaching began in Cambridge a few years before James Mirrlees, with renewed vigour, set up the new B.Phil. (later the M.Phil.), B.Litt. and D.Phil. programmes in Oxford in 1969–70.

By retaining the names of the grant recipients quoted above and those put forward by Carlo Casarosa (2004, 550–53) and by Vera and Stefano Zamagni (2002), and yet others discovered in the *Oxford University Calendar* and *Gazette*, we may identify a number of (but not all!) scholars according to their Italian alma mater:

1. *From the Catholic University of Milan*: Carlo Beretta, Vittorio Conti (1968), Angiola Contini (1972–04), Carlo Dell'Aringa, Piero Ferri, Giacomo Vaciago (1965 and 1992), Vera Negri-Zamagni (1970–73), and Stefano Zamagni (1970–73);
2. *From the Universities of Rome*: Lucio Izzo (1955), Romano Pantanali (1958), Paolo Miurin (1963), Rainer S. Masera (1966); Stefano Mieli (1973), Leonardo Becchetti, Pierluigi Ciocca (1967–69, supervisor R.C.O. Matthews); Lorenzo Infantino, Alberto Lupoi, Luciano Milone, Paolo Piacentini, Michele Morciano, Vincenzo Patrizi, Carlo Pietrobelli, Francesca Sanna-Randaccio, Eutimio Tiliacos, Gian Cesare Romagnoli (Trinity College);
3. *From the University of Milan and Bocconi University*: Giampaolo Arachi, Carlo Bertoletti, Carlo Mortara, Claudio Lupi;
4. *From the University of Ancona*: Pietro Alessandrini (1969) (Ancona and Urbino), Renato Balducci (ditto 1973), Riccardo Mazzoni, Mauro Marconi, Paolo Pettenati (1971–72);

5. *From the University of Turin*: Alessandro Vercelli (1973), Lia Fubini, Astrig Tasgian, Stefania Zotteri;
6. From the *University of Pisa*: Carlo Casarosa (1978–80), Alberto Chilosi (1975–06);
7. *From the University of Naples*: Antonio di Maio, Fausto Domenicantonio (1970–02), Antonio M. Nucifora;
8. *From the University of Bologna*: Roberto Scazzieri (1975–80), Vincenzo De Nicolò, Flavio Delbono, Giulio Ecchia, Gianluca Fiorentini, Luca Lambertini, Paolo Onofri, Gianpaolo Rossini, Bruno Salituro, Carlo Scarpa, Alessandro Zanello (1975–77);
9. *From the University of Parma*: Mario Biagioli (1977), Augusto Schianchi (1974–07), Roberto Violi, Marco Ziliotti, Luciana Rocca (1973–76);
10. *From the University of Siena*: Renzo Azelio Castelnuovo (1962–63); Daniele Castelnuovo (1973); Massimo Di Matteo (1974–76, Hartford College);
11. *From other universities*: Florio Gradi (1951; Florence), Davide Croff (1972; Venice); Vinicio Guidi (1977; Florence); Luigi Spaventa (Perugia 1968–69); Giuseppe Mazzarino (1971–2010; LSE and Milan); Daniele Giovanni Zizzo (Palermo, 1988), Michele Bernasconi (Pavia 1992);
12. *From Canton Ticino, Switzerland*: Mauro Baranzini (Fribourg and Zürich, at Queen's 1971–85), Roberto F. Cippà (Fribourg, Queen's 1977–82).

As we have noted, we are well aware that this is only a partial list.

2.2 Luigi L. Pasinetti: The Frontrunner at Oxford. Studentship and Research Fellowship at Nuffield College, 1959–60 and 1960–61

Luigi Pasinetti graduated from the Catholic University of Milan in February 1955. At the end of the academic year 1958–59, he had behind him three academic years abroad: two in Cambridge, at Gonville and Caius, and one at Harvard. At that point, having studied for the required nine terms in order to submit his Ph.D. at Cambridge, he did consider returning to his home country. Siro Lombardini, his mentor at the Catholic University of Milan, had put Luigi's name up for a lectureship in economics (*economia politica*). However, the Chairman of the Faculty, Francesco Vito, did not take up the proposal, maintaining that Pasinetti should teach econometrics, or mathematics for economists, or something in this area.[1]

> Without an official appointment, or another concrete alternative, I remained quite hesitant. It was at that moment that Robin Marris, who in those years was a sort of deputy director of the research seminar in Cambridge, momentarily replacing Piero Sraffa, told me that the Nuffield College in Oxford had advertised a limited number of 'studentships'. [...] I applied, giving Nicholas Kaldor and (probably) Robin Marris as referees, and was awarded one. (Pasinetti, interview with Baranzini, August 2000)

So, in September 1959 Luigi Pasinetti moved from Cambridge to Oxford. During his stay at Nuffield (September 1959–August 1961), Pasinetti published a paper entitled 'A Mathematical Formulation of the Ricardian System' in *The Review of Economic Studies*, which appeared in February 1960. In 1960, he also published 'Cyclical Fluctuations and Economic Growth' in the *Oxford Economic Papers*; the Italian version of which was first published in the same year in *L'Industria*. In 1961, this was followed by 'Cyclical Fluctuations and Economic Growth: A Reply to Mr. Neisser' in the *Oxford Economic Papers*. Additionally, a long paper, written jointly with Luigi Spaventa, appeared in the 1960 September–October issue of the *Rivista di Politica Economica*. Most of these contributions were mainly written, if not fully completed, in Oxford. During his stay at Harvard in 1957–58, under the supervision of Wassily Leontief, Pasinetti had drafted an essay entitled 'On Concept and Measures of Changes in Productivity', published in the

[1] Francesco Vito's position was, of course, ill-founded; however, in the long term, for Pasinetti it turned out to be a lucky escape. In this way, he stayed on for nearly two decades in Oxbridge. He was hence able to influence the Cambridge School of Economics much more than would have been possible in Milan.

1959 August issue of *The Review of Economics and Statistics.* It was the first controversy that he would engender, since it led Robert M. Solow, at the Massachusetts Institute of Technology, to write a long 'Comment' (in the same issue) that attempted to rebuke Pasinetti's arguments. Pasinetti's paper expressed a deep dissatisfaction with the way in which technical progress was handled by the marginalist school in general, and by Robert Solow in particular. Pasinetti, who in this context asserts the prominence of technical progress over capital accumulation, had noted that: 'the whole neo-classical movement and the increasing modern application of mathematics, which have contributed so much to improving the tools of economic analysis and to conferring rigor and definiteness on economic thought, have preferred to leave technical progress aside' (Pasinetti 1959, 270). Pasinetti would return on this issue 15 years later:

> Technical progress has been a much harder phenomenon to incorporate into economic analysis. This is paradoxical. In a period in history which has witnessed the most surprising and unprecedented advances in technology and their application to production, the established economic theory has proceeded for more than a century [now nearly a century and a half] on the amazingly myopic assumptions of no change in technical knowledge. So pervasive has been the influence of the law of diminishing returns on the whole way of economic thinking! Even today this 'law' is still haunting economic theorists in all sorts of devious ways. When faced with an increase in production per man, [...] any economic theorist subservient to tradition will be unable to begin doing anything unless he proceeds first to break down the change into two different types of changes: changes due to a variation of the proportions of 'factors', *at diminishing returns*; and changes due to a 'shift' of the (otherwise assumed to be rigidly fixed in shape) technical functions. (Pasinetti 1974, 91–92)

> [In] my own discussion with Solow [...] I have pointed out that, according to Solow's own findings, the aggregate capital-output ratio in the U.S. economy was lower in 1949 that in 1909. It could therefore be argued that, during that period, the overall capital intensity of the U.S. production

> processes, very far from increasing (as Solow's 'moving along the production function' would suggest), has in fact decreased. (Pasinetti 1974, 92n)

It is interesting to note how Nicholas Kaldor described the reaction of Robert Solow and his MIT colleagues to Pasinetti's paper. In fact, he writes as follows to Pasinetti at Nuffield on 16 February 1960, from Berkeley:

> I much enjoyed also reading your controversy with Bob Solow. When I went to M.I.T. my first impression was that all these objections to their prevailing approach left them quite unaffected—it was like pouring water on a duck's back. However, my impression afterwards was that they are really more uneasy about the whole thing than they could care to admit. […] Yours, Nicholas Kaldor

Pasinetti's early work on Ricardo, 'A Mathematical Formulation of the Ricardian System', shows his mastery of the interconnections between value, distribution and growth. He had been at Oxford for a full term when this work was published in February 1960 in *The Review of Economic Studies*. As pointed out in Baranzini and Harcourt (1993, 7–8), the principal object of the paper was to show how an analytical model could capture the ingredients of Ricardo's system and (re)produce his results. The model contains the essence of Ricardo's theory of value—that it was principally embodied labour that, in practice, determined the natural exchange ratios of reproducible commodities. It also highlighted Ricardo's own stress on persistent and permanent or dominant factors at work in the economy, which expressed themselves in the forces which determined natural prices. Pasinetti relegated the short-term factors associated with supply and demand and the determination of market prices to a secondary position. No more so was this the case than in Ricardo's theory of the natural wage and changes in population *cum* labour force, with which was associated his theory of accumulation. Pasinetti's model of Ricardo's system treats the Malthusian principle of population (which Ricardo adopted) as though it works instantaneously, so that the wage is *always* at its natural level even though accumulation is occurring. (As with Ricardo, Pasinetti does *not* suppose the natural wage to be a physiologically determined subsistence wage; habit and history also influence its size.) This simplification allows a much more clear-cut picture of the accumulation process and the approach to the stationary state.

We may anticipate that, in the late 1970s and early 1980s, a number of authors (Hicks, Hollander and Casarosa) suggested a model of the Ricardian theory of distribution and economic growth, which, contrary to the Sraffa-Pasinetti interpretation, gives emphasis to the forces of supply and demand for the determination of the wage rate. Pasinetti (1982) challenged this version. (We reconsider this aspect below.) While at Oxford, Pasinetti also published 'Cyclical Fluctuations and Economic Growth', which appeared in the *Oxford Economic Papers*. In fact, on 16 February 1960, from Berkeley, Nicholas Kaldor writes to Pasinetti at Nuffield College, Oxford, as follows:

> My dear Luigi,
>
> Many thanks for your letter and for sending me your paper on 'Cyclical Fluctuations and Economic Growth' which I really think is first-rate. I hope you won't mind if I have some copies made, and distribute it among a small discussion group here, so that we can discuss it. I can't pretend I have another go at it, and may to offer some points you make towards the end of your paper about the investment function are most important, and have so far been entirely ignored in macro-economic models. I should go, however, rather further in suggesting that the non-proportional nature of investment demand is not solely or even mainly due to the Engel curve, but to the fact that technical progress leads constantly to the invention of new products which did not figure in the consumers' preference function simply because they did not exist. [...] Yours, Nicky Kaldor

On the same day, 16 February 1960, Kaldor wrote a letter of reference on behalf of Luigi Pasinetti to the Warden of Nuffield College. Among other things, Kaldor commented: 'The only thing that I can add to my reference about him sent to you last year is that he has recently sent me a paper on "Cyclical Fluctuations and Economic Growth" (which originally appeared in *L'Industria*, in Italian) which I regard as absolutely first-rate, and shows him to be far ahead of everybody working in this field [...].'

On 29 February 1960, Pasinetti wrote a letter to Nicholas Kaldor with a few comments on his previous paper on cycles and growth. He writes at the end of the letter: 'To clarify the mathematics of the paper various graphical devices may be used. Prof. Hicks was insisting a few days ago on a particular graphical representation which he was suggesting. I prefer however the diagram which I reproduce here [...]' L.P. (Luigi Pasinetti). This proves, then, that Pasinetti was in touch with John Hicks. On 15 March 1960, Pasinetti writes a four-page letter to Kaldor with various important comments on the mathematics of Kaldor's draft 'Capital Accumulation and Economic Growth'. The letter closes as follows:

> Just before closing I am glad to give you a good news. I have been elected a Research Fellow of Nuffield College. The news is not official as yet because the election has to be confirmed by the Governing Body, but I have no reason to suppose that it will not be. My best wishes and regards to all. Yours, Luigi Pasinetti.

In the spring of 1960, Pasinetti was appointed to an assistant lectureship in the Faculty of Economics and Politics at the University of Cambridge and lecturer and fellow of King's College, the appointment starting from1 October 1961. However, for the academic year 1960–61, he remained at Nuffield for a second year.

2.3 Italian Economists and John Hicks

2.3.1 Introduction

John Hicks (1904–89) was, without doubt, a leading economic theorist of the twentieth Century; together with Kenneth Arrow, he was awarded the Nobel Prize in 1972. His work was mainly on 'pure economic theory', in the fields of value, money, capital, growth and distribution. In 2004, the 'invisible college of former colleagues and pupils' gathered in Bologna for the meeting 'John Hicks: One Hundredth Anniversary Workshop'. Roberto Scazzieri, Amartya Sen and Stefano Zamagni, the editors of *Markets, Money and Capital. Hicksian Economics for the*

Twenty-First Century, edited the papers presented at this workshop. According to Scazzieri and Zamagni:

> Hicks's contributions often address contentious issues, and sometimes suggest unconventional and controversial points of view. In John Hicks, we see economic theorizing at its most fundamental, almost formative, stage. In his writings, economic theorizing strives, and succeeds in maintaining, a balance between the requirements of analysis and the explicit recognition of the relevance of history and institutions. In short, Hicks's contribution to economics belongs *both* to the so-called 'mainstream' and to its critique. (Scazzieri and Zamagni 2008, 1)

Pasinetti and Mariutti maintain that 'Hicks was, and remained, an independent thinker. He paid a high price for this independence, by being surrounded by an atmosphere of solitude both in Cambridge and in Oxford—the two places that housed him in the critical moments of his academic life. […] It is in fact not surprising that, unlike many of his colleagues, Hicks did not claim to belong to a specific school of thought; even less that, he should aim at founding one. This was in line with his introverted character, and even more so with his methodological stand. He has left us a remarkable example of scientific honesty in not hiding the "structural break" that took place in his way of doing economics.' (Pasinetti and Mariutti 2008, 69–70) In their thought-provoking essay 'Italian Economists and Linacre College', Vera and Stefano Zamagni maintain that Ursula and John Hicks were a powerful magnetic force, attracting young Italian scholars to Oxford—and, in particular, to Linacre College—from the second half of the 1960s to the early 1980s and beyond.

> The question naturally arises as to why so many Italian economists were drawn to Linacre,—what was the decisive factor? We believe we can say without fear of contradiction that it was the intellectual fascination, and their great love for Italy, of one of the best known scholarly husband and wife teams of the University of Oxford: John and Ursula Hicks. Ursula was fellow of Linacre College, while John was full professor, teaching in the then [and still now] impenetrable (especially for women!) All Souls College, but the pair was so close, and All Souls so withdrawn into its circle of male

dons, that John too finished up by sharing his 'social life' and skills with the postgraduate students of Linacre College'. (Vera and Stefano Zamagni 2002)

We should say that Italian research students working for an Oxford higher degree (M.Phil., M.Litt. or D.Phil., together with with a very low number of undergraduates) were not confined to Linacre. Other colleges—such as Queen's, Lincoln, Nuffield, Pembroke, St Antony's, Hertford, Christ Church and many others—did enrol Italian speaking pupils. Nevertheless, let us quote again Vera and Stefano Zamagni:

> How did this link with Linacre unravel? Essentially through word of mouth. It began with a generation mainly connected to the Bank of Italy, when the Director of the *Servizio Studi* of the 1960s Francesco Masera, who knew the Hickses, had his son Rainer go to Linacre, while Pierluigi Ciocca, Alessandro Vercelli, Lionello Punzo and others came into contact with John Hicks through other Oxford Colleges. [...] In a period of around fifteen years, a good forty-six Italian economists (including the undersigned) passed through Linacre, an extraordinary phenomenon, perhaps unique of its kind. (Vera[2] and Stefano Zamagni 2002)

Not surprisingly, the first centennial celebrations of the birth of John Hicks took place at the University of Bologna; a selection of the papers was edited by Roberto Scazzieri, Amartya Sen and Stefano Zamagni and published by Cambridge University Press. Eighteen out of twenty-eight contributors to that volume are, or have been, associated with Italian universities. This is a proof of the profound impact that Hicks had on more than one generation of Italian economists.

[2] In this chapter, we shall not deal with contributions in the area of economic history. However, it is worth pointing out that Vera Zamagni-Negri, now Professor of Economic History at the University of Bologna, was with her husband Stefano at Oxford between 1969 and 1973; she was awarded an Oxford D.Phil. few years later. She is one of the most authoritative scholars of Italian and European economic history, and has published and edited important works; *Economic History of Italy 1860–1900* was first published by Clarendon Press, Oxford, in 1993. The volume provides a scientific and painstaking reconstruction of Italy's path from a largely rural economy to a fully industrialized nation, with strong private and public sectors. It also offers, as she points out 'an extensive resource of quantitative data, based on original field work by the author and the many detailed but small scale studies existing in Italian'.

2.3.2 Rainer Stefano Masera

One of the earliest Italian research students of John Hicks at Oxford was Rainer Stefano Masera, who was at Linacre College from 1967 to 1970. His D.Phil. thesis was published in 1972 by Clarendon Press with the title *The Term Structure of Interest Rates: An Expectations Model Tested on Post-War Italian Data*. In this work, Masera maintains that, in the presence of differentiated interest rates due to a different maturity of the debt, decisions relative to short-term interest rates may have different significances according to general macro-economic expectations (see also Costabile and Scazzieri 2012, 744). Masera's volume was reviewed in *The Economic Journal* by Nicholas H. Dimsdale (Keynes's nephew), then fellow of The Queen's College, Oxford, who argues that 'once we move away from models with a single rate of interest, we need a theory of the term structure which will explain the observed pattern of market rates. In this book Masera develops a theory of the term structure and then tests his model using Italian data.' Masera first provides an 'admirably clear survey' of the literature on term structure, and then embraces the 'expectational theory'. As Dimsdale points out, Masera 'is not impressed by the market segmentation theory and points out that, if long and short rates are determined in separate markets, the relevant supply and demand schedules should in principle be identifiable'. This was an important original contribution to the literature (including the works of John Hicks), since the followers of the market segmentation approach had not, at least until the early 1970s, provided empirical evidence to support their thesis. Dimsdale also argues that:

> Masera develops an alternative version of the expectation theory in which forward rates reflect market expectations of the future spot rate for a wide range of maturities for a short-time horizon. He is following a suggestion of Hicks in *Value and Capital* that the expectations theory can be expressed in terms of expectations about the future long rate. [...] According to Masera forward rates are revised on the basis of forecasting errors for the whole range of maturities, which seems a more plausible approach. [...] In the final version of the model, which is tested using monthly data, the results are improved by including the normal level of the rate of interest. (Dimsdale 1973, 570)

At the end of his review Dimsdale (1973, 571) concludes that Masera's work is a 'valuable contribution to a subject of continuing interest to monetary specialists'.

2.3.3 Stefano Zamagni

Stefano Zamagni's scientific contribution is certainly impressive and we cannot consider all venues here. As far as Hicks's programme is concerned, we refer to Zamagni (1973, 1983, 1984), Casarosa and Zamagni (1985) and also Scazzieri and Zamagni (2008). John Hicks, in his *Causality in Economics*, underlines the role of asymmetric relationships in the explanation of economic history; he calls attention to the fact that chains of events often have to be interpreted in terms of 'sequential causality'. *A* causes *B* on condition that *A* happens before *B*, and also on condition that there are sufficient reasons for maintaining that all intermediate events are causally related to one another so as to produce the final effect *B* during the given time interval (see Hicks 1979b, 87–88). However, Hicks does not mention the existence of a causal ordering on the recursive type. In fact, recursivity and sequentiality might appear to be quite independent of each other. The reason for this is that sequentiality is a property of the actual process by which *A* produces *B*, whereas recursivity may be considered as a logical property of theory independent of the actual process of causation. However, as Zamagni (1983) and Harré and Madden (1975) argue, the recursive ordering may be linked with the process of causation through time, if one accepts the realistic view that the causal structure of any given theory reflects the way in which causation takes place.[3] Another important contribution by Stefano Zamagni is connected with the dynamization of Hicks's analysis, and to the study of the 'traverse'; that is, the transition from one steady-state to another. His paper was published in the *Oxford Economic Papers* in 1984, and then reprinted in a volume edited by D. A. Collard, D. R. Helm, M. Fg. Scott and A. K. Sen. As pointed out in the introduction to *Markets, Money and Capital. Hicksian Economics for the Twenty-First Century*:

[3] This point has been expounded in Baranzini and Scazzieri (1986, 46–47).

> In short, there is a plurality of ways in which time can be conceptualized in economics, and each one answers peculiar cognitive questions. It follows that there will be a multitude of different methods, each one able 'to cast light upon some aspects of the phenomena' (Hicks 1965, v). This implies that *the* dynamic method does not exist. Indeed, there are two wide varieties of dynamics: 'expectational' and mechanical. In the former, expectations play a fundamental role in explaining the economic process—i.e. in dealing with the specific role of history in economic affairs. This is not so in mechanical dynamics models, where change consists only of 'locomotion'—that is, is an analogue of a simple change of place. It is within such a cognitive frame that one can understand the specific meaning of Hicks's traverse analysis. By drawing attention to deviations between the actual position of the economic system and its corresponding long-period (steady-state) position, the study of traverse provides a case for the *counterfactual* approach to sequential causality—the cause being a change in technology occurring at a certain point of time (the 'impulse'), the effect being the entire difference between the traverse path and the path the economy would have followed in the absence of such disturbance. (Scazzieri and Zamagni 2008, 8)

The contribution by Zamagni has extended the frontiers of Hicks's work; Hagemann (1990, 166n) maintains that Zamagni's 'intention is to show the richness and potentialities of the Hicksian traverse as a method for dynamic analysis', where, for dynamic analysis and due to a structural change, it is the intended passage from one steady state to another. In 1959, John Hicks had stated: 'I am very sceptical of the importance of [...] "steady state" theory. The real world (perhaps fortunately) is not, and never is, in a steady state; it has adventures which are much more interesting' (Hicks 1959, iii, 8; quoted in Collard 1984, 6). The steady state may be defined as a state with a given composition of the capital stock 'appropriate to the new technology and compatible with the labour and savings flows' (Zamagni 1984, 135–36). The results obtained by Zamagni in this fixed-wage setting are quite interesting, and are compared with those sketched by a number of classical scholars. Nevertheless, even more interesting are his conclusions:

1. First, concerning convergence analysis, according to Zamagni (1984, 148) the problem of convergence to a new steady state is quasi-irrelevant. At best, he writes, it usually would take a long

time; but it could also happen that 'a myriad of phenomena of various kinds' would shake the very bases of the economy and make convergence difficult to study. 'Indeed, the rate at which technologies, endowments, and institutional constraints change is so rapid in modern times, relative to the rate at which an economy adjusts to any set of underlying institutional and structural factors, that any inherent convergence tendencies are of very secondary importance and interest. [...] Here lies the basic difference between stability analysis and traverse analysis: since it is only in the late phase that any question of convergence to equilibrium can arise, traverse analysis is in any case capable of telling us about the short-run effects of a technical change, a task which cannot be accomplished by stability analysis' (Zamagni 1984, 148). This is also the lesson that we have personally learned from Joan Robinson—that outside the steady-state equilibrium anything can happen, and that the institutional, behavioural and technical setting comes to complicate the picture.

2. The second conclusion by Zamagni is even more stimulating. He argues that, in his model, capital markets adjust instantaneously to the new technical conditions, and entrepreneurs exhibit the same mode of behaviour as that adopted in the previous situation. He rightly argues that:

> This is clearly unsatisfactory. The innovative process has some rules of its own which cannot be described as simple and flexible adaptations to changes in market conditions. Why is it that capitalists should continue to choose the optimal technique only on the basis of profit rate maximization, without paying any attention to the volume of profits accruing to them over a certain time span? Why should capitalists maintain during the entire traverse the same consumption pattern as that of the reference path, when it is known that they will meet capital losses and gains? Finally, why is it that all capitalists will be able, instantaneously and simultaneously, to introduce the innovation which becomes available at T=0? [...] It is a remarkable feature of Hicks's traverse theory that it provides a vantage point allowing us to put the historical dynamics of technical change into perspective. (Zamagni 1984, 149)

2.3.4 Mario Amendola

Another scholar of Hicks's works is Mario Amendola, who spent two years in Cambridge from 1962 to 1964. Amendola, jointly with Jean-Luc Gaffard of the French University of Nice, has dedicated most of his scientific research to the extension of the steady-state analysis of John Hicks to a dynamic path, often labelled, as said, as 'traverse analysis'. From the numerous contributions by Amendola and Gaffard we have chosen three as being representative of the way in which they extend John Hicks's research programme. This is what they write at the beginning of their volume *Out of Equilibrium* published by Clarendon Press in 1998: 'This book is essentially devoted to "continue with continuation—into the future", a task to which John Hicks called others at the end of the last paper he wrote before his death. We believe that the best way to do this is to build a comprehensive analytical approach for out-of-equilibrium economics. This has required a long-time, a massive effort, and much help from others.' (Amendola and Gaffard 1998, v) The two scholars refer to John Hicks's last paper 'The Unification of Macroeconomics' published in *The Economic Journal* in 1990. In their volume *Out of Equilibrium*, Amendola and Gaffard start by explaining that 'general equilibrium models' focus on interdependence among all variables; such an inter-dependence is 'instantaneously obtained' via an equilibrium system of prices which, after all, represents the only inter-dependence link. Hence in this framing a simultaneous (or contemporaneous) causality is established. Instead, Amendola and Gaffard focus their attention on *interdependence out-of-equilibrium*, which is represented by a 'feedback mechanism over time'. According to them:

> Different types of disequilibria follow from this and interact with each other sequentially. Different evolution paths of the economy may thus be associated with any kind of original shock. The model proposed is a heuristic tool that makes it possible to explore them. What we are after is not mimicking reality, though. Rather we want to be able to unveil sequential causality relations which represent the backbone of processes of economic change. Unlike in the equilibrium approach, these processes are not sketched out by the 'fundamentals' of the economy but are rather the

> outcome of what happens on the way; this may change according to the decisions taken and the policies followed sequentially. (Amendola and Gaffard 1998, 259)

The two authors maintain that one of the main goals of economic analysis is to suggest policy strategies. In the 'general equilibrium approach', these recommendations are built on the belief that economies are always in a state of equilibrium 'so that it is the world that adjusts to the model, not vice versa' (Amendola and Gaffard 1998, 259). Instead, they firmly believe that policy recommendations will be valid only if the dynamics mechanisms, which describe the 'genesis of economic phenomena', to use their terminology, are explained. This is exactly what their out-of-equilibrium analysis tries to describe. Its implications for policy strategies may differ from the traditional ones. In their previous volume—*The Innovative Choice. An Econometric Analysis of the Dynamics of Technology*, published in 1988—Amendola and Gaffard had already pointed out that the neo-Austrian theory put forward by John Hicks offers a representation of the production process that takes explicit account the phase of construction of new plant—and, hence, of the productive capacity—as the physical expression of the specificity of new techniques, and 'at the same time to consider the implications of technical intertemporal complementarity of a process thus defined' (Amendola and Gaffard 1988, ix). Ivano Cardinale and Roberto Scazzieri have recently explored the connections between Amendola's neo-Austrian treatment of the production process and a more detailed representation of production activity in terms of tasks and productive functions. Finally, in their paper 'Sequential Analysis and Out-of-equilibrium Paths', written for the meeting 'John Hicks: One Hundredth Anniversary Workshop' held in Bologna in 2004, Amendola and Gaffard consider the relationship between the monetary and technical features of production along sequential adjustment paths. They argue that the main issue in this framework is that of the harmonization of the construction and utilization phases along such an adjustment path. The two authors draw their paper to a close in the following way:

> When we move from the consideration of the behaviour of an economy during a given period to a process taking place over time, investment and consumption are more realistically interpreted as the construction and utilization of production that take place over a sequence of related periods, and hence their relation is considered to be one of inter-temporal complementarity rather than of substitution. John Hicks's conclusions concerning Smith and Keynes with reference to a single period of finite length are confirmed, but other, more illuminating, conclusions can also be reached. Specifically, that the reallocation of financial resources from unproductive consumption to investment (or vice versa) sooner or later brings about a distortion of productive capacity, resulting in a breakdown of the coordination of economic activity and a threat to the viability of the economy. Different kinds of external interventions—concerning financial resources, human resources, and final demand—are then required to interact dynamically in order to make the expansionary process associated with a structural modification viable. (Amendola and Gaffard 2008, 403–4)

There is no doubt that the works of Amendola and Gaffard, together with those of Stefano Zamagni, Roberto Scazzieri, Alberto Quadrio Curzio, Carlo Casarosa, Rainer Masera, Augusto Schianchi and Piero Ferri, as well as many other non-Italian scholars such as Amartya Sen, Christopher Bliss, Roberto Cippà, Harald Hagemann and so forth, have extended the frontiers of Hicks's work. One may also add that there may also be endogenous forces at work to ensure the viability of the expansionary process associated with a given structural change. It is a matter that is to be found in the background of long-term analysis—that of the endogenous formation and dispersion of socio-economic classes. This may influence not only the level of savings of the system, but also the composition of consumption mentioned by Amendola and Gaffard (2008). This issue is present in most of Hicks's works on economic growth—especially in *Capital and Growth*, as well as *Methods of Dynamic Economics*; however, the matter has not been explicitly taken up in the vast literature in this field. There exist a number of elements that are continuously at work in the determination of the progressive concentration or dispersion of wealth—which, in the long run, is the very basis of the strength of socio-economic classes. (On this, see Baranzini 1991a, 2008.)

2.3.5 Piero Ferri

Piero Ferri, who was at Linacre College from 1968 to 1971, wrote his D.Phil. thesis on 'Some Aspects of Unemployment in Italy: 1951–68' under the supervision of John Hicks. The aim of the thesis was that of reconsidering the peculiarity of the Italian labour market, in general, and the complex nature of its unemployment—in particular, within a process of growth. While different interpretations were taken into consideration, an alternative suggestion was offered. Piero Ferri set himself to overcome previous investigations of the Italian economy that had focused on the decisive role of wages in deepening the Italian dualism between regions and therefore hindering the overall process of growth (see, in particular, Vera Lutz 1962 and Hildebrand 1965). These analyses were mainly based on Hicks's *Theory of Wages* (1932), which he wrote before World War II and that he had revised in 1963. Piero Ferri maintains that Hicks was unsatisfied with this work and therefore encouraged Piero to search for alternative routes and interpretations. The period considered in Ferri's thesis was characterized by deep structural changes and by a new macroeconomic environment. After years of heavy unemployment, some northern Italian regions were very close to full employment. In this context, the strength of the unions seemed to have increased substantially. This was in line with the tenets of a then recently discovered Phillips curve. Within this perspective, recent facts seemed to support Lutz-Hildebrand thesis: the cost pressure (pushed by unions) seemed to reignite the old process of capital deepening and so hampering both the regional divide and the process of growth itself. As far as the first aspect was concerned (i.e. wage pressure), a different perspective consisted in considering the heterogeneity of the labour market. The distinction between a primary and a secondary market, a classification that became popular later on (see Hicks 1974), justified both the presence of full employment problems, epitomized by the Phillips curve, and the persistence of a quantity adjustment mechanism based on an abundant labour supply. This distinction implied a methodological suggestion based on the co-existence of price and quantity adjustment (see Hicks 1965). In fact, even if some sectors reached full employment and this situation strengthened both unions and wage dynamics, it remained true that Italy continued to enjoy an abundant labour supply. Lewis (1954) and Kindleberger (1967) stressed the role of this aspect in the process of growth and it was considered a decisive factor of growth. In this sense, the working of the labour market could only be fully understood within a growth perspective, as is stressed in the Italian translation of the thesis (see Ferri 1971). As far as the capital substitution process is concerned, this process did not find much econometric support in the analysis carried out along the lines suggested by Salter (1961). To the contrary, the emphasis was more on the accumulation process that could explain the overall pattern of growth along with its structural problems. Hicks (1974) subsequently reconsidered some aspects of this dual labour market in his *Crises in Keynesian Economics*: a book that did not come as a surprise to his former D.Phil. student Piero Ferri. Piero Ferri was rector of the University of Bergamo from 1984 to 1999.

2.3.6 Annalisa Cristini

We should also mention Annalisa Cristini, a promising pupil of Piero Ferri. Now Professor and Dean at the University of Bergamo, while in Oxford Cristini earned her M.Phil. in 1987 and D.Phil. in 1990 with a thesis on 'OECD activity and commodity prices', an updated version of which was published in 1999 by Palgrave Macmillan with the title *Unemployment and Primary Commodity Prices: Theory and Evidence in a Global Perspective*. This volume, writes Cristini, discusses the links between primary commodity prices and the OECD rate of unemployment. A descriptive account of the main facts and a VAR analysis help define the essential features of the macroeconomic model, which constitutes the core of the essay. The model simultaneously determines the industrialized countries' economic activity, primary commodity prices, the world real interest rate and Less Developed Countries (LDC) external debt. It hence tries to assess both the impact of primary prices on the OECD economy as well as the feedback running from the primary commodity to the industrialized economies. Dynamic simulations of oil price shocks elucidate the propagation mechanism of the system and the specific contribution played by each factor in transmitting the shock. From 1988 to 1989, Cristini was research assistant to Prof. Nickell at Nuffield College; she has written extensively, though not exclusively, on labour economics.

2.3.7 Carlo Dell'Aringa

Another Italian research student that was in Oxford between 1967 and 1970 is Carlo Dell'Aringa, who was later to become full Professor of Labour Economics at the Catholic University of Milan before taking up various ministerial roles in Italy's government, as a specialist of labour economics and relations. Dell'Aringa earned his D.Phil. in Oxford in 1970 with a thesis written under the supervision of John Hicks on 'Employment, Wages, Prices, and Distribution of Income in the Italian Industry, 1953–1967'.

2.3.8 Augusto Schianchi

Another dedicated scholar of Hicksian economics is Augusto Schianchi (1946). A pupil of Luigi Frey and Stefano Zamagni, Schianchi graduated in economics in 1970 from the University of Parma and, from 1974 to 1977, he was an M.Phil. student at Linacre College where he was in receipt of a research scholarship. He was supervised by Robert Bacon, then a fellow of Lincoln College. After earning his Oxford higher degree, he went back to Parma in 1978 where he combined a prominent academic career with various scientific and high-ranking executive duties: from 1984 to 1987 he was the economic adviser to the Italian Treasury Minister Giovanni Goria. Since 2004, he has been a full Professor at Parma. He has worked and published with Robert Bacon, Flavio Delbono, Andrea Mantovi and various other economists. His fields of research include econometric models, financial theory and applications, industrial economics and the theory of demand. Schianchi, during his stay in Oxford, became involved in Hicksian economics. Recently, he has written two papers (jointly with Andrea Mantovi). The first 'A gamer-theoretic traverse analysis: Price competition and strategic investment' is a strategic model of transitional dynamics, in which the traverse path is driven by the properties of the competitive setting. Specific 'master integrals' allow for the study of the neo-Austrian effects occurring along the traverse path, and thereby reduce the problem to the form of the elementary problem of optimal investment timing; structural change is then addressed along the lines of modern strategic investment problems.

The second paper has the title 'A neo-Austrian perspective on the value of growth prospects'. Here, the valuation framework inherent to the neo-Austrian theory of capital set forth by Hicks (1973) is discussed in terms of a fundamental formula which disentangles the profitability associated with the prospect scale of operation from the internal rate of return of the production process. The formula is employed to tailor a perspective on the value of investment prospects, meant to complement the insights embodied by Tobin's *q metric.*

2.3.9 Roberto Cippà and Vinicio Guidi

Yet another line of research in the vast field of Hicksian economics attracted a good deal of interest in the 1980s and 1990s. This related to the micro-foundations of macro-economics, which was taken up by Christopher Bliss and Roberto Cippà.[4,5] More precisely, in the belief that

---

[4] Roberto Cippà (1953) holds a *licence en sciences économiques* and a doctorate of the University of Fribourg, Switzerland. In September 1977, (with the support of a Swiss Science Foundation fellowship), he was admitted as a graduate student to The Queen's College, Oxford, where he wrote a D.Phil. under the supervision of Christopher Bliss. After finishing his Oxford D.Phil. in economics, he joined the Swiss National Bank and became Executive Director of the IMF (2000–06). He has now returned to Zurich, where he is Director of External Relations of the Swiss National Bank.

[5] This research line reflects another important outcome of Anglo-Italian scientific cross-fertilization. At The Queen's College, Oxford, between Michaelmas Term 1976 and Trinity Term 1983, the first author of this volume organized an economic theory and econometrics seminar. The participants were scholars who were, or had been, associated with the University of Oxford. The topics of the seminar covered a wide spectrum, ranging from classical, marginalist and Keynesian economics to the problems of general equilibrium and quantitative methods. Roberto Cippà (Queen's), Roberto Scazzieri (Linacre) and the first author of this essay (Queen's) were the convenors of the scientific meetings. The institution at which the seminars took place was no casual choice. Since 1969, The Queen's College had sponsored the Florey European Studentship Scheme, originally planned by Lord Howard Florey, provost of the college and Nobel laureate for the therapeutic discovery of penicillin. Lord Florey's aim was twofold: to invigorate the College and Oxford by bringing to them the best research graduates from continental European universities, and to strengthen the ties of international cooperation in most fields of academic research. Between 1976 and 1983, The Queen's College became a place of meeting and discussion for a number of British and continental research students, also including academic visitors, and led to the publication of the volume *Advances in Economic Theory*, published by Basil Blackwell, Oxford, and edited by the first author of this volume. Contributors were Roberto Scazzieri, Christopher J. Bliss, Roberto F. Cippà, Carlo Casarosa, Alvaro Cencini, Bernard Schmitt, Megnad Desai, Roy McCloughry, Nicholas Dimsdale, Mario Biagioli, Luigi Pasinetti, Mauro Baranzini, Heinrich Bortis, Pietro Balestra, Giuseppe Mazzarino and Augusto Schianchi. From the mid-1980s to the end of the 1990s, The Queen's College seminar moved to the Continent. Courtesy of the the Swiss Science Foundation of Berne and a number of Italian universities, an annual International Workshop on the 'Wealth of Nations in Economic

the distinction between macroeconomics and microeconomics is highly artificial, most of the literature (at least until the 1980s) was concerned with the construction of models that incorporate Keynesian features inside a general equilibrium framework. For this task, the extreme assumptions of the Walrasian models make them an inadequate tool. In fact, the complete information that characterizes general equilibrium analysis is obviously in contrast with the idea, underlying Keynes's theory, that economic units have imperfect knowledge of their future environment. This explains the revival of temporary equilibrium analysis, first enunciated by Lindahl (1939) in his *Studies in the Theory of Money and Capital* and then developed by John Hicks (1939) in his *Value and Capital.* Temporary equilibrium models may be conceived either in postulating price flexibility or, as developed by the French school, following the fixed-price method and assuming that adjustments are made by quantity rationing. Neither approach is complete, nor pretends to give an exhaustive explanation of the real world. Bliss and Cippà (1982) put forward a competitive temporary equilibrium model that enquires into the consequences of economic agents having different and inconsistent price expectations. In their words:

> This paper is concerned with the temporary equilibrium approach to economic theory, with some of the possibilities of extending that approach and with some of the problems that the approach gives rise to. 'Temporary equilibrium' is a term coined by Hicks (1939), but it could be extended to cover a number of models that are not as complete and formal as his Walrasian type of model but which nevertheless are situated in the short run. We here include most attempts to give a formal expression in terms of a closed model to Keynes's theory. [...] Since Hicks first introduced it, the temporary equilibrium approach has proved to be enormously fruitful.

Theory' was held. Roberto Scazzieri (Padua and Bologna), Ferdinando Meacci (Padua), Pierluigi Porta (State University of Milan), Heinrich Bortis (Fribourg) and the first author of this essay (Verona and, subsequently, Lugano, Switzerland) organized these workshops, which were held alternately in Switzerland and Italy. A number of Oxbridge economists, or economists with Oxbridge connections joined these intensive meetings; to mention a few, Izumi Hishiyama, Francis Seton, Michael A. Landesmann, Richard Arena, Florian Fleck, Mark Perlman, Prue Kerr, Bernard Schmitt, Alvaro Cencini, Harald Hagemann, Mario Amendola, Heinrich Bortis, Gianni Vaggi. Nicholas Georgescu-Roegen joined a special meeting in Engelberg, Switzerland, in March 1990.

[...]. The present paper represents an extension of the approach along new lines. (Bliss and Cippà 1982, 45–46)

Bliss and Cippà conclude that the capital market in an uncertain world ought to be seen as imposing quantity constraints on agents' actions, even if all prices are flexible and all markets are perfectly efficient. This particular 'rationing scheme' allows Bliss and Cippà to deal with the problem of the consistency of future plans and to define a new notion of temporary equilibrium with rationing: the *consistent temporary equilibrium,* that is, a situation in which all existing markets 'clear', and where every virtual demand equals the corresponding supply. Bliss and Cippà conclude that:

> One way of introducing changes in consumers' tastes is to consider the model inside a stochastic context, where preferences and agents' endowments are defined as random variables depending on the state of the economic environment. Since the occurrence of a particular state is determined according to the probability law, subjectively defined, it is logical to conceive that the expected prices differ from $\mathbf{p}_1$ [a set of reference prices which reflect the market opinion about what the future will be], and that at the same time they are seen by the agents as future equilibrium prices. When eventually the economy moves to the next period, the values of the new equilibrium price vector will depend on which specific expectations have been fulfilled. These considerations stimulate us to generalize the analysis and focus our attention on the conditions for which an equilibrium at one date gives rise to an environment compatible with an equilibrium at the next date. The analysis becomes sequential and more difficult. Pre-existing contracts and spot markets at every date are no longer compatible with the above simple formalization of the model, but at the same time strengthen the reasons for which the method proposed can be justified, reducing considerably the 'quasi-perfect' information about future plans that the market can perceive in the simple two-period model. (Bliss and Cippà 1982, 65)

Along similar lines in the same volume, we find a contribution by Roberto Cippà and Vinicio Guidi (1982)[6]. They start with a discussion of

---

[6] *Vinicio Guidi* (1948) earned a degree in economics in Florence in 1973. Between 1975 and 1978, following a year in the army, he carried out research in his alma mater under the supervision of

the general equilibrium model, in which they critically analyse the main assumptions that limit the possibility of studying important economic realities. From this point of view, they consider the extensions of the original model of Arrow and Debreu; in particular, they concentrate on the temporary equilibrium models with quantity rationing as developed by Drèze and Benassy.

2.3.10 Carlo Casarosa

A line of inquiry taken up by Hicks was that of 'capital and dynamics', with contributions in the field of economic growth, income distribution and capital accumulation, in which 'repercussions of economic change' cannot be confined to the single period (Hicks's 'week'). In this frame, another important link between the Oxford school in general, and John Hicks in particular, with the Italian school of economics of the second half of the twentieth Century is represented by the early scientific contributions of Carlo Casarosa. Between 1976 and 1978, Casarosa was an academic visitor in Oxford on sabbatical leave from the University of Pisa, and he worked in close contact with John and Lady Ursula. This link concerns the so-called 'New View' of Ricardo's theory of growth and distribution, and the role of price rigidities and of money wages in Keynes's work. From the late 1970s onwards, Hicks and Hollander (1977) and Casarosa (1978a, 1982a), quite independently, came to the same conclusion on a fundamental point of Ricardian theory. These works referred to an analysis by Samuelson (1959). The Hicks-Hollander-Casarosa 'New View', contrary to the traditional (i.e. Sraffa-Pasinetti) interpretation, gives emphasis to the forces of supply and demand for the determination of the (Ricardian) wage rate. Within the framework of the Hicks-Hollander-Casarosa model, different aspects are discussed, and the notion of a dynamic equilibrium path is used to describe the movements of the system over time. The main feature of such a dynamic path is that the wage rate is, in general, above its natural level and coincides with it only in the stationary state. Casarosa argues that the 'New View'

Piero Tami. During the academic year 1978–79, he undertook research work in Oxford under the supervision of Amartya Sen. Since 2001, he has been a full professor of economics in Florence.

allows for an elucidation of all Ricardo's propositions concerning the tendencies of the wage rate and of the rate of profits during the process of growth. More precisely, Casarosa shows that, although the Ricardian economy cannot move along a steady growth path because of decreasing returns, the notion of dynamic equilibrium turns out to be quite useful for restricting the possible trajectories that the economic system might follow during the process of growth. Moreover, if the marginal product of labour decreases slowly enough, the actual path of the economic system is likely to remain in close proximity to the dynamic equilibrium path most of the time, so that one should be able to describe the notion of the system as if it followed the dynamic equilibrium path. As the author points out, the role played by the dynamic equilibrium path in this case is exactly the same as that played by the natural equilibrium path in Pasinetti's model.

In response to this 'new formulation', Pasinetti (1982) replies by challenging some of the propositions put forward in separate papers by Samuelson, Hicks-Hollander and Casarosa. More precisely, for Pasinetti the interpretation of the Ricardian system followed by Casarosa simply belongs to a stream of economic thought (which goes back to Marshall) that tries to incorporate the basic proposition of Ricardo into the analytical framework based on the working of supply and demand. Thus, following Pasinetti, a formalization of Ricardo's analysis that emphasizes his hints at the forces of supply and demand is not new at all, since the pre-Sraffa economic literature includes several attempts that had been written with the purpose of reconciling Ricardo with marginal economic theory. Pasinetti adds:

> By concentrating all emphasis on the Ricardian notion of *market* wage rate, Casarosa's approach is open to the danger of neglecting—or reducing to irrelevance—the much more fundamental notion of a *natural* wage rate. This is in fact the trap into which—it seems to me—Hicks and Hollander (1977) have fallen. In their analysis, the 'natural' wage rate plays no role. To begin with, they confuse it with the 'subsistence' wage; and second, they relegate the latter to play the external role of a boundary 'floor'. All their attention is concentrated on the *market* wage rate. (Pasinetti 1982, 241)

2.3.11 Andrea Maneschi

Andrea Maneschi enrolled at University College, Oxford, in the Michaelmas Term of 1955; he stayed until 1959 and later became a distinguished economist in the USA. He does not fully take sides with Pasinetti on this issue. Immediately after high school, Maneschi left his native Milan for Oxford, where he took a B.A. in Engineering Science in 1958, followed by a Diploma in Economics in 1959. He then went on to Johns Hopkins University in Baltimore where, in 1964, he obtained a Ph.D. in Political Economy. From 1965 to 1967, he was assistant professor of economics at Yale; he subsequently moved to the Vanderbilt University, where he was initially Associate Professor, later on becoming full Professor of Economics, and is now Emeritus Professor. He has written extensively on Ricardo, on Kaldor, and, in general, on the theory of international trade and the history of economic thought. He has also written papers on the post-Keynesian theory of profit determination and income distribution. In 1993, he reconsidered the Hicks-Hollander-Casarosa versus Pasinetti controversy. With respect to the papers of Hicks and Hollander (1977) and Casarosa (1978a, 1982a), papers he writes:

> In both their [Hicks-Hollander's and Casarosa's] models there is a clear tendency for the economy ultimately to attain the stationary state, in which the market wage is reduced to the level of the natural wage. Although Pasinetti's formalization of the Ricardian system does distinguish between market and natural wage rates, Caravale and Tosato (1980) correctly point out that his analysis is not a fully dynamic one in the sense that much of it is in fact conducted—as he himself states—*as if* the wage rate were as its natural level, which would then make it impossible for capital accumulation to lead to a rise in population. (Maneschi 1993, 126)

2.3.12 On Carlo Casarosa Again

On another line of research, Casarosa (1978b, 1981, 1982b, 1984) maintains that the conventional presentation of Keynes's aggregate analysis requires rethinking, due to its considering the aggregate expected demand as a function that reflects the entrepreneurs' expectations about aggregate expenditure. Casarosa's aim is to show that this view has no microeconomic foundations in an atomistic framework, and that Keynes's aggregate expected demand and supply analysis is simply an extension of the analysis of the firm to the whole economy. Hence, according to Casarosa and contrary to Patinkin's view, Keynes's statement—according to which at every point of effective demand entrepreneurs' expectations of profits are maximized—is correct. Casarosa summarizes his arguments as follows:

1. The Keynesian short-run theory of the firm is a reformulation, in terms of aggregate supply and expected demand functions for the firm, of the Marshallian theory of the competitive firms.
2. The theory of effective demand extends the analysis under (1.) to the systems as whole.
3. Keynes's claim that at the point of effective demand 'the entrepreneurs' expectation of profit will be maximized' is correct; however, profit expectations are realized only when the economic system is in short-run equilibrium.
4. The point of effective demand (or 'daily' equilibrium) of the economic system is attracted towards the short-run equilibrium position, which is determined by the aggregate supply and expenditure functions.
5. The aggregate expected demand function for the economy as a whole is *not* the producers' guess of the expenditure function; the two functions are distinct even when the entrepreneurs' expectations are right. (Casarosa 1982b, 77–78)

Casarosa finally maintains that the mix-up between the 'expected demand function' and the 'expenditure function' has probably been caused by the formulation that we find in *General Theory*, where John Maynard Keynes uses the same wording 'aggregate demand function' for both concepts. 'But, whatever Keynes's responsibility, the notion that the expected demand function is the producers' estimate of the expenditure function is clearly a theoretical aberration which has strangely survived' (Casarosa 1982b, 77). There are points of agreement and disagreement between John Hicks's programme and Casarosa's research programme. A point of agreement concerns the interpretation of the Keynesian hypothesis of the relative downwards rigidity of money wages. Ever since *Value and Capital* (1939), Hicks had maintained that an economic system with flexible prices and money wages (i.e. quite sensitive to disequilibria between supply and demand) is highly unstable; hence the rigidities, especially of money wages, maintained by Keynes have a stabilizing role in the economic system. Since his early works, written in the mid-1960s, Casarosa has always stressed the role of downwards rigid money wages in the presence of unemployment in order to return to full employment. In any case, this rigidity does provide flexibility to the economic system, even if full employment is not reached. Full employment may also be reached by means of an increase in aggregate demand for goods and services. In a letter to the present author, Casarosa however admits that his position differs from that of John Hicks on one specific point. More precisely, he maintains that Sir John had always assumed, in order to understand Keynes's work, that markets of goods and services are of the fixed-price type, and not flex-price. However, according to Casarosa, in order to explain the fundamental mechanisms of Keynesian economics, it is sufficient to assume downwards rigidity *only* for money wages. According to him, 'I am convinced that a relevant feature of the General Theory is the consistence of its fundamental outcomes with a high degree of freedom of entrepreneurs' behaviour (in the case of perfect and imperfect competition, mark-up strategies, and so on)' (Casarosa, in a letter to the first author of this volume in May 2013).

Finally, among the pupils of John Hicks we should mention Giacomo Vaciago and Alessandro Vercelli.

2.3.13 Giacomo Vaciago

Giacomo Vaciago graduated at the Catholic University of Milan in 1964 and enrolled at Linacre College, Oxford, in 1965. In 1968 he was awarded an M.Phil. in economics with a thesis written under the supervision of John Hicks. He came back to Christ Church College in 1992–93 having being elected to a Fowler Hamilton visiting fellowship

(Peter Oppenheimer and Michael Bacharach were the two economics 'students'—i.e. fellows—of the College at that time). During that stay, he delivered the first Fowler Hamilton Lecture on 'Public vs private debt' which was published in *Moneta e Credito* in September 1993.Vaciago was first full Professor of Economics at Ancona before being called back to his alma mater, the Catholic University of Milan. He has held various senior ministerial posts in Rome. His early research and publications were in the field of long-run growth and productivity (Verdoorn-Kaldor's Law) which led, inter alia, to the publication in the *Oxford Economic Papers* in July 1975 of the paper 'Increasing Returns and Growth in Advanced Economies: A Re-Evaluation'. His main field of research, however, remains that of monetary theory and policy.

2.3.14 Alessandro Vercelli

Alessandro Vercelli graduated in political science in 1969 at the University of Turin and, for the years 1969–72, was a research fellow of the Einaudi Foundation. In 1972–73, he was a junior research fellow at St Antony's College, Oxford. His 1991 volume *Methodological Foundations of Macroeconomics: Keynes and Lucas*, in which he carries out an investigation of the methodological and epistemological foundations of modern macroeconomic theory, with specific reference to the approach of J. M. Keynes and R. Lucas, is an outcome of his research activity. In the last two decades, he has extended his interest to the topics of the environment, sustainability and inequality. With Partha Dasgupta and Karl-Göran Mäler, he has edited a volume entitled *The Economics of Transnational Commons* that stresses the relevance of shared natural resources, and of the links between poverty and environmental degradation. More recently, in 2008 and jointly with Simone Borghesi, he published a volume with Palgrave Macmillan entitled *Global Sustainability: Social and Environmental Conditions*, wherein they explain the extent to which the recent process of globalization may be considered consistent with sustainable development.

2.4 Building on the 'Exchange' and 'Production' Paradigm: Alberto Quadrio Curzio and Roberto Scazzieri

Along the lines of thought sketched by John Hicks and Luigi Pasinetti, we also find the contributions by Alberto Quadrio Curzio and Roberto Scazzieri. In fact, Hicks (1976, 1986) did consider the characteristics of research lines in economic theory, maintaining that each line involved a selective concentration of attention. This seems for him to be the distinctive characteristics of any given research line in economic theory, rather than the consideration of a particular 'ideal' model. He suggested that it is no longer possible to see the development of economic theory as a linear evolutionary process from the mercantilists to contemporary economics; rather, a number of alternative 'paradigms' characterize the past and present situations of our science. Quite independently, and almost simultaneously, both Hicks (1976) and Pasinetti (1963, 1965a, b), who had left Oxford just few terms earlier, seemed to agree on a fundamental distinction between the theories centred on the analysis of the production phenomena and the theories centred on the analysis of exchange. Hicks, in order to emphasize the distinction, labels 'political economy' as the first group of theories, and 'catallactics' as the second.

Hicks's and Pasinetti's viewpoints complement each other. Hicks stresses how changes in economists' concentration of attention may also be independent of changes in the basic ingredients of economic life. See, for instance, his explanation of the 'triumph of catallactics' which runs in terms of the intellectual superiority of the exchange over the production research line at the time when this change took place in the 1870s (Hicks 1976, 214–15). Pasinetti, on the other hand, highlights the influence of external events on the internal dynamics of economic theory.

Alberto Quadrio Curzio and Roberto Scazzieri[7] were the first to study the implications of such a proposal and its application to the documentation of a particular period in the history of economic analysis

[7] In particular, we may mention the five-volumes work *Protagonisti del pensiero economico*, edited by Quadrio Curzio and Scazzieri (1978–83); see Baranzini (1979), Baranzini and Scazzieri (1986) and Quadrio Curzio (1993a, b).

and economic history. This is seen especially in their introduction to the four volumes on the leading economists since David Ricardo (1977–82, 1983). In fact, they attempted a thoughtful and original reconstruction[8] of the history of economic theory in which the relative strength or weakness of the exchange and production research lines depends on a special interplay of 'internal' or 'external' history. Changes in the organization of economic life are considered influential, particularly when they determine a change in the relative importance of two distinct aspects of productive activity: (1) the production of commodities by means of commodities; and (2) the transformation of primary resources into final consumption goods. In this interpretation, economists tend to be more interested either in (1) or in (2), depending on whether their description of the productive system is framed in terms of inter-industry relationships, or in terms of vertically integrated sectors, respectively. The structural dynamics of the economic system may thus influence the evolution of economic thought. As noted, Alberto Quadrio Curzio and his then pupil Roberto Scazzieri were the first to make an in depth study of the implications of the dichotomy production/exchange in economic analysis, and its fruitful application for the history of economic analysis. The volume *Foundations of Economics* published in 1986, which contains the contributions of renowned scholars, has been the inspiration of numerous works that have subsequently taken up this issue.

In the same volume, Pasinetti (1986) argues that the exchange-production duality may be traced back to a deeper dichotomy in the theories of value. In fact, many precious insights are to be gained from the pre-theoretical stages of the discussions on value, where diverging principles become acceptable when considered within a normative framework. Pasinetti identifies in the works of A. Smith and W. S. Jevons the reference points for discussing two alternative paradigms. Smith presents the *pure-preference model* (or pure-exchange model), which looks at all economic problems as if they were problems of the optimal allocation of resources, and where prices are determined by individuals' preferences and resource endowment. Jevons is a proponent of a *pure-labour economy model*, where production and exchange are inherently linked by labour

[8] Quadrio Curzio and Scazzieri's seminal work was also well-received in France: see Lutfalla (1983).

specialization and where prices emerge from the necessity of an extensive division of labour. In particular, Pasinetti stresses the relevance for each paradigm of developing its basic structure ('first skeleton') by concentrating on one single principle. This basic structure may be unfolded, in spite of successive generalizations of each paradigm, by identifying what is essential and cannot be omitted from the theory under consideration. Examination of the distinct ways in which prices are determined and of the way in which the two lines of research are successful in integrating exchange and production leads Pasinetti to maintain that alternative visions of economic life may be associated with different goals of analysis. This ought to ensure a degree of autonomy for alternative frames of analysis (see Baranzini and Scazzieri 1986, 77).

2.5 Italian Economists on Roy Harrod

If we were to consider, at least partially, Richard M. Goodwin to be an Italian economist, then we should mention that Roy Harrod supervised him for one year while he was a Rhodes Scholar at St John's College, Oxford (1934–37). Harrod's tutoring naturally had a lasting influence on him. It seems that Harrod even passed to Goodwin for reading the proofs of *The General Theory*, sent to Harrod by Keynes.

Daniele Besomi is a Swiss-Italian economist who has dedicated several years of research to the interpretation of Harrod's works and to the editing of his unpublished interwars essays and correspondence. After earning a first degree at the University of Pavia, Besomi spent one year in Cambridge, where he gained an M.Phil. in economics in 1987. Then, supported by a variety of research grants, he spent various periods of time researching in Cambridge, Oxford and at Chiba University, Japan, where most of Harrod's papers are now. In 1997, Besomi received the Joseph Dorfman Best Dissertation Prize from the History of Economic Society; this was for his Ph.D. dissertation on *The Making of Harrod's Dynamics*, submitted at the University of Loughborough. A book bearing the same title was awarded a prize for the 'best book in the history of economic thought' by the European Society for the History of Economic Thought. Harald Hagemann endorsed Besomi's *The Collected Interwar*

Papers and Correspondence of Roy Harrod—a monumental edited work in three volumes comprising almost 1700 pages and published in 2003—as follows:

> Roy Harrod (1900–1978) was an eminent economist who made seminal contributions to several fields, most notably to business cycle theory and modern growth theory in the 1930s and 1940s. He also was official biographer of Keynes and served Churchill as a statistical adviser at the beginning of World War II. Daniele Besomi (born 1960) is the author of *The Making of Harrod's Dynamics* (1999) and an impressive number of journal articles which have illuminated Harrod's work from various perspectives. For this scholarly work Besomi received the highest honours from the two leading international associations for the history of economic thought. This three-volume collection of Harrod's interwar correspondence and papers, edited by Besomi, is fascinating reading. It is a presentation of a rich set of correspondence between Harrod and other leading economists of his time and a collection of formerly relatively inaccessible essays and press items which are a gold-mine for every scholar interested in the genesis of modern growth economics or Harrod's role as a public intellectual. (Harald Hagemann, University of Hohenheim, Germany; endorsement of Besomi's edited work)

Nevertheless, Besomi's contribution has gone well beyond the editing of Harrod's works. In *The Making of Harrod's Dynamics*, Besomi has inquired into the origin and early development of Roy Harrod's notion of economic dynamics. It examines how Harrod gathered the analytical, methodological and epistemic components of his theory, and how these are logically connected. It shows that the organizing concept is the instability principle, by stating that in order to provide an endogenous explanation of movement a destabilizing factor must be *ex-ante* introduced. In this way, it represents an epistemic premise rather than an outcome of Harrod's trade cycle theory. Besomi also considers the relationship of Harrod's dynamics with the 'orthodox theory' and with the alternative approaches to dynamics—in particular, the 'time-lag theories of the cycle'. The point of 'divergence' was the instability principle, which Harrod saw as a rejection of the traditional assumption of the stability of equilibrium.[9]

[9] These points have been pointed out to us in a letter by Daniele Besomi himself.

Among other Italian scholars that have researched Harrod's works are Bruno Miconi (1967), Maurizio Pugno (1992), Massimo Di Matteo (2010) and Bruno Soro (2012). Pierpaolo Varri, who also was at Cambridge in the early 1970s, has written an introduction to Harrod's *Dinamica economica* published by Il Mulino in 1990, and has also written a paper on 'Harrod's Dynamic Economics and Joan Robinson's Generalization of the General Theory' (1996). In 1979, Alfredo Medio in 1979 published a volume on *Harrod e il problema della dinamica economica.* Finally, we should not forget Gianni Vaggi on this topic. We are aware that numerous other Italian scholars have written on Harrod, but we wanted to confine ourselves to former Oxbridge scholars. As far as Besomi recalls, the only conference on Roy Harrod was convened in Genoa in 1996 (for the 60th anniversary of the publication of his *Trade Cycle*). *Economic Dynamics, Trade and Growth: Essays on Harrodian Themes* (1988) presents the papers given at that conference, which were edited by G. Rampa, L. Stella and A. Thirlwall.

2.6 Italian Graduate Students at Nuffield College (1970–95)

2.6.1 Imperfect Competition and General Equilibrium Models

In 1969, James Mirrlees arrived at Nuffield College from Cambridge with a chair that later would be called the Edgeworth Chair of Economics. Together with Nicholas H. Stern, John S. Flemming (1940–2003), Christopher Bliss and several other economists, Mirrlees would soon strengthen the teaching (and research) in economics at Oxford. In particular, he set up a new B.Phil. degree (later to be an M.Phil.) that ran for six terms (two years), with a number of qualified teachers. In 1977, due to Mirrlees, Amartya Sen arrived—first, as Professor of Economics at Nuffield, before being appointed to the Drummond Professorship of Political Economy at All Souls College, following the resignation of Joseph Stiglitz who returned to the USA. Professor Sen's arrival from the

LSE was announced during a 'historical' sub-Faculty meeting at St Cross Building. In the late 1970s, 1980s and early 1990s, a number of new distinguished fellows, readers and professors were appointed, either at Nuffield or in other Oxford colleges. While the old 'guard' had, in general, concentrated its attention on macro-economic variables, on classical and Keynesian models, and the history economic analysis, the younger generation of Oxford economists were, in general, always more involved in micro-economic topics, in the general equilibrium (micro-founded) models and in applied economics. Professor John Vickers, now Warden of All Souls, formerly Drummond Professor of Political Economy 1991–2008, is probably the best example; competition and regulation are his main research interests. This general trend also affected Cambridge and most other English speaking universities. Casarosa (2004, 551–3) maintains that this tendency had connections with the disillusionment of the scientific community with the politically saturated Marxist and Sraffian theories that in Cambridge and elsewhere, but not in Oxford, had dominated the academia of economics. However, we are not sure that this is the correct interpretation. In any case, we must admit that the scientific output of the second generation of Italian young economists who arrived in Oxford to work especially (but not exclusively) in the field of micro-economics after 1985 is impressive, to say the least. Several of them came from Bologna and were, inter alia, direct or indirect pupils of Stefano Zamagni. Others came from Rome, Siena, Parma and the Catholic University of Milan. Most of them then returned to distinguished academic careers in Italy or elsewhere; in particular, in Bologna. We cannot mention them all; we shall mention some of those who, in due course, took Oxford higher degrees. The list is certainly much longer. We will consider them according to seniority and then consider a couple of representative works published in learned journals.

2.6.2 Carlo Luigi Beretta

Carlo Luigi Beretta is now full Professor of Economics in the Faculty of Political Science of the Catholic University of Milan, where he has also been Chairman of the Faculty for several years, following the 21 years of

Quadrio Curzio's service in that role. Beretta earned a First degree in the same university. He then spent three years as a research student at Oxford, where, in 1977, he gained his D.Phil. with a thesis on 'Monopoly in General Equilibrium Theory'. After a number of years at the University of Bergamo and the University of Parma, he returned to the Catholic University. He has been widely published on game and decision theories, on general economic equilibrium and welfare theory with application to institutional settings, as well as on international trade theory with reference to factor movements.

2.6.3 Gianpaolo Rossini

Gianpaolo Rossini gained his First degree in political science (major economics) at the University of Bologna; from 1978 to 1980 he was a research student al Linacre College, Oxford, where he earned his M.Phil. degree in economics. Since 1997, he has been full Professor at the University of Bologna. Rossini has published widely on the mechanisms of price formation, on game theory, on the theory and policy of international trade, and on the role of uncertainty and risk, especially in entrepreneurial decisions. He has also published on practical questions of economic policies, on monetary policies, and on current account composition and the sustainability of external debt in various nations. Some of his research works have been co-written, in particular with Michele Moretto, Luca Lambertini, Andrea Mantovani and Paolo Zangheri.

2.6.4 Flavio Delbono

Flavio Delbono studied economics at the University of Parma, graduating in 1982. He then earned a Ph.D. in economics at Siena in 1986. In 1984, he enrolled at Linacre College, Oxford; this was made possible by a variety of grants, one of which was a British Council Scholarship. In December 1988, he earned his D.Phil. degree with a thesis on 'Technological Change and the Behaviour of Firms'. In his first terms at Oxford, Delbono studied under Professor Amartya Sen, who left Oxford for Harvard in 1986. Delbono has published extensively in learned journals, inter alia, in the field of technological change, strategies of public enterprises in non-competitive markets, on the various forms of oligopolies and duopolies. Recently, he has taken up the issue of cooperative firms, as well as poverty and human development indices.

2.6.5 Vincenzo Denicolò

Vincenzo Denicolò is Professor of Economics at the University of Bologna and has, for some time, been a professor at the University of Leicester. As he points out in his personal page of the University of Bologna, 'his main research interest currently is the economics of innovation and intellectual property, but he works, more broadly, on industrial organization and competition policy and maintains an interest in social choice theory, in which he has also published extensively in the past. He has been visiting fellow at Clare Hall (Cambridge) and visiting professor at the European University Institute and the University of Paris II. He served as co-editor of the *International Journal of Industrial Organization* and as head of the Bologna Doctoral School in Economics and Statistics.' He has published extensively in respected economic journals, including the *Quarterly Journal of Economics*, the *Journal of Economic Theory* and the *RAND Journal of Economics*.

2.6.6 Gianni De Fraja

Gianni De Fraja is the William Tyler Professor of Economics in the University of Leicester. He attended the Scuola Superiore Sant'Anna in Pisa, where he graduated in 1982. He then took his Ph.D. at the University of Siena with a thesis on 'Game Theory'. Following this, he went to Linacre College, Oxford, where he earned his D.Phil. on oligopolistic competition. Since leaving Oxford, he has taken up academic positions in the universities of Leicester, Bristol and York. Between 1999 and 2005, he was managing editor of the *Bulletin of Economic Research*. His research interests are in the areas of public economics, the economics of education, regulation, and game theory. He has published papers, among others, in the *Oxford Economic Papers*, *Review of Economic Studies*, *Economic Journal*, *Journal of Public Economics*, and *Journal of Political Economy*.

2.6.7 Luigi A. Franzoni

Luigi A. Franzoni is full Professor in the Faculty of Economics of Bologna. He received his D.Phil. from Nuffield College, Oxford, and has been published in leading journals on the economic theory of settlements, law enforcement, tax amnesties and intellectual property.[10] He is author of a well-received introduction to law and economics (*Introduzione all'economia del diritto*).

2.6.8 Carlo Scarpa

Carlo Scarpa is now a full Professor of Economics at the University of Brescia. After being awarded a laurea in economics at the University of Parma, he received a research doctorate in economics from the University of Bologna. He then enrolled as a research student at Oxford, where he obtained a Ph.D. in economics working at Nuffield College. He has specialized in industrial economics, and has carried out research and published widely on industrial economics, antitrust and regulation, as well as on energy, local public services and intellectual property rights.

2.6.9 Luca Lambertini

Luca Lambertini, before completing his Ph.D. at Bologna in 1994 with a thesis on 'Product Differentiation and Strategic Behaviour', enrolled at Linacre College, Oxford. There, he submitted a D.Phil. thesis under the supervision of Martin Slater on 'Strategic Interaction under Endogenous Product Differentiation'; the higher degree was officially awarded to

[10] This information is presented on his personal page at the University of Bologna.

him in May 1996. He is now full Professor of Political Economy at the University of Bologna, Faculty of Social Studies. His research interests cover the fields of game theory, imperfect competition, product differentiation with particular emphasis on vertical and spatial differentiation, labour-managed enterprises vs profit-seeking enterprises, and international trade and policies coordination. He has published widely in high-ranking journals.

2.6.10 Gian Cesare Romagnoli

Gian Cesare Romagnoli took a First degree in economics at La Sapienza, Rome, and then spent a long period of research at Trinity College, Oxford. He was later a Research Fellow at the Institute of Economics of the University of Pennsylvania. He is now Professor of *Politica Economica* in the Faculty of Political Science, Università Roma Tre, and was awarded the Ezio Vanoni Prize of the *Presidenza della Repubblica* for his contribution to public finance.

2.6.11 On Some Analytical Results

We now make reference to two works of the economists quoted above. They seem to us to represent the scope and method of the wider research programme carried forward in Oxford, or immediately afterwards, by the group of economists mentioned above. We may recall that numerous papers written by 'Oxford educated' Italian economists were published in the *Oxford Economic Papers*, which represents a distinctive feature. We start with Delbono and Denicolò's (1991) paper on 'Incentives to Innovate in a Cournot Oligopoly', which appeared in the *Quarterly Journal of Economics.* By retaining the basic framework of analysis of Lee and Wilde, Delbono and Denicolò show that '(a) an increase in the number of firms may result in a decrease in the equilibrium R&D effort of each firm and in the equilibrium total effort; (b) in equilibrium there may be under-investment with respect to a social optimum' (Delbono and Denicolò 1991, 952). In 1993, the two authors published the paper 'Regulating Innovative Activity. The Role of a Public Firm' in the *International Journal of Industrial Organization*. The authors prove that, under general conditions, there is over-investment in R&D in a 'non-cooperative equilibrium due to duplication of effort'. Hence, a public firm may be instrumental as a regulator to shrink 'the market of R&D and the socially optimal level' (Delbono and Denicolò 1993, 46). The authors show that, in a mixed duopoly, each firm invests less in R&D than in a private duopoly and that 'although the expected time of innovation is postponed, social welfare is higher than in a private duopoly' (ibid., 35). This, hence, has wider implications in a mixed duopoly, as it is the case with many industries at the beginning of the twenty-first century due to a spate of privatizations. We report finally on Vincenzo Denicolò's (2002) paper 'Sequential Innovation and the Patent-Antitrust Conflict', published in the *Oxford Economic Papers*. In this paper, Denicolò focuses on the intrinsic strain between patent and antitrust rules. In order to do this, he dissects a two-stage patent race model, where competition among the patentees may lead to profit erosion. He concludes that collusion, in this framework, stimulates investment in second-generation innovation, which improves welfare if their social gains exceed private gains (or returns). 'However, it discourages investment in first-generation innovations. Thus, for the pooling of subsequent patents to be beneficial, the non-appropriable returns from the second innovation must be large and it must be costly to achieve by comparison with the first' (Denicolò 2002, 649).

The above fields of research lead us to mention here a Cambridge educated scholar who has worked since the early 1990s in the fields of taxation, micro-economics and, recently, finance.

2.6.12 Elettra Agliardi

Elettra Agliardi gained a First degree in economics at Bologna in 1986, an M.Phil. in economics at Cambridge in 1989, a Ph.D. in economics at the European University Institute in 1990 and, finally, a Ph.D. in economics at Cambridge in 1992. For the years 1990–92, she was a research officer in the Department of Applied Economics at Cambridge, and from

1990 to 1995 she was a college lecturer in economics and fellow (title A) of Churchill College. She is now full Professor of Economics of the University of Bologna. Since 2012, she has been on the editorial board of the journals *Finance* and *Economic Notes*. Agliardi's papers are often cited in the literature; in particular, her paper in the *Australian Economic Papers* (2001) on 'Taxation and Investment Decisions: A Real Options Approach'. According to her, the paper aims to analyse 'the impact of the tax system on the firm's incentives to invest and disinvest in an uncertain environment. This paper follows the real options approach, which allows us to investigate the value to a firm of waiting to invest and/or disinvest, when payoffs are stochastic and investments partially reversible. The implications for the magnitude and directions of the effects of tax policy are studied; also the case of tax policy uncertainty is examined.'

2.6.13 Models of Saving and Accumulation: The Flemming-Mirrlees (-Hicks-Kaldor-Pasinetti) Approach

As previously mentioned, in the early 1970s Oxford teaching and research were undergoing progressive and important reform in the field of economic theory. On the one hand, the influence of the 'old guard' was losing ground. John Hicks, the pupils of Roy Harrod, Walter Eltis and Maurice F. G. Scott, David Soskice, Andrew Glyn, Michael Bacharach, Francis Seton, Nicholas H. Dimsdale and many other distinguished scholars represented the 'old guard'. At the same time, the 'Nuffield school' was gaining impetus, with the appointments of James A. Mirrlees, John S. Flemming, Nicholas H. Stern, Maurice F. G. Scott and many others who were more neo-classical and micro-economic minded. For those who had interest in the macro-economic theories of income and wealth distribution before coming to Oxford, the moment was ripe for working on the micro-foundations of macro-economics. This was undertaken in order to build a bridge between the two approaches, following a suggestion formulated by John Hicks (1965) and Samuelson and Modigliani (1966). This is exactly what the first author of this volume set himself to develop when he arrived at The Queen's College in 1971 with a Florey

European scholarship awarded to him by the college. The starting points were the works of John Hicks, James E. Meade, and Anthony B. Atkinson, by keeping them in the frame of the macro-economic post-Keynesian theory of income and wealth distribution.[11]

The 'bridge' between the two research programmes is well-represented by Chap. XXI ('Optimum Saving') and Appendices D and E of Hicks's (1965) *Capital and Growth*, where a (social) utility function is postulated in order to find the level of consumption that maximises total utility and, at the same time, yields the level of consumption and savings that allows the system to place itself on a given growth path with well-defined properties. In this sense, Hicks has anticipated a wide literature on growth and optimal savings, which would proliferate in the late 1960s, 1970s, 1980s, and even later. It might be argued that Chap. XII of Hicks's *Capital and Growth* ('The Model in Outline', 131–47) represents a remarkable exception in John Hicks's way of working; for him to graft his growth model into the Cambridge theory of distribution is very unusual. In fact, where 'other writers feature mainly in footnotes', as Bliss (1987, 642) has it, here Hicks shares an approach that has a clear Cambridge post-Keynesian imprint. Post-Keynesian, neo-Ricardian as well as neo-classical two- (or multi)-class models consider a class of 'pure' capitalists whose income is derived entirely (or mainly, in certain cases) from capital, and a class of workers whose income is derived from both work and accumulated savings. As discussed at length in Baranzini (1991a) and Baranzini and Mirante (2013), the main features may be summarized as follows: (a) the savings ratio of the two classes is exogenously given and, hence, independent, for instance, of the rate of interest earned on savings (both life-cycle and inter-generational); (b) little attempt is made to explain the 'historical' importance of the inter-generational bequest of the system; and (c) the equality that may be observed in the long-run equilibrium between the rate of profit earned by the entrepreneurs and the rates of interest earned by the other classes on their accumulated savings.

The research line focuses on the patterns of accumulation of capital in a two- or multi-class model incorporating the basic ingredients of the life-cycle theory and the possibility of the existence of an inter-generational

[11] See, in particular, Baranzini (1976, 1991a, 2008).

bequest. This is not incompatible with the macro-economic analysis since, with appropriate mathematical tools, it is possible to aggregate individuals and to consider classes of individuals characterized by a homogeneous economic behaviour and propensity to transmit wealth to their heirs. In this context, the life-cycle theory may provide:

1. Greater insight into the determination of the distribution of income among classes and into the determination of the equilibrium variables of the model;
2. An understanding of the sort of reasons that may lead to historical class differences, to a different accumulation of capital (both life-cycle and inter-generational), and to the particular conditions under which a class may start (or stop) accumulating inter-generational assets;
3. An assessment of the relative strength of the life-cycle vs the inter-generational capital stock and the conditions, which favour one or the other of the capital stocks.

The results obtained throw additional light on the behaviour of consumers and, more importantly, on the process of capital accumulation. In particular, they show that in the very long run the system may explain the evolution towards a two-class (or multi-class) society of financial capital owners. In the case in which all classes may pass on a financial bequest (excluding education) to their children, in order to have a steady-state path, the capitalists must have a much stronger will to bequeath capital to their children than the other dynasties or classes. It is only in such a situation that all classes will hold a positive share of the total capital stock. Can this analytical result be reconciled with common sense and economic reality? The answer is bound to be positive, since: (a) the working class, by definition, derives a high proportion of its income from human capital stock, so this class may be inclined to discount its inter-generational bequest at a rate lower than average; and (b) it is not unrealistic to posit a situation where, in general, low-income families give higher priority to life-cycle consumption and, consequently, a lower one to the inter-generational capital stock. On the other hand, from a long-term perspective, those classes that derive a high proportion of their income from inter-generational wealth (and the remaining part from life-cycle savings) are bound to give weight to the accumulation of such wealth, by discounting it at a rate higher than average. As already pointed out, several scholars have already explored a differentiated propensity to leave a bequest to the next generation. The general outcome of these studies is that bequests appear to be luxury goods, both with respect to permanent income and wealth of the donors. The 'permanent' income elasticity of bequests, according to Menchik and David, is always positive and ranges from about 0.3 for persons with a low income to 2.7–4.75 for high-income earners. Not surprisingly, indeed.

2.7 Italian Economists at Oxford Building on Production Theory

2.7.1 Introduction

We report now on works elaborated and published by Italian research students and scholars at Oxford in the field of the theory of production during the years 1975–2000. At that time, various distinguished economists could provide supervision in the field of the investigation of production processes, both at the conceptual and analytical levels. A non-exhaustive list would include Alan C. J. Brown, Francis Seton, Michael O. L. Bacharach, John Enos and Amartya K. Sen, as well as John Hicks himself.

2.7.2 Roberto Scazzieri

One research student who took up this line of research was Roberto Scazzieri, who came to Linacre College, Oxford, in January 1975. Another graduate of Bologna, Alessandro Zanello, arrived at the same time. He had come to Oxford after working at Bologna, under Quadrio Curzio's supervision, on a dissertation on Leonid Kantorovich's value theory, and was later to join the International Monetary Fund.[12] Scazzieri

[12] Alessandro Zanello, under the supervision of Hywel Jones, earned a B.Phil. degree at Oxford in 1977. He then moved on to the USA where, under the supervision of Edwin Burmeister, he wrote

has turned out to be one the most prolific scholars to have pursued the production theory line of research in his first years at Oxford. More generally, over the years, he has pursued several research lines of the Italian-Oxbridge school of economics. They were connected, in particular, with the research programmes of John Hicks, Piero Sraffa and Luigi Pasinetti in Oxbridge and with those of Alberto Quadrio Curzio, Paolo Sylos Labini and Giorgio Fuà in Italy. His works belong, at the same time, to the best tradition of the modern school of Italian Economic Thought and to the best of the modern Oxbridge schools of economics. In fact, both schools emphasize the long-run changes of economic systems, undergoing processes of structural change. Since January 1975, Scazzieri has been closely associated first, with the University of Oxford and, since the late 1980s, with the University of Cambridge. Apart from Sraffa, he is probably the Italian economist who has had the most long-lasting, intense and fruitful involvement with Oxbridge. Scazzieri is son of an electrical engineer whose university education was deeply influenced by a meeting with Guglielmo Marconi and the early development of communication technology. He took a laurea in Economics and Politics with first class honours at Bologna with a dissertation on 'Productivity Laws and Price Determination' written under the supervision of Alberto Quadrio Curzio. He was then awarded a Stringher scholarship and, in January 1975, he enrolled at Linacre College, Oxford. For five years, he worked on an M. Litt. thesis on 'Scale and Efficiency in Classical and Post-Classical Models of Production', first, under the supervision of David Soskice and, thereafter, Michael Bacharach. He then worked under the supervision of Michael Bacharach on a D.Phil. thesis on 'Tasks, Processes and Technical Practices: A Contribution to the Theory of the Scale of Production'.

Scazzieri's research in Oxford initially dealt with foundational aspects of production theory; in particular, considering the relationship between scale, the efficiency ranking of technical practices, and the overall efficiency of production structures. In this way, Scazzieri took up an important research line that was being kept alive at Oxford by a number of people: John Hicks (in his *Capital and Time*); Francis Seton (in his

a Ph.D. on multi-sector models of growth. During part of his career, he was associated with the Department of Economics of Dartmouth College.

works on the structural theory of value); J. A. C. Brown; another Oxford research student, Michael A. Landesmann (in his works on production analysis and structural dynamics); and Amartya K. Sen, who was, at that time, Drummond Professor at All Souls. His interests in production theory had originally been fundamentally stimulated by his former mentor at Bologna, Alberto Quadrio Curzio, especially though his volume *Accumulazione del capitale e rendita* published in 1975. The friendship with Michael A. Landesmann played a pivotal role in the evolution of Scazzieri's interests at Oxford, as he himself points out:

> The first friend that I should recall [...] is perhaps Michael A. Landesmann, a graduate from the University of Vienna who was then at Balliol. We first talked to each other in the tower of Nuffield College library and we soon discovered that we had many interests in common: essentially history and philosophy. We also found ourselves sharing the belief that economic theory should be primarily concerned with historical dynamics of forms of organization, particularly in the production sphere. Already at that time, Michael was a tireless organizer of meetings and 'private seminars', and his room became one of the most intellectually lively places for young economists in Oxford. (Scazzieri 1993b, 105)

When Scazzieri started his research at Linacre College in January 1975, the study of the relationship of output to productive efficiency was deeply rooted in the history of economic theory. Nonetheless, there would have been few economists satisfied with the state of the arts in this field. The reason is that economic theory did not seem to provide a satisfactory explanation of phenomena of 'increasing and diminishing returns', 'economies and diseconomies of scale' and so on. Scale-efficiency relationships provided a fertile arena in which heated debates took place, often starting with differences in basic definitions and hypotheses. The original discussion took place mainly in *The Economic Journal*, among John Clapham, Cecil Pigou, Dennis Robertson, Piero Sraffa and others, during the 1920s. Another important debate developed in the late 1940s between Chamberlin, Hahn and McLeod in the *Quarterly Journal of Economics*. This debate was concerned with the issue of input divisibility in relation to increasing returns to scale (Scazzieri 1982, 19–42).

In fact, as Scazzieri maintains, scale-efficiency relationships are treated in a distinctly different way depending on whether we consider the classical or the 'post-classical' theory of production. The main dissimilarity is to be found in the fact that decreasing and increasing efficiency by the classics were treated as the outcome of producers' behaviour, vis-à-vis technical alternatives—in particular, under constraints relative to the scarcity of inputs (such as land) or the indivisibility of given production processes. On the other hand, in the 'post-classical', or modern theories, scale-efficiency relationships decreasing or increasing efficiency are the direct outcome of technological laws, and no longer connected to variations of scale affecting producers' choices. This might appear a paradox in the evolution of production theory, for the view of scale of scale-efficiency phenomena accepted by neo-classical economists severs the link between such phenomena and technical decisions; and such an outcome seems to contrast with the pervasive role of choice in the neo-classical view of the productive world. Scazzieri, in the final part of his paper, discusses the general 'philosophy' of the two approaches and concludes that the classical approach can provide a useful starting point for the formulation of an economic theory of scale-efficiency phenomena.

> The point of view chosen by post-classical [i.e. neo-classical or marginalist] writers implies that only an extra-economic explanation is possible. However, such an outcome is not a necessary consequence of admitting that scale-efficiency phenomena can partly be explained by laws independent of producers' choices. The reason is that, at least in principle, it is possible have an economic theory of such phenomena and also to allow natural or technological laws to play a part in their determination. If one accepts the latter point of view, the analytical representation of production technology can no longer be based on the linearity assumption, unless *ad hoc* qualifications are introduced. Additionally, it will be possible to deal with the cases in which scale-efficiency phenomena arising from producers' choices appear in conjunction with nonlinearities based on natural or technological laws. (Scazzieri 1982, 40)

In 1993, Scazzieri published with the Clarendon Press a volume that was the result of nearly ten years of research in Oxford: *A Theory of Production. Tasks, Processes, and Technical Practices*:

> The aim of this study is to consider the structure of productive processes within a general description of human, technical, and environment capabilities and their utilization in 'supporting' networks of productive tasks. As a result of this investigation, the view will emerge of the overall economic system as a set of interdependent funds (such as workers, machinery, natural resources) executing, according to a co-ordinated pattern, a certain transformation or set of transformations. Such patterns will affect the physical characteristics of the material environment and/or capabilities of the funds involved in productive activity. (Scazzieri 1993a, 1)

Clearly, Scazzieri's work fills an important gap in the existing theoretical literature on production structures. Unsurprisingly, in the mid-1980s the editors of *The New Palgrave Dictionary of Economics* asked Scazzieri and Luigi Pasinetti to write the entry 'Structural economic dynamics'. In this way, Scazzieri remains one of the few economists to have published a joint paper with Luigi Pasinetti. We may add that in Landesmann and Scazzieri's (1996) edited volume on *Production and Economic Dynamics* this research line has been further refined. The volume, as Landesmann and Scazzieri point out, takes into account two different research programmes. The first considers the issue of structural economic dynamics based on the interlocking research lines of John Hicks on traverse analysis, Luigi Pasinetti on non-proportional growth models, and Richard M. Goodwin's methods of dynamic decomposition and economic fluctuations. The second research programme is that started by Nicholas Georgescu-Roegen in the field of the organization of production as a field characterized by 'the interrelationship between tasks, fund factors and material transformations'. According to Landesmann and Scazzieri:

> This volume proposes a new approach in the analysis of structural dynamics, in which a comprehensive view of the dynamics of the whole economic system is associated with the decomposition of the latter into subunits (such as processes, industries, integrated sectors, eigensectors) in order to represent the disaggregated dynamics of structural adaptation and compositional change. On the other hand, a detailed representation of micro-organisational features leads to the analysis of networks and networking processes within and amongst such subunits. (Landemann and Scazzieri 1996, xv; 2nd edn, 2009)

This is the extent to which Scazzieri examined the foundational aspects of production theories during his Oxford years. Later, we shall introduce the research programme he carried out while at Cambridge.

2.7.3 Mario Morroni

Another Italian scholar worth mentioning here is Mario Morroni, with his two Cambridge University Press volumes: the first, published in 1992 under the title *Production Process and Technical Change*; the second, published in 2006 under the title *Knowledge, Scale and Transactions in the Theory of the Firm*. Morroni is life member of Clare Hall, Cambridge, where he spent several terms; in 1992, he was awarded the Myrdal Prize of the European Association for Evolutionary Political Economy. The purpose of Morroni's first book is to present a 'consistent scheme capable of unifying the economic analysis of the production process in order to understand the effects of technical change' (Morroni 1992, 1). As the author further points out, the study may be carried out along two lines: either (a) defining a scheme of relations among the economic variables of the production processes, variables that may be varied by institutional aspects such as industrial relations changes, or changes in expectations; or (b) as an empirical *methodology* that may allow for the study of the economic implications of changes in techniques. The inclusion of temporal and organizational aspects allows the author to examine the analytical implications of recent research on the nature of firms and the characteristics of technical change, while the model is used to analyse technical changes that involve variations of scale or degrees of flexibility. Industrial economics and management studies are therefore brought together in a new way. Nathan Rosenberg of the University of Stanford, reviewing Morroni's 2006 Cambridge University Press volume, writes that 'Morroni writes with refreshing analytical clarity on the current status of the theory of the firm. His book provides a masterful re-examination of neo-classical theory at a time when academic economists have been challenged to integrate such intractable forces as internal economies of scale, high transaction costs, and radical uncertainties into their theoretical models. His book is an invaluable guide to all who share these concerns.'

2.7.4 Antonio Andreoni

As Roberto Scazzieri moved to Cambridge towards the end of the 1980s, the line of research on production theory also moved, at least partially, to the Cam. The issues of production and structural analysis—or, better, of the structural analysis of production processes and economic dynamics—have been recently taken up by Antonio Andreoni. Formerly a research associate at the Centre for Science, Technology and Innovation Policy, at the Institute for Manufacturing, Department of Engineering, University of Cambridge, Andreoni has been since 2014 at the School of Oriental and African Studies (SOAS), University of London. He holds a B. Sc. and M. Sc. from the University of Bologna, where his supervisor had been Roberto Scazzieri, and an M.Phil. and a PhD. (obtained in 2013) in Development Studies from the University of Cambridge. His Ph.D. Dissertation on 'Manufacturing Development: Structural Change and Production Capabilities Dynamics' was supervised by Ha-Joon Chang, a former pupil of Bob Rowthorn and also an associate of Ajit Singh. His research areas cover manufacturing and industrial systems, the political economy of manufacturing development, structural economic dynamics and intersectoral linkages, industrial competitiveness and skills: metrics and benchmarking, and industrial and innovation policies evaluation. He has written various papers in his research areas. In a paper on 'Structural Learning: Embedding Discoveries and the Dynamics of Production', an effort is made to open the 'production black box' by proposing the analytical map of production as a tool for disentangling the set of interdependent relationships among capabilities, tasks and materials. The concept of structural learning is introduced to identify the continuous process of structural adjustment triggered and oriented by existing productive structures at each point in time. The author maintains that structural learning trajectories allow for the transformation of structural constraints, such as bottlenecks and technical imbalances, into structural opportunities. In addition, complementarities, similarities and indivisibilities are essential focusing devices for activating compulsive sequences of technological change, as well as for discovering structurally embedded opportunities. The paper finally investigates the tension between structure and agency present in structural learning trajectories, and examines the form it takes in different productive organizations. (This research programme builds on a research line initiated by Scazzieri 1981, 1993a.)

In another paper written for the *Oxford Review of Economic Policy*, written jointly with three of his colleagues, with the title 'What is New in the New Industrial Policy?', Andreoni explores the recent evolution of manufacturing-related policies in leading OECD economies–Germany, Japan, the United Kingdom and the United States. A new framework, the industrial policy matrix, is used to illustrate and compare policy approaches in terms of factor inputs, intervention levels and degrees of coordination. In yet another highly technical paper, 'International Industrial Policy Experiences and the Lessons for the UK' (written with H.-J. Chang and M. L. Kuan), Andreoni reviews a diverse set of countries with the most successful industrial policy experiences since the Second World War—the USA, Germany, Japan, Italy, Finland, (South) Korea, Singapore, China and Brazil—with a view to deriving lessons for the UK. The picture that emerges is an alarming one, in which the UK's industrial performance distinguishes itself for being the worst and for getting worse all the time. In another paper written with M. Gregory, 'Why and How Does Manufacturing Still Matter: Old Rationales, New Realities', Andreoni calls for 'the renaissance of a manufacturing oriented view of the economic system'. He begins by providing a critical review of the main turning points in the manufacturing versus services debate evaluating the analytical and empirical arguments deployed in favour of each view. He then goes on to describe the profound transformations in industrial systems and the redistribution of manufacturing production across countries over the last two decades, which challenge some of the assumptions on which the service-oriented view is built. The paper ends by investigating the negative consequences of de-linking manufacturing production from services (off-shoring) are explored by highlighting the systematic disruption of the bundle of technological linkages constituting the industrial commons. Finally, we should mention the important paper 'Triggers of Change: Structural Trajectories and Production Dynamics', written jointly by Andreoni and Scazzieri (2013) for the *Cambridge Journal of Economics*. The paper concentrates on production processes as principal loci of structural economic dynamics along increasing and decreasing returns trajectories. According to the authors, these trajectories are triggered by structural opportunities and constraints embedded in production systems, and their historical realization is subject to different institutional configurations. This approach suggests the governance of economic dynamics via structural policies working both on the technological and organizational conditions of production. The authors finally stress that capitalist economies have to rely on a mix of coordination devices across different production units and aggregation levels in order to capture structural opportunities and thus avoid structural constraints. These works surely represent a continuation and progress of the long-standing tradition of the Italian and Oxbridge school of economic thought.[13] Since his appointment at the Cambridge Institute for Manufacturing in 2013, Andreoni has promoted the Babbage Industrial Policy Network and the associated Babbage Lecture Series. The aim of the Network is to stimulate the exchange between production economists and technologists, and Lecture Series has hosted presentations by leading thinkers, among whom have been Mike Gregory, Ha-Joon Chang, Mario Sergio Salerno, Patrizio Bianchi, Ken Warwick, Bob Rowthorn, Lord Sainsbury, Lord Adonis, Michael Best, Philipp Shapira, Giovanni Dosi, Thomas Kurfess and Mariana Mazzucato. Andreoni, now at SOAS, University of London, is also a Member of the Global Young Academy.

2.8 Italian Scholars at Michael Bacharach's Bounded Rationality in Economic Behaviour Unit

Michael O. L. Bacharach, student (i.e. fellow) of Christ Church since 1969 and university professor from 1996 until his death in 2002, founded the Oxford Laboratory in Experimental Economics and the Bounded Rationality in Economic Behaviour Unit. It attracted a number of distinguished scholars, among whom we would like to mention Daniele Giovanni Zizzo and Michele Bernasconi, who have both published scientific papers jointly with Michael Bacharach.

[13] Andreoni confirmed a number of the above points in a letter to the present authors.

2.8.1 Daniele Giovanni Zizzo

Daniele Giovanni Zizzo is now Dean of Research and Innovation in the Faculty of Humanities and Social Sciences at Newcastle University, as well as a Professor of Economics in the Newcastle University Business School. He graduated from the University of Palermo and earned an M.Phil. and D.Phil. in Oxford. Zizzo was a stipendiary lecturer at Brasenose College, a junior research fellow, and, from 2001 to 2004, a student (i.e. fellow) of Christ Church College and a university lecturer. As he points out in his personal page, while in Oxford he 'was an acting director of BREB (*Bounded Rationality in Economic Behaviour Unit*) and experimental laboratory coordinator, managing the research unit and convening research workshops and conferences'. From 2004 to 2008, he was at the University of East Anglia, where he was promoted to full Professor. He considers himself 'primarily an experimental and behavioural economist. His research is motivated by the search for more realistic empirical and theoretical foundations of economic decision-making, using mainly experimental, but also analytical and computational methods as required'. According to his personal page, Zizzo considers himself 'a mainstream economist, but one interested in pushing forward the boundaries of mainstream economics, and one firmly committed to a wider perspective as an interdisciplinary social scientist'. In fact, he has published in top scientific journals, and in 2004 edited, inter alia, with Palgrave Macmillan the volume *Transfer of Knowlegde in Economic Decision Making*.

2.8.2 Michele Bernasconi

Michele Bernasconi is now Professor of Public Finance at the University of Venice 'Cà Foscari'. His fields of research include economics and psychology, experimental economics and public finance. He holds a Ph.D. in economics from the University of Pavia (1993) and a Ph.D. in economics from the University of York (1992). At York, he wrote a thesis on 'Non-conventional Decision Analysis: Theories, Evidence and Implications'; and he was a recipient of various research fellowships: a Mortara fellowship from the Bank of Italy (1986), a Luigi Einaudi research fellowship

(1987), an Ellis Hunter teaching fellowship from York (1987–88) and a British Academy Postdoctoral fellowship (1983). In 1992, he was a research officer of the Institute of Economics and Statistics at Oxford and, in 1997, together with Michael Bacharach, he published a paper on 'The Variable Frame Theory of Focal Points. An Experimental Study' in *Games and Economic Behavior*.

2.9 Other Distinguished Italian Scholars Who Undertook Research at Oxford

As observed in the Introduction to this volume, we cannot report on all the Italian economists who have studied at Oxford. However, we would like to mention Pierluigi Ciocca and Stefano Mieli, as well as Renato Balducci, Francesca Sanna-Randaccio, Mario Biagioli, Paolo Piacentini-Karnizawa, Michele Morciano, Bruno Salituro and Lia Fubini.

2.9.1 Pierluigi Ciocca

Pierluigi Ciocca (1941) graduated in law from the Sapienza Universities of Rome in 1965 and, for the next two years, he undertook graduate work at the Institute for Studies and Economic Researcy (ISRE) in Rome under the guidance of Bruno de Finetti, Paolo Sylos Labini, Luigi Spaventa and Sergio Steve. With the support of a Luigi Einaudi fellowship, he enrolled at Balliol College, Oxford, between 1967 and 1969 and undertook research work under the supervision of John Wright and Robin Matthews. While at Balliol, he took part in seminars organized by John Hicks, Roy Harrod and Robert Solow. Having returned to Rome, he began a prominent career at the Bank of Italy, where he attained the position of Deputy Director General (1995–2006). In 2005, he was shortlisted for the position of *Governatore della Banca d'Italia* but, due to the opposition of the then Italian prime minister, his name was not put forward for selection. He has taught in various universities and has published extensively in the fields of monetary theory, policy and regulation.

Particularly well-known is the volume *Money and the Economy: Central Bankers' Views*, which he edited in 1987 (Macmillan/St. Martin's).

2.9.2 Stefano Mieli

Stefano Mieli (1947) graduated in Rome in 1973. Between 1973 and 1975, with a Stringher grant from the Bank of Italy, he undertook post-graduate work in Oxford. In 1975, he entered the Bank of Italy where he pursued a prestigious career, reaching the rank of *direttore centrale*. He has published in the field of finance regulation and has taught in the universities of Reggio Calabria and Florence.

2.9.3 Renato Balducci

Renato Balducci (1947) is now Emeritus Professor at the University of Ancona (now the *Università Politecnica delle Marche*). He graduated in 1972 in economics from Ancona with a thesis on '*Aggiustamento della bilancia dei pagamenti, liquidità internazionale e inflazione*', supervised by Fausto Vicarelli. Giorgio Fuà encouraged him to apply for a Mortara grant in order to pursue his academic development abroad. The grant that he duly obtained allowed him to spend a considerable period in Oxford, from 1973 onwards, before returning to teach at Ancona. In 2005, with Neri Salvadori, he jointly edited the volume *Innovation, Unemployment and Policy in the Theories of Growth and Distribution* (Edward Elgar). As the author has confirmed to us in a recent correspondence, the volume integrates the analytical methods and the research themes of New Growth Theory into the cultural tradition of the classical and post-Keynesian economists. It provides a new insight into the processes of the growth of modern economies, which highlights the interdependence between distribution and growth. The contributions show that 'political and social stability, security of property rights, efficiency of the capital market, research, education, investment in physical and human capital, public spending and taxation policies are all necessary for the success and stability of a country's development process'.

2.9.4 Francesca Sanna-Randaccio

Francesca Sanna-Randaccio is full Professor of Economics at the Faculty of Engineering, La Sapienza, Rome. In 1971, she graduated in political science at La Sapienza; in 1973, she earned an M.A. in International Relations at Johns Hopkins and, in 1980, an M. Litt. in economics at Oxford. She has published especially in the fields of international and industrial economics, and in economics of the firm. She has published in the *Journal of International Economics*, *Review of International Economics*, *International Journal of Industrial Organisation* and *Journal of International Business Studies*.

2.9.5 Mario Biagioli

Mario Biagioli (1946) earned a degree in economics in Rome in 1969 and a post-degree diploma in economic development in Naples in 1971. He was admitted to Linacre College in 1976 and, in 1980, obtained an Oxford M. Litt. with a thesis on the 'Sources of External Imbalance and Demand Management Policies in Italy during the Seventies' (he was supervised by Andrea Boltho, and his examiners were David Soskice and Peter Oppenheimer). He has since that time been associated with the University of Modena (1975–96) and with the University of Parma (1996–2016), where he has been full Professor of Economic Policy since 2001. He had focused on labour economics and on exchange rate mechanisms. One of his earliest fields of research concerned the effects of the flexible exchange rates of 1970. In a paper presented at the economic theory and econometric seminar at The Queen's College, Oxford, in 1979 he concluded that, when the hypotheses made by the monetary approach hold (i.e. full employment of all productive resources and clearing of all markets):

> there are two main implications of the monetary approach for policy-making. First, the only possible remedy to external imbalances (either deficits in external payments or a depreciation of the exchange rate) is a reduction of the rate of credit expansion. Second, exchange rates changes are assumed not to have any long-lasting effects on real variables. Then,

> exchange rates changes *per se* are regarded as an ineffective means to improve the external position of a country. However, the contribution of flexible exchange rates advanced by monetarist authors is usually positive, since they regard floating as a "second best" measure for restoring the possibility of decreasing real wages when nominal wages are sticky. (Biagioli 1982, 219–20)

A third conclusion indicated in the thesis is that those indications do not apply when the economy does not fulfil the conditions requested by the monetary approach, and the economy works under Keynesian conditions, as had been the case with Italian experience since that period. In this situation, the economy is subjected to a balance-of-payments restraint of the kind studied by Harrod and by Thirlwall, among others; other kinds of policy remedy are required. These conclusions were a clear warning for the years of financial international disorder that were to follow and for the adoption of a common currency, the Euro, which characterized the macroeconomic policies adopted by European policy-makers thereafter. Most of the scientific work generated by Biagioli in the 35 years (1980–2015) that have passed since his studies in Oxford was aimed at broadening and developing the ideas first expounded while at Oxford. In the field of labour economics, he focused his studies along three lines: first, the evolution of Italian pay systems and wage differentials and the problems these posed to macroeconomic policies. Second, he considered the economics of 'profit-sharing', with the aim of examining the situations in which profit-sharing might increase productivity and economic performances, both at the micro- and macroeconomic levels. His third line of study was the econometric estimations of the theory of human capital.

2.9.6 Paolo Piacentini-Karnizawa

In 1971, Paolo Piacentini-Karnizawa (1948) earned a First degree in economics at La Sapienza in Rome; in the mid-1970s he moved to Oxford where, in 1978, he was awarded an M. Litt. degree with a thesis on the economics of Georgescu-Roegen. He is now full Professor at La Sapienza in Rome. He has published in various fields; his early interest was in the representation of production processes and technical progress, with particular reference to the extension and application of the 'flow-fund' approach.

2.9.7 Michele Morciano

Michele Morciano, after obtaining a laurea in economics at La Sapienza in Rome, applied and was admitted to Trinity College, Oxford, where he obtained an M. Litt. in economics with a thesis on the dynamics of relative prices and income distribution in an input-output model (written under the supervision of Alan Brown). Returning to Italy, after a period of research and teaching, he entered the banking sector and, later on, the field of public administration.

2.9.8 Bruno Salituro

Bruno Salituro holds a degree in economics from the University of Bologna (1974). From 1976 to 1978, Salituro was a research student at Linacre College, Oxford, where he obtained a B.Phil. degree in 1978. He has published a successful textbook of macro-economics with Anna Soci, and has researched and published in the field of monetary theory (national and international), as well as labour economics. He is now Professor in the Department of Economics of the University of Bologna.

2.9.9 Lia Fubini

Lia Fubini is full Professor of Labour Economics in the University of Turin. She graduated in economics from Turin in 1972, was a research fellow at the Einaudi Foundation 1972–73 and undertook research in Oxford, at Linacre College, in 1973–74 and 1976–78. There, she focused on multinational firms and on issues of monetary economics. On her return to Italy in 1978, she began work on industrial economics and vertical integration. Since the mid-1990s, she has switched her focus to macro- and labour-economics. She has mainly published in the field of labour market flexibility. In her (2003) paper on 'Women's Unemployment in Italy' she stresses that 'the low employment rate of married women and the high unemployment rate in Southern European Countries seem to provide important indications of labour market and a social system that do not provide enough flexibility for women to combine work with demanding family activities.'

Bibliography

Agliardi, E., & Agliardi, R. (2008). Progressive taxation and corporate liquidation policy. *Economic Modelling, 25*(3), 532–541.

Amendola, M., & Gaffard, J.-L. (1988). *The innovative choice, an econometric analysis if the dynamics of technology*. Oxford: B. Blackwell.

Amendola, M., & Gaffard, J.-L. (1998). *Out of equilibrium*. Oxford: Clarendon Press.

Amendola, M., & Gaffard, J.-L. (2008). Sequential analysis and out-of-equilibrium paths. In R. Scazzieri, A. Sen, & S. Zamagni (Eds.), *Markets, money and capital. Hicksian economics for the twenty-first century, op. cit.*, pp. 382–404.

Andreoni, A., & Scazzieri, R. (2013). Triggers of change: Structural trajectories and production dynamics. *Cambridge Journal of Economics, 38*(6), 1391–1408.

Baranzini, M. (1976). *On the distribution of income in two-class growth models*. D. Phil. thesis, The Queen's College, Oxford.

Baranzini, M. (1979). Review of *Protagonisti del pensiero economico*, Vol. I: *Nascita e affermazione del marginalismo* (1871–1890); Vol. II: *Tradizione e rivoluzione in economia politica* (1890–1936). In A. Quadrio Curzio, & R. Scazzieri (Eds.), *Economic Journal, 89*(3), 480–482.

Baranzini, M. (1991a). *A theory of wealth distribution and accumulation*. Oxford: Clarendon Press.

Baranzini, M. (2000). Luigi Lodovico Pasinetti. In P. Arestis & M. Sawyer (Eds.), *Biographical dictionary of dissenting economists* (2nd ed., pp. 417–24). Cheltenham: E. Elgar.

Baranzini, M. (2008). Flexible saving and economic growth. In R. Scazzieri, A. Sen, & S. Zamagni (Eds.), *Markets, money and capital. Hicksian economics for the twenty-first century, op. cit.*, pp. 287–308.

Baranzini, M., & Harcourt, G. C. (Eds.). (1993). *The dynamics of the wealth of nations: Growth, distribution and structural change: Essays in honour of Luigi L. Pasinetti*. Basingstoke/New York: Macmillan/St. Martin's Press.

Baranzini, M., & Mirante, A. (2013). The Cambridge post-Keynesian school of income and wealth distribution. In G. C. Harcourt, & P. Kriesler (Eds.), *The oxford handbook of post-Keynesian economics, op. cit.*, Vol. I, pp. 288–361.

Baranzini, M., & Scazzieri, R. (Eds.). (1986). *Foundations of economics. Structure of inquiry and economic theory.* Oxford/New York: Basil Blackwell; and 'Knowledge in economics: A framework', 1–87.

Besomi, D. (1999). *The making of Harrod's dynamics.* London: Macmillan.

Biagioli, M. (1982). A monetary model of exchange-rate determination applied to the Italian experience with flexible exchange rates. In M. Baranzini (Ed.), *Advances in economic theory, op. cit.*, pp. 207–224.

Bliss, C. J. (1987). Hicks John, Richard (1904–89). *The New Palgrave: A Dictionary of Economics,* Vol. 2, 641–46, Macmillan.

Bliss, C. J., & Cippà, R. (1982). Temporary equilibrium with rationed borrowing and consistent plans. In M. Baranzini (Ed.), *Advances in economic theory, op. cit.*, pp. 45–66.

Caravale, G. A., & Tosato, D. A. (Eds.). (1980). *Ricardo and the theory of value, distribution and growth.* London/Boston: Routledge & Kegan Paul.

Casarosa, C. (1978a). A new formulation of the Ricardian system. *Oxford Economic Papers, 30*, 38–63.

Casarosa, C. (1978b). Un contributo all'analisi dei fondamenti microeconomici della teoria keynesiana della domanda effettiva. *Rivista di politica economica, 68*(11), 1371–1409.

Casarosa, C. (1981). The microfoundations of Keynes's aggregate supply and expected demand analysis. *Economic Journal, 91*(361), 188–194.

Casarosa, C. (1982a). The new view of the Ricardian theory of distribution and economic growth. In M. Baranzini (Ed.), *Advances in economic theory, op. cit.*, pp. 227–239.

Casarosa, C. (1982b). Aggregate supply and expected demand analysis in Keynes's general theory: An essay on the microfoundations. In M. Baranzini (Ed.), *Advances in economic theory, op. cit.*, pp. 67–79.

Casarosa, C. (1984). The microfoundations of Keynes's aggregate supply and expected demand analysis: A reply. *Economic Journal, 94*(376), 941–945.

Casarosa, C. (2004). Gli studi nel Regno Unito della seconda generazione. In G. Garofalo, & A. Graziani (Eds.), *La formazione degli economisti in Italia (1950–1975), op. cit.*, pp. 535–554.

Casarosa, C., & Zamagni, S. (1985). Sir John Hicks: il pensiero e l'opera. *Studi Economici, 27*, 3–75.

Cippà, R. F., & Guidi, V. (1982). Temporary equilibrium with rationing. In M. Baranzini (Ed.), *Advances in economic theory, op. cit.*, pp. 90–112.

Collard, D. A. (1984). The ascent of high theory. A view from the foothills. In D. A. Collard et al. (Eds.), *Economic theory and Hicksian themes* (pp. 1–10). Oxford: Clarendon Press.

Costabile, L., & Scazzieri, R. (2012). Il pensiero economico nei decenni successivi al secondo dopoguerra. In V. Negri Zamagni, P. L. Porta, L. Costabile, R. Faucci, C. Perrotta, R. Scazzieri, & G. Todeschini (Eds.), *Il contributo italiano alla storia del pensiero. Economia* (pp. 739–765). Rome: Enciclopedia Italiana di Scienze, Lettere ed Arti.

Delbono, F., & Denicolò, V. (1991). Incentives to innovate in a Cournot Oligopoly. *Quarterly Journal of Economics, 106*(3), 951–961.

Delbono, F., & Denicolò, V. (1993). Regulating innovative activity: The role of a public firm. *International Journal of Industrial Organization, 11*(1), 35–48.

Denicolò, V. (2002). Sequential innovation and the patent-antitrust conflict. *Oxford Economic Papers, 54*(4), 649–668.

Di Matteo, M. (2010). On Harrod's model and instability once again. *Studi e Note di Economia, 15*(2), 285–295.

Dimsdale, N. H. (1973). Review of R. S. Masera's *the term structure of interest rates: An expectation model tested on post-war Italian data. Economic Journal, 83*(330), 569–571.

Ferri, P. (1971). *La disoccupazione in un processo di sviluppo economico*. Milan: Giuffré.

Ferrulli, S. (2012). *Economisti italiani a Cambridge (1960–1980). Processi formativi, aggiornamenti teorici e nuovi orientamenti di politica economica*. Ph. D. thesis, Rome Tre.

Fubini, L. (2003). Women's unemployment in Italy. In D. Del Boca & M. Repetto-Alaia (Eds.), *Women's work, the family & social policy* (pp. 109–123). Berne/Frankfurt: P. Lang.

Goodwin, R. M. (1982b). In M. Palazzi (Ed.), *Intervista a un economista: Richard M. Goodwin*. Bologna: Clueb.

Hagemann, H. (1990). The structural theory of economic growth. In M. Baranzini, & R. Scazzieri (Eds.), *Foundations of economics, op. cit.*, pp. 144–171.

Harré, R., & Madden, E. H. (1975). *Causal powers*. Oxford: B. Blackwell.

Hicks, J. R. (1939). *Value and capital: An inquiry into some fundamental principles of economic theory*. Oxford: Oxford University Press.

Hicks, J. R. (1959). *Essays in world economics*. Oxford: Clarendon Press.

Hicks, J. R. (1965). *Capital and growth*. Oxford: Clarendon Press.

Hicks, J. R. (1973). *Capital and time: A Neo-Austrian theory*. Oxford: Clarendon Press.

Hicks, J. R. (1974). *The crisis in Keynesian economics*. Oxford: B. Blackwell.

Hicks, J. R. (1976). "Revolutions" in economics. In S. J. Latsis (Ed.), *Method and appraisal in economics* (pp. 207–218). Cambridge: Cambridge University Press.

Hicks, J. R. (1979b). *Causality in economics*. Oxford: B. Blackwell.

Hicks, J. R. (1986). Is economics a science? In M. Baranzini, & R. Scazzieri (Eds.), *Foundations of economics. Structure of inquiry and economic theory, op. cit.*, pp. 91–101.

Hicks, J. R., & Hollander, S. (1977). Mr. Ricardo and the moderns. *Quarterly Journal of Economics, 41*, 351–369.

Hildebrand, G. H. (1965). *Growth and structure in the economy of modern Italy*. Cambridge, MA: Harvard University Press.

Kindleberger, C. P. (1967). *Europe's postwar growth. The Rome of labor supply*. Cambridge, MA: Harvard University Press.

Landesmann, M. A., & Scazzieri, R. (Eds.). (2009). *Production and economic dynamics*. Cambridge: Cambridge University Press (1st ed. 1996).

Lewis, W. A. (1954). Development with unlimited supplies of labour. *Manchester School, 22*(2), 139–191.

Lindhal, E. (1939). *Studies in the theory of money and capital*. New York: Rinehart.

Lutfalla, M. (1983). Review of A. Quadrio Curzio and R. Scazzieri (Eds.), *Protagonisti del pensiero economico*, t. 3, *Rivoluzione industriale e economia politica (1817–1848)* and t. 4, *Struttura produttiva, scambio e mercati (1848–1872)*. Bologna: Il Mulino (1982), *Revue d'économie politique, 93*(4), 610–611.

Lutz, V. (1962). *Italy: A study in economic development*. Oxford: Oxford University Press.

Maneschi, A. (1993). Ricardian comparative advantage and the perils of the stationary state. In M. Baranzini, & G. C. Harcourt (Eds.), *The dynamics of the wealth of nations: Growth, distribution and structural change. Essays in honour of Luigi L. Pasinetti, op. cit.*, pp. 124–146.

Miconi, B. (1967). On Harrod's model of instability. *L'industria, 19*(4), 455–478.

Morroni, M. (1992). *Production process and technical change*. Cambridge: Cambridge University Press.

Morroni, M. (2006). *Knowlegde, scale and transactions in the theory of the firm*. Cambridge: Cambridge University Press.

Pasinetti, L. L. (1959). On concepts and measures of changes in productivity. *The Review of Economics and Statistics, 41*(3), 270–282.
Pasinetti, L. L. (1963). A multi-sector model of economic growth. Revised Ph.D. Diss., King's College, Cambridge.
Pasinetti, L. L. (1965a). Causalità e interdipendenza nell'analisi econometrica e nella teoria economica. In *Annuario dell'Università Cattolica del Sacro Cuore 1964–65* (pp. 233–250). Milan: Vita e Pensiero.
Pasinetti, L. L. (1965b). A new theoretical approach to the problems of economic growth. *Pontificiae Academiae Scientiarum Scripta Varia, 28*, 572–696.
Pasinetti, L. L. (1974). *Growth and income distribution: Essays in economic theory.* Cambridge: Cambridge University Press.
Pasinetti, L. L. (1982). A comment on the "new view" of the Ricardian theory. In M. Baranzini (Ed.), *Advances in economic theory, op. cit.*, pp. 240–242.
Pasinetti, L. L. (1986). Theory of value – A source of alternative paradigms in economic analysis. In M. Baranzini, & R. Scazzieri (Eds.), *Foundations of economics., op. cit.*, pp. 409–431.
Pasinetti, L. L., & Mariutti, G. (2008). Hick's "conversion" – From J. R. to John. In R. Scazzieri, A. Sen, & S. Zamagni (Eds.), *Markets, money and capital. Hicksian economics for the twenty-first century, op. cit.*, pp. 52–71.
Pugno, M. (1992). *Roy F. Harrod: dall'equilibriodinamico all'instabilità ciclica.* Bologna: Il Mulino.
Quadrio Curzio, A. (1993a). On economic science, its tools and economic reality. In M. Baranzini, & G. C. Harcourt (Eds.), *The dynamics of the wealth of nations: Growth, distribution and structural change. Essays in honour of Luigi L. Pasinetti, op. cit.*, pp. 246–271.
Quadrio Curzio, A. (1993b). Distribuzione della ricchezza e del reddito. In *Enciclopedia delle Scienze Sociali* (pp. 194–207). Rome: Istituto della Enciclopedia italiana Treccani.
Salter, W. E. (1961). *Productivity and technical change.* Cambridge: Cambridge University Press.
Samuelson, P. A. (1959). A modern treatment of the Ricardian theory. *Quarterly Journal of Economics*, 1–35 and 217–31.
Samuelson, P. A., & Modigliani, F. (1966). The Pasinetti paradox in neoclassical and more general models. *Review of Economic Studies, 33*(4), 269–301.
Scazzieri, R. (1981). *Efficienza produttiva e livelli di attività. Un contributo di teoria economica.* Bologna: Il Mulino.

Scazzieri, R. (1982). Scale and efficiency in model of production. In M. Baranzini (Ed.), *Advances in economic theory, op. cit.*, pp. 19–42.

Scazzieri, R. (1993a). *A theory of production: Tasks, processes and technical practices*. Oxford: Clarendon Press.

Scazzieri, R. (1993b). Action, processes and economic theory. In A. Heertje (Ed.), *The makers of modern economics* (Vol. I, pp. 84–114). Aldershot/Brookfield: E. Elgar.

Scazzieri, R., & Zamagni, S. (2008). Between theory and history: On the identity of hicks's economics. In R. Scazzieri, A. Sen, & S. Zamagni (Eds.), *Markets, money and capital. Hicksian economics for the twenty-first century, op. cit.*, pp. 1–37.

Soro, B. (2012). Harrod, Kaldor, and the idea of the "foreign trade *multiplier*". *Economia Internazionale, 65*(1), 173–187.

Zamagni, S. (1973). Struttura del capitale e crescita non uniforme, Appendix to J. R. Hicks. *Capitale e tempo. Una teoria neo-austriaca* (pp. 247–286). Milan: Etas Libri.

Zamagni, S. (1983). Strumentalismo causale *versus* realismo causale in economia. In M. C. Galavotti & G. Gambetta (Eds.), *Causalità e modelli probabilistici* (pp. 111–146). Bologna: CLUEB.

Zamagni, S. (1984). On Ricardo and Hayek effects in a Fixwage model of traverse. In D. A. Collard et al. (Eds.), *Economic theory and Hicksian themes* (pp. 135–151). Oxford: Clarendon Press.

Zamagni, V., and Zamagni, S. (2002) Italian Economists and Linacre College, The Linacre Journal, *6*, 25–38.

3

The Cantabrigiensis-Italian School of Economics (1950–1990)

3.1 Who's Who

By collating the names of the recipients of the Stringher and Mortara grants, those put forward by Carlo Casarosa[1] (2004, 550–53), by Fernando Vianello (2004), by Pierluigi Ciocca (2008) and by other sources, we may identify, according to their Italian alma mater, a number of scholars who went to Cambridge for the period 1950–75. We also provide the year of matriculation, or the year in which a grant was awarded. However, the list is not exhaustive:

1. *From the Universities of Rome*: Paolo Sylos Labini (1949); Mario Lombardo (1953); Luigi Spaventa (1957 and 1958–60); Giovanni Caravale (1958, n.a.; 1959, 1960); Paolo Leon (1958); Luigi Marini (1959); Ferruccio Marzano (1958, 1962); Duccio Cavalieri (1959;

[1] Carlo Casarosa (2004, 547), after quoting the Italians of the first generation who went to Cambridge, adds: 'In the early 1970s a new generation of young Italian economists arrives in Cambridge; among these Antonietta Campus, Giorgio Gilibert, Alessandro Roncaglia, Mario Tonveronachi, Giovanni Vaggi and Pierpaolo Varri.' Vianello (2004, 484–7) cites Michele Salvati, Salvatore Biasco, Sebastiano Brusco, Giorgio Fodor, Giancarlo de Vivo and himself as being in Cambridge from the 1960s onwards.

M. Baranzini, A. Mirante, *A Compendium of Italian Economists at Oxbridge*, DOI 10.1007/978-3-319-32219-3_3

2nd MIT); Antonio Pedone (1959); Salvatore Biasco (1959); Mario Amendola (1960, 1962); Domenico Mario Nuti (1962, 1964); Giuseppe Campa (1962, 1965); Bruno Miconi (1962, 1963); Roberto Ruberti (1963–65); Ezio Tantarelli (1965); Giorgio Questa (1966); Fernando Vianello (1966–68); Giovanni Carosio (1968); Orietta Vito Colonna (1969); Alessandro Roncaglia (1970, 1971–73); Riccardo Parboni (1972); Maurizio Franzini (1973); Stefano Vona (1975), Paolo Garonna (1973); Joseph Halevi (1974); Fabrizio Barca (1978); Roberto Ciccone (1979);

2. *From the Catholic University of Milan*: Nino Andreatta (Easter Term, 1956); Luigi L. Pasinetti (1956, n.a.; 1957); Terenzio Cozzi (1962); Alberto Quadrio Curzio (1962); Luciano Boggio (1967); Pierpaolo Varri (1970); Giancarlo Graziola (1971); Graziella Marzi (1971); Daniele Schilirò (1979);
3. *From the University of Milan and Bocconi University*: Ezio Lancellotti (1960, 1962); Giovanni Maria Ciocca (1962–63); Rolando Valiani (1964–65); Giovanni Maria Bernareggi (1965); Carlo Boffito (1969, Bocconi); Ferdinando Targetti (1972, Bocconi); Anna M. Carabelli (1973), Termini Ferrari (1975, Bocconi); Franco Donzelli[2] (1974, Bocconi); Pier Angelo Mori (1976, Bocconi); Fabio Ranchetti (1979, Università degli Studi);
4. *From the University of Naples*: Bruno Trezza (1961); Neri Salvadori (1977); Lilia Costabile (1979); Fabio Petri (1972); Carlo Panico (1978; Ph.D. 1983);
5. *From the University of Bologna*: Luca Meldolesi (1963); Giovanni Palmerio (1964, Bologna); Massimo Ricottilli (1972); Silvia Giannini (1978); Francesca Bettìo (1978); Giuliana Campanelli (1979); Elettra Agliardi (1987); Roberto Scazzieri (1992);
6. *From the University of Pavia*: Piero Garegnani (1953); Francesco Volpi (1955); Mario Sarcinelli (1956); Franco Romani (1957); L. E. Ongaro (1962); Michele Salvati (1960, 1965); Giorgio La Malfa (1961, 1966); Guido Montani (1967–68); Giovanni Vaggi (1971);
7. *From the University of Siena*: Mario Tonveronachi (1970); Ugo Pagano (1974); G. Cifarelli (1976);

---

[2] Laurea Bocconi (1973), Ph.D., Faculty of Economics and Politics, Cambridge 1990.

8. *From other universities*: Onorio Gobbato (1955, Venice); F. Buffoni (1961, Sassari); Paolo Pettenati (1961–62, Florence); F. Gallo (1961, Catania); Andrea Saba (1961, Catania); Sebastiano Brusco (1962 and 1965, Sassari); Marcello De Cecco (1964, Parma); Rieser Vittorio (1966, Turin); Antonella Picchio del Mercato (Padua); Giorgio Gilibert (1968, Turin); Amedeo Amato (1970, Genoa); Marco Eller Vainicher (1971, Florence); Antonietta Campus (1971, Sassari); Alfredo Medio (1971, Genoa); Antonio Sassu (1972 Cagliari); Annamaria Simonazzi (1976, Modena); Maurizio Zenesini (1976, Trento); Giancarlo De Vivo (1979 and 1991, Florence); Lilia Costabile (1979, Florence); Diego Gambetta (1979, Turin); Sergio Destefanis (1980, Fribourg); Gloria Vivenza (2001, Verona), Alberto Chilosi (1976–67, Pisa);
9. *From Canton Ticino* (Italian speaking Switzerland): Angelo A. Rossi (1967, Freiburg im Üechtland); Mauro Baranzini (1976: Zurich and Freiburg im Üechtland), Daniele Besomi (1986: Pavia), Marcello Corti (1980: Freiburg im Üechtland).

3.2 Piero Sraffa: The Neo-Ricardian School and the Capital Controversy

3.2.1 Introduction

The neo-Ricardian school is mainly built on the seminal works of David Ricardo and Piero Sraffa. Sraffa's seminal work *Production of Commodities by Means of Commodities* represents a critique of marginalist (i.e. neo-classical) economics and his influence has been a turning point of the 'two Cambridges capital debate'. The controversy began with Joan Robinson, Ruth Cohen and David Champernowne in the early 1950s (see Harcourt 2006, 2012a), and was taken up by the neo-Ricardian and post-Keynesian scholars, especially in the 1960s and 1970s. The unquestionable leader of the neo-Ricardian school has been Piero Sraffa, but it must be said that he often preferred to remain in the background. The list of prominent neo-Ricardians that were not Italian-born includes, in alphabetical order, Gilbert Abraham-Frois, Krishna Bharadwaj,

Avi Cohen, Maurice Dobb, John Eatwell, Christian Gehrke, Heinz Kurz, Izumi Ishiyama, Murray Milgate, Gary Mongiovi, Joan V. Robinson, Bertram Schefold, Franklin Serrano and Ian Steedman. A non-exhaustive list of Italian-born prominent neo-Ricardians, also in alphabetical order, includes Roberto Ciccone, Terenzio Cozzi, Giancarlo De Vivo, Pierangelo Garegnani, Giorgio Gilibert, Giorgio Lunghini, Roberto Marchionatti, Domenico Mario Nuti, Sergio Parrinello, Luigi Pasinetti, Fabio Petri, Massimo Pivetti, Fabio Ravagnani, Alessandro Roncaglia, Neri Salvadori, Mario Tonveronachi, Fernando Vianello. There are many more who it is not possible to mention here. Luigi Spaventa, Michele Salvati and Alberto Quadrio Curzio remain somewhat apart, as will be discussed. (The school partially overlaps with other schools of economic theory, as post-Keynesian and neo-Marxian economics.) The Italian academia is well-represented and at least ten of the scholars we have mentioned here have had strong connections with Cambridge. Unfortunately, we cannot consider them all. Nevertheless, we know that the school has grown thanks to the contributions of the whole scientific community.

3.2.2 Piero Sraffa

Piero Sraffa (Turin 1898, Cambridge 1983) was born into an affluent and cultured Jewish family. After attending the prestigious Liceo Massimo D'Azeglio, he enrolled in the Faculty of Law at the University of Turin in 1916. In 1917, he was conscripted into the Italian army and he graduated in 1920 with a thesis on Italian inflation. From April 1921 to June 1922, he was in London where, inter alia, he attended some courses at the LSE and was impressed by Edwin Cannan's lectures on classical theories of production and income distribution. He also participated in the activities of the London Labour Research Department. In the summer of 1921, during a short visit to Cambridge, he went to see Keynes

> for a meeting that turned out to be crucial for the whole of his future career. At that time, Keynes was editing a series of articles for a monthly supplement (entitled *Reconstruction in Europe*) to the weekly *Manchester Guardian Commercial.* Keynes [...] thought immediately to put young Sraffa to the test. He asked him to write an article [...] on Italy's financial

> crises. The young man felt flattered. He went back to Italy and started working on it, very hard. He wrote the article (in Italian) in a very short time, had it translated into English by a London friend, and sent it to Keynes, who realized immediately that the article was so well argued and documented as to be suitable for a scientific journal, not for a newspaper. (Pasinetti 2007, 138)

Hence, the paper was published in *The Economic Journal* (Sraffa 1922a) and a much simpler version in the *Manchester Guardian Supplement* (MGS) on 7 December 1922.

Unfortunately, 'The [MGS] article received the attention of Benito Mussolini, who, within days of its publication, sent a telegram to Angelo Sraffa, labelling Piero's article "an act of true and real sabotage of Italian finance". [...] On this occasion, Keynes suggested that Sraffa might temporarily work in England' (Porta 1984b, 15–16). Sraffa's father, who was then Rector of the Bocconi University, having received a request of abjuration by Mussolini, suggested to his son that he leave Italy in order to let things cool down. Piero went to stay[3] for a while in Lugano, Switzerland; after a couple of weeks, following his father's advice, he took a train to Calais. Nevertheless, at Dover he was denied entry to the UK as persona non grata, 'and could not be admitted into England until after the Labour Government came into office' (Porta 1984b, 16n). In 1923, Sraffa was appointed *libero docente* at Perugia and, in 1926, full Professor at Cagliari. In the same year, he published a paper in *The Economic Journal* on 'The Laws of Returns under Competitive Conditions' which challenged Marshall's theory of prices. In July 1927, Sraffa accepted an invitation by Keynes to take up a lectureship at Cambridge, a place that he would not leave until his death in 1983. Initially, he was at King's and, in 1939, he was elected to a fellowship at Trinity.

Sraffa's scientific contribution was mainly pursued along three major research lines. His first line of research was the rediscovery, reconstruction and re-evaluation of the classical approach with his edition of Ricardo's *Works and Correspondence*. The second research line was the rejection of the marginalist theory (especially Marshall's and Hayek's versions). His

[3] As he repeatedly told the first author of this volume; however, we were not able to find an entry of the Lugano hotels or accommodations.

third line of research was his analysis of value and distribution, which was firmly rooted in the classical framework of analysis. More generally, Sraffa's work, especially through his *Production of Commodities by Means of Commodities*, has often been seen as the trigger for the Cambridge neo-Ricardian school and of the 'capital theory controversy', as Geoff Harcourt has repeatedly pointed out. In this chapter, we shall consider a number of Sraffa's Italian pupils or scholars who arrived in Cambridge from the early 1950s onwards and who may be considered as belonging to the Cambridge neo-Ricardian school. Some of them were supervised or coached by him; some were supervised by other scholars, but kept in close touch with Sraffa. Some of them arrived in Cambridge after his death in 1983. Among these we might mention, in no particular order: Pierangelo Garegnani, Alessandro Roncaglia, Domenico Mario Nuti, Salvatore Biasco, Giorgio Gilibert, Giancarlo De Vivo, Antonietta Campus, Fabio Petri, Mario Tonveronachi, Roberto Ciccone and Fabio Ranchetti. Michele Salvati, Luigi Spaventa, Luigi Pasinetti (who is more of a post-Keynesian than a neo-Ricardian). Alberto Quadrio Curzio, who belongs in this list, will be considered separately later in the chapter. Finally, it is worth quoting Jean-Pierre Potier in his *Piero Sraffa, Unorthodox Economist: A Biographical Essay* (1987, 65):

> By the early sixties, Sraffa was beginning to feel that he could no longer devote himself to continuous research. In spring 1967 he told Luca Meldolesi that he had put together the scattered writings of Saint-Simon, whose work, according to him, largely anticipated Marx's political theory, but that he did not have the strength to carry through a complete edition of his works. [...] He was at the time working on the *General Index* of his edition of Ricardo's *Collected Works*, Volume XI of the series, with the help of Arnold Heertje. [...] During the sixties, many researchers were eager to meet Sraffa and to seek his advice. They were always warmly received in the bachelor's rooms, in Nevile's Court, which he had been given for life by Trinity College. [...] The young economists who came from Italy to see him included Salvatore Biasco, Sebastiano Brusco, Giorgio Gilibert, Alfredo Medio, Luca Meldolesi, Guido Montani, Domenico-Mario Nuti, Alessandro Roncaglia and Fernando Vianello. Researchers from other countries included Amit Bhaduri, Krishna R. Bharadwaj, Arun Bose and Bertram Schefold. (Potier 1987, 65)

3.2.3 Pierangelo Garegnani

Pierangelo Garegnani (1930–2011) may be considered one of the foremost pupils of Piero Sraffa; he was defined by Murray Milgate as 'a leading figure of the Cambridge School'. In the autumn of 1953, having been awarded the laurea in political science at Ghislieri's College of Pavia, he went up to Trinity College, with the support of scholarships from Trinity, Ghislieri and the British Council. At Trinity, he was officially supervised by Maurice Dobb, but he was in close contact with Piero Sraffa, also at Trinity. In December 1958, he submitted his Ph.D. thesis 'A Problem in the Theory of Distribution from Ricardo to Wicksell'; the viva took place the following year, with Joan Robinson and Lionel Robbins as his examiners. Murray Milgate, in the obituary written for the *Royal Economic Society*, maintains that the main ingredients of Garegnani's contribution are to be found in three papers: the first on heterogeneous capital in the *Review of Economic Studies* (1970), the second in the two papers in the *Cambridge Journal of Economics* (1978–79) on consumption, investment and effective demand; and the third on the classical economists and Marx in the *Oxford Economic Papers* (1984). 'These papers capture, respectively, his critique of neoclassical theory, his approach to the theory of effective demand, and his account of the theoretical core of classical economic analysis' (Murray Milgate). From 1961 to 1962 Garegnani was a Rockefeller Fellow at the *Massachussetts Institute of Technology*, and a Fellow (title F) at Trinity College in 1973–74. As he points out in *Who is Who in Economics*:

> [M]y early work was based on the distinction between the rediscovered 'classical' approach to distribution in Quesnay, Smith and Ricardo and later theory. This work was an attempt to trace in both approaches the same unsolved problem of 'measuring' capital independently of distribution. [...] From this basic, later work proceeded along three lines. The first pursued the criticism of the conception of capital in modern explanation of distribution by the demand and supply of the factors of production in terms of their reciprocal 'substitutability'. This work dealt with the implications of the 'reswitching' of techniques and 'reverse capital deepening'[4]

[4] On this point see Sect. 3.3.1.7.

> [...] The second line consisted of a clarification of the alternative classical analysis. This brought into focus its characteristic separation between the determination of relative prices and profits and that of real wages, output and technical conditions of production. This separation contrasts sharply with modern simultaneous determination. The third line used results from the previous two in order to set Keynes's propositions on the determination of aggregate output on a more solid base, thus allowing for their application to long-period theory. (Garegnani 1999, 415)

At the institutional level, Garegnani held posts at Sassari (1962–66), Pavia (1966–70), Florence (1970–74), La Sapienza, Rome (1974–92) and Roma Tre (1992 onwards). He was the director of the *Centro di Ricerche e Documentazione 'Piero Sraffa'*, and also the literary executor of the works, documents and papers left by Sraffa to the Wren Library of Trinity College, Cambridge. The *Royal Economic Society* has published an account of his scientific contribution signed by Murray Milgate.

3.2.4 Alessandro Roncaglia

Alessandro Roncaglia (1947) is correctly considered one of the most distinguished scholars of Sraffian economics and of the Cambridge school of economics of the twentieth century: he has published a large number of influential contributions dealing with his Master's works and 'the latter's resurrection of the classical approach to the theory of value and distribution' (Kurz 2002, 119). Alessandro Roncaglia was a researcher in Cambridge from 1971 to 1973, on leave from the University of Perugia, with a grant from the Italian Consiglio Nazionale delle Richerche (CNR).[5] He did not enrol for a Cambridge higher degree as he wanted to work under the guidance of Piero Sraffa (who was at that time Marshall Librarian), whom he met weekly, even outside term time, either in his office at the Marshall Library,[6] or in his quarters at Trinity. Sraffa provided

[5] It was Luigi Spaventa that 'urged me to plan (and helped me organise) a period of study at Cambridge' (Roncaglia 2013, 173).

[6] In the late 1960s and 1970s, the Librarian's office was on the upper floor of the Marshall Library; you could reach it by walking upstairs from the Library desk, or through an open passage linking the Department of Applied Economics and the upper floor of the Library. When Sraffa retired, the

him with a pass for the Marshall and University Libraries. He recalls that he attended lectures by Kaldor, Goodwin, Kahn, Dobb, Hahn and others. He had already been at Cambridge as a summer visitor at King's in 1970—together with Mario Tonveronachi and Mario Draghi—and for shorter visits to Sraffa in 1973–78. At the institutional level, he has been Professor of Economics at La Sapienza, Rome, since 1981. For many years, he has been the editor of *Moneta e Credito*, and *PSL Quarterly Review* (previously *BNL Quarterly Review*), member since 1998 of the Accademia Nazionale dei Lincei and President of the *Società Italiana degli Economisti* (2011–4). Among his publications, *The Wealth of Ideas: A History of Economic Thought* earned him in 2002 the *Blanqui Prize* of the *European Association for the History of Economic Thought*.

Roncaglia's thought has been condensed in his volume on *Piero Sraffa* published in 2001, which provides a comprehensive overview of Sraffa's life and his influence on politicians, economists and philosophers such as Gramsci, Keynes and Wittgenstein. In this long and much thought-out essay, Roncaglia closely examines Sraffa's ideas and theoretical contributions, from the critique of the Marshallian theory of the firm to his revival and reinterpretation of the classical approach. According to the author, the explicit aim of the volume is to consider 'the explosive potential of Sraffa's celebrated work *Production of Commodities by Means of Commodities*. This work provided both the solution to the problems left open by the classical theory of value and the foundations for a critique of marginalist-neo-classical theory of capital and distribution.' Roncaglia illustrates how Sraffa aimed at a complete turn-around of economic theory, from the dominant neo-classical-marginalist approach to a classical-Keynesian one. Additionally, *Production of Commodities by Means of Commodities* discusses present trends of research within this latter approach, the full impact of which has not been understood by mainstream economics. 'I enjoyed reading the book and consider it a valuable source of information and welcome contribution to the ongoing discussion', points out Heinz D. Kurz (2002, 119) in his review of Roncaglia's essay.

Office was taken up by E. A. G. Robinson. In the 1980s, the passage between the Department of Applied Economics and the upper Marshall Library was closed.

3.2.5 Domenico Mario Nuti

Domenico Mario Nuti (1937) graduated cum laude in Rome with a thesis supervised by Giuseppe Ugo Papi, and was placed in the queue for a Bank of Italy scholarship to study abroad. While waiting to go to Cambridge, he joined the Warsaw School of Planning and Statistics with a Polish Academy of Sciences fellowship. In Warsaw he was taught by Oskar Lange, Michal Kalecki, Wlodek Brus, Kazimierz Laski and others. From Warsaw, he went to King's College, Cambridge in 1962 as a research student

> where I was to remain, in various capacities, for the next 17 years. I was taught first by Nicky Kaldor, a most inspiring lecturer, 'maestro' and challenger of orthodoxies. I shone in the Cambridge Tripos and began work on a Ph.D. thesis on 'Problems of Investment Planning in the Socialist Economies'. By virtue of being a leading specialist in my chosen field, Maurice Dobb soon replaced Kaldor as my supervisor. My first research output on socialist economies—three essays on enterprise incentives, investment criteria and inflation—gained me the Stevenson Prize (1965) and a Research Fellowship at King's, followed by a tutorship, teaching lectureship and directorship of studies accompanied, from 1970, by a parallel appointment at the Faculty of Economics. (Nuti 2000, 463)

As had many others, Nuti had arrived in Cambridge just before the initial skirmishes of the 'two Cambridges controversies' on income distribution and on the theory of capital erupted between, on the one side, the neo-classical or marginalist school of thought, and, on the other side, the Marxian, Ricardian and post-Keynesian schools of thought. According to Nuti:

> A major issue was the measurability of capital, capital malleability and substitutability, the shape and very existence of aggregate production functions. The questions may seem highly esoteric but have devastating policy implications: an innocent-looking assumption of a Cobb-Douglas aggregate production function implicitly leads to assertions that income distribution is given by 'God and the engineers' (Joan Robinson) and cannot

and should not be altered; that unemployment is not due to Keynesian deficit demand but to excessive high real wages; that investment mistakes can be costlessly rectified. Like me, many knew that this was not and could not be the case and clung to the promises of any seemingly plausible alternative approach, like Piero Sraffa's *Production of Commodities by Means of Commodities*, neo-Marxian and neo-Ricardian cost-based prices, or neo-Keynesian propositions about income distribution and their possibly micro-economic extensions. (Nuti 2000, 463–64)

Nuti's main contributions, mainly completed or initiated during his 17 years at King's, first explore and develop the Austrian theory of capital and time leading to a strong criticism of the aggregate production function. Within this frame, he considers in particular the steady-state or equilibrium relationships among the wage rate, the interest rate, consumption and growth. Second, he carries out an extensive analysis of the criteria at the basis of the investment strategy in socialist countries, and he tries to construct a model of economic fluctuations and crises in the same type of economies. He has also studied macro-economic policies and the process of accumulation in planned economies—in Poland, in particular.

3.2.6 Salvatore Biasco

Salvatore Biasco (1939), after earning a degree in statistics in Rome, moved to Cambridge in 1959, where he remained for at least three years. In Italy, he was a pupil of Paolo Sylos-Labini and, in 1968, he published a volume where, inter alia, he compares the distribution theory of post-Keynesian and Sraffian models. Together with a number of distinguished colleagues, he founded the 'Modena School of Economics' where he remained until 1983, when he took up a chair of *Economia Internazionale* at La Sapienza, Rome. He was also Deputy President (1992–95) of the Società Italiana degli Economisti and, in 1982, he was awarded the Saint-Vincent Prize for economics for his volume *L'inflazione nei paesi capitalistici industrializzati*. As an Italian MP, he took a very active part in the rewriting of corporate taxation.

3.2.7 Sebastiano Brusco

Sebastiano Brusco (1934–2002) earned a degree in Agricultural Science at Sassari in 1960 and, three years later, a B.A. in economics at Cambridge, where he attended tutorials and lectures from 1961 to 1963. He then went back to Cambridge from 1965 to 1968 as a research student. In 1980, he was appointed full Professor in the Faculty of Economics at Modena, which he had contributed to setting up years earlier. Brusco has been a distinguished scholar in the fields of industrial economics and policy, regional development and industrial districts. His younger colleagues Margherita Russo and Anna Natali (2008, 2) stress, as follows, the ground-breaking contribution of Sebastiano Brusco on two related fields: 'theory and tools for analysing the industrial structure and for designing development policies. […] In Brusco's thought, a central role is played by knowledge, competence, information, education and training: as far as small firms productive systems, industrial districts, and also less developed areas are concerned. An innovative approach to policy design and intervention stems from this view, stressing mechanisms able to diffusely affect capacity, learning and perception of opportunities.' Sebastiano Brusco is also widely acknowledged for having been a pioneer of the debate on the dynamic interaction between social integration, labour market and productive set-ups at the local level (see his paper 'The Emilian Model: Productive Decentralization and Social Integration' in the 1982 issue of the *Cambridge Journal of Economics*).

3.2.8 Giorgio Gilibert

Giorgio Gilibert (1944–2016) was a full Professor of Economics at Trieste. After graduating at the University of Turin, he enrolled at Cambridge in 1968. His fields of interest included the theory of capital, economic history, and the history of economic thought. In 2003, he published a paper 'The Equations Unveiled: Sraffa's Price Equations in the Making' in *Contributions to Political Economy*. This is how he summarized his paper:

> In the first part of *Production of Commodities by Means of Commodities*, four equation systems are introduced: three are drawn up in order to solve the

> problem of relative prices; the last one is devised to define a suitable standard of prices. The book was published in 1960, but—as we are told in the preface—its 'central propositions' and a first version of the price equations had been originally conceived and written more than 30 years before, when the author was still in his twenties. Having access now to the Sraffa Papers, preserved in the Wren Library, we can ascertain the intellectual origin of the equations. In this paper the analytical path that led to the final draft of the price equation is followed, step by step, and the link between these equations and Sraffa's quest for an 'invariable standard of value' is clarified.

Gilibert's wide-ranging knowledge of classical economics and of the history of economics analysis, together with his strong Cambridge connections, led the editors of the 1987 *New Palgrave Dictionary of Economics* to ask him to write the following three entries: 'circular flow', 'revenue, gross and net' and 'production: classical theories'; two of them were retained for the 2008 edition of the *Dictionary*.

3.2.9 Giancarlo De Vivo

Giancarlo De Vivo (1946) earned his degree in law in 1968 at the University of Naples. He continued his graduate studies in economics (1971–73) at Florence, under the supervision of Pierangelo Garegnani. In the academic year 1979–80, he was senior visiting scholar at the Faculty of Economics in Cambridge, where he taught as an affiliated lecturer in the M.Phil. in economics for a number of years. In 1991–92, he was back in Cambridge as a Visiting Fellow of Trinity College. Since 1982, he has edited, jointly with John Eatwell and Murray Milgate, the journal *Contributions to Political Economy*, published by *Oxford University Press* for the Cambridge Political Economic Society. Additionally, he has contributed to the *New Palgrave Dictionary of Economics* with seven entries, among which the entry on David Ricardo is surely a masterpiece. In 2015, he was awarded the Feltrinelli Prize for social and political sciences by the *Accademia Nazionale dei Lincei* for his contribution to the reappraisal and modern revival of the classical theory of value and distribution (in particular, the physiocrats, Ricardo and Marx) and, for its modern formulation (in particular, in Keynes, Sraffa and the post-Keynesians). He has also contributed in the field of 'economics bibliography'—in particular, in his 'Adam Smith and his books' (2001b) and his *Catalogue of the Library of Piero Sraffa* (2014b). In 2000, he edited the *Collected Works of Robert Torrens* in eight volumes (edited and introduced, with a bibliography).

3.2.10 Antonietta Campus

Antonietta Campus arrived in Cambridge in 1971 from the University of Sassari. She attended lectures by Joan Robinson, Nicholas Kaldor, Maurice Dobb and Richard F. Kahn, and became acquainted with John Eatwell and Piero Sraffa. She wrote the entry 'marginalist economics' for the 1987 *New Palgrave Dictionary of Economics*—an entry that has been highly praised for providing a systematic coverage of the various strands and interpretations of marginalist economics. Professor Campus was also one of the founding members of the School of Modena. Her name is mentioned in the archive of the papers of Piero Sraffa in relation to four documents that she sent him between 1972 and 1979.

3.2.11 Fabio Petri

Fabio Petri (1949) first earned a degree in political science at Naples with a thesis on *The Cambridge Capital Controversies in Capital Theory*. After a year at the Faculty of Economics at Siena, from 1974 to 1979 he undertook post-graduate studies at Trinity College. He was then called back to Siena where, in 1990, he was appointed full Professor of Economics. He has contributed widely, inter alia, in the fields of the theory of value, capital and distribution; and also in the theory of aggregate investment, and Sraffian and Marxian economics. He wrote two entries in the 1987 *New Palgrave Dictionary of Economics*: on the 'rate of exploitation' and on 'long run and short run'. Petri's views on the present state of economic theory are best made clear in his 2004 volume *General Equilibrium, Capital and Macroeconomics*. In fact, the volume has been promoted by stressing

> that the shift in general equilibrium theory, from its early long-period to the modern very-short-period versions, has had very important

consequences which are insufficiently appreciated by large parts of the economics profession. This shift has produced new difficulties, and has undermined central tenets of neoclassical macroeconomic theory (such as the negative dependence of aggregate investment on the interest rate, or the existence of a downward-sloping demand curve for labour) which had their basis in the long-period versions where capital was treated as a single factor.

3.2.12 Mario Tonveronachi

Mario Tonveronachi has served for many years as a professor of Financial Systems in the University of Siena. He graduated at Siena in 1970, subsequently attending Trinity College, Cambridge, as a graduate student from 1971 to 1974. At Cambridge during this time many young Italian economists were undertaking research work, among whom, according to Casarosa (2004, 547), were Antonietta Campus, Giorgio Gilibert, Alessandro Roncaglia, Gianni Vaggi, Piepaolo Varri and Mario Tonveronachi himself. Tonveronachi has been a member of the editorial board of *PSL Quarterly Review*, *Moneta e Credito* and the *Journal of Post-Keynesian Economics*. He has written books and articles on Keynesian and Post-Keynesian theory, financial systems, crises and regulations, as well as on growth and distribution. He has also published extensively with Alessandro Roncaglia since the 1970s. This is how Roncaglia and Tonveronachi (2014) introduce their paper 'Post-Keynesian, Post-Sraffian Economics: An Outline', written for the *Essays in Honor of Jan A. Kregel* (himself a post-Keynesian economist):

> The authors of this chapter belong to the so-called Anglo-Italian school, being Italian economists educated at Cambridge. They were accordingly nourished with Keynesian and Sraffian ideas (plus the capital theory debate and Sylos Labini's oligopoly theory), and their initial research work was in this field, producing an interpretation of Sraffa's economics (Roncaglia 1975; see also Roncaglia 2009) and an interpretation of Keynes' economics (Tonveronachi 1983). In both cases, our interpretations differ from 'orthodox' ones—namely, from interpretations [...] relying on notions of 'long-period equilibrium' for the economy as a whole or

> ignoring the microfoundations of macro-economics or presenting unemployment as a short-period phenomenon belonging to the theory of the trade cycle. As it became clear to both of us in the fullness of time, and as we shall try to illustrate below, this is connected to methodological choices and to a different interpretation of some basic concepts. In this, we were helped by two different kinds of influences: Sylos Labini on the side of method and the Anglo-American blend of Keynesianism represented by Jan Kregel. By Anglo-American Keynesianism, we mean a unique and fruitful blend of Cambridge ideas pointing to the compatibility of the Keynesian and the 'classical' approach and of American Post-Keynesian ideas (Minsky, Weintraub) stressing the non-ergodic nature of the economy, uncertainty and the role of money and finance. (Roncaglia and Tonveronachi 2014, 40)

3.2.13 Roberto Ciccone

Roberto Ciccone earned a first degree in economics at La Sapienza in Rome and, in 1978, enrolled at Cambridge, where he earned a Diploma in economics. He is now full Professor in the Department of Economics of Roma Tre. From 1985 to 1990, he was member of the editorial board of *Political Economy. Studies in the Surplus Approach.* During his research career, he has focused on the resumption and reinterpretation of the classical theory of distribution, profit determination and relative prices. He has also contributed to the critique of marginalist (or neo-classical) economics and to the extension of the Keynesian model in order to include the dynamics of capital accumulation. Ciccone is to be accounted among the finest scholars of Sraffian economics. We should also mention his volume on *Public Debt, Aggregate Demand and Accumulation*, published in 2002.

3.2.14 Fabio Ranchetti

Fabio Ranchetti (1948) holds a degree in philosophy (Milan 1973) and an M.Phil. in economics (Trinity College, Cambridge, 1980). In Cambridge, with the support of a CNR scholarship, he wrote a dissertation 'On tâtonnement', under the supervision of Frank Hahn and Richard M. Goodwin. He is at present full Professor of Economics at the University of Pisa. His fields of research include the history of economic thought, the distribution of income, Sraffian and Keynesian economics, post-Keynesian distribution theories, and monetary economics.

***

We refer now to two distinguished scholars, whom it is difficult to classify as straight Sraffian or neo-Ricardian authors. The first is Michele Salvati. As he told us in a recent letter (dated 1st January 2016), during the first part of his academic career he was a supporter of Sraffa's approach (along the line of thought of his colleague Marco Lippi, as he adds). However, as time passed, Salvati grew progressively disenchanted with his early beliefs. This was for a variety of reasons: first, according to him, too much effort was taken up by the issue of relative prices and reswitching, and too little effort was being dedicated to the forces that determine growth, activity levels, and income and wealth distribution. In other words, Salvati is convinced that it is not possible to replace a wrong (but complete) theory with just half a theory (even better, half a 'critique'). Additionally, Salvati is convinced that the economic system cannot be easily expressed and generalized with quantitative formulae such as in the case of the natural sciences, and mathematics, in particular. For him, the role of history and institutions is too important. The second economist too difficult to label is Luigi Spaventa, who may be defined as 'Sraffian' until his 1982 U-turn, to which we shall refer later.

Michele Salvati (1937) graduated in law from Pavia (Collegio Borromeo) in 1960; in October of the same year, he enrolled at Cambridge, where he gained a BA in economics in 1965. Salvati is one of the very few to have earned a BA at Oxbridge. After one further year in Cambridge, he returned to Italy in 1966. With Fernando Vianello, Sebastiano Brusco, Andrea Ginzburg and Salvatore Biasco, he laid the foundations of the Faculty of Economics of the University of Modena and Reggio Emilia. Subsequently, he moved to the State University of Milan; he also took an active part in politics as an Italian MP (1996–2001). Salvati's research interests have moved from industrial economics and the theory of the firm in the early part of his career, to labour economics in the 1980s. In the 1990s, his main publications concerned the political economy of labour policy and the history of postwar Italian economic policy. Salvati has written 12 books and around 60 major papers, mostly in Italian. Since his return to the State University of Milan in 2001, Salvati's work shifted further towards political economy, history and political science. The turn towards a more principled blending of economics, history, political science and political philosophy—one of the many possible versions of 'political economy'—is the prominent feature of his publications of the last ten years.[7] An (almost) complete bibliography of Michele Salvati's writings up until 2006 has been assembled by Marco Leonardi: *Bibliografia degli scritti di Michele Salvati*, in G. Dosi and M. C. Marcuzzo (eds) *L'economia e la politica. Saggi in onore di Michele Salvati*, Bologna: Il Mulino 2007, 317–46.

Luigi Spaventa[8] (1934–2013) earned a degree in law at La Sapienza in Rome in 1957, with a thesis written under the supervision of Giuseppe Ugo Papi on 'La teoria delle forme di mercato'. He applied for and immediately obtained a Bonaldo Stringher research grant from the Bank of Italy, which allowed him to spend a year as a research student at King's College (1957–58), where he arrived in November 1957 together with Mario Sarcinelli. He came back to Cambridge for two years in 1959, having been awarded a senior Stringher grant by the Bank of Italy. At King's, he was supervised by Robin Marris and Nicholas Kaldor; he was also informally supervised by Piero Sraffa at Trinity. In the Sub-faculty of Economics, he obtained a B.A. degree. In 1960, jointly with Luigi Pasinetti, Spaventa published the paper 'Beyond Aggregate Models in the Theory of Economic Development'. After a critical analysis of the aggregate development models formulated by Harrod-Domar, Solow and Kaldor, in the two closing sections Pasinetti pointed out the line of enquiry he had started and would be following in the future (the dynamic analysis of disaggregated economic systems with full employment, cf. Pasinetti 1981),

[7] These are concepts drawn from Salvati's personal page at Unicreditanduniversities.eu; the whole text of his entry has been submitted and discussed with him.

[8] Guarini (2013, 249–50) points out that Luigi Spaventa's mother, Lydia De Novellis Spaventa (who died in 2000), graduated in 'lettere e filosofia' (with Gianni Gentile) and in 'political science'. She had started her academic activity with Corrado Gini, who, in 1936, founded the 'Facoltà of scienze statistiche, demografiche ed attuariali' at what would later be named La Sapienza. In 1966, she was awarded 'La libera docenza' in social statistics, a type of exam for future professors.

while Spaventa sketched out an analysis of the case of economic systems in intermediate stages of development (Roncaglia 2013, 177). In the following years (1960 to 1969–70), Spaventa's contribution is very much in line with those of Sraffa, Garegnani, Pasinetti, Harcourt and many others in carrying out the controversy against Cambridge, MA, in the capital theory debate. In the academic year 1968–69, he was Visiting Fellow at Oxford, where he attended Hicks's lectures and seminars. A first reordering of Spaventa's scientific strategy was in sight:

> Spaventa's 1970 article in *Oxford Economic Papers* represented not only a resumption of the 'Sraffian' criticism of neoclassical distribution theory, but also—perhaps above all—an attempt to take it in a different direction, as indicated by Hicks in *Capital and Growth* [...]. It is a line of analysis that in some respects shows certain affinities [...] with that adopted by Kaldor (1956) and then by Luigi Pasinetti [...]: working on the basis of different saving propensities of capitalists and workers, it forges a link between the rate of growth and rate of profit. (Roncaglia 2013, 194)

During the 1970s, according to Roncaglia:

> Spaventa continued to follow the developments in the theory of capital, reading and discussing the various contributions made by others, but showing an increasing scepticism towards Sraffian modelling, eventually losing patience with it, given the urgency of the material problems of economic life. In his research activity, which played such an important part in his professional life, Spaventa provided some highly significant contributions in various fields: to the theory of economic development (and dualism), the pure theory of capital and distribution, the framing of economic policy, the connection between inflation and income distribution, the political economy of public debt, and the sequence of monetary regimes within the EU. (Roncaglia 2013, 194)

The second, and more strident, reordering of Spaventa's scientific strategy came in 1982, when he published a paper with the title 'A U-turn in Economic Theory'. Essentially, Spaventa called for the reconstruction of economics also via a number of postulates of the neo-classical synthesis, since 'the neo-Ricardian approach has, at least in some of its extreme formulations, ended up by throwing away with so much dirty water also creatures of vital utility for analysis', and consequently confining it 'to a useless limited scope, in which demand, money, financial assets and even the dynamics find no room'.[9] In the middle of a distinguished academic career (at Palermo, Perugia and La Sapienza, Rome), from 1976 to 1983 Spaventa was a member of the Italian parliament. In 1988–99 he was Treasury Minister, and in 1993–94 Budget Minister. From 1998 to 2003, he was chairman of CONSOB, the Italian public authority responsible for the Italian securities market. He was a member of the editorial board of the *Banca Nazionale del Lavoro Quarterly Review* and *Moneta e Credito*, where he played an active part, providing appraisal of articles submitted for publication, offering suggestions and critical observations, and publishing himself at least 13 papers (three of which he co-authored).

3.3 Luigi L. Pasinetti: Back to King's College from Oxford, October 1961

From October 1961 to September 1976, Luigi Pasinetti primarily worked and taught in Cambridge. Pasinetti's main scientific output consists of some 120 papers, mainly published in international journals and in four volumes published by *Cambridge University Press*. His scientific programme may be divided into six separate but strongly inter-related strands. They represent ground-breaking contributions in the fields of the theory of structural change, growth, value, income distribution, capital accumulation and technological change. We shall, of course, consider these issues with respect to the whole contribution of the Cambridge school of economics, and by bringing some of them together. Two strands of Pasinetti's scientific programme—the measurement of productivity changes; and Ricardo and classical political economy (in particular, the Ricardian model of growth and distribution)—have already been considered (see Section 2.2 above) since, in part, they were developed and published while he was at Nuffield College, Oxford. However, the following strands were developed while he was back at Cambridge:

[9] Quoted in Roncaglia (2013, 189–90), his translation. He then adds: 'This seems to me a bit too extreme'.

- The first two Cambridges controversy: on profit determination, income distribution and capital accumulation;
- The second two Cambridges controversy: on capital theory;
- On structural dynamics and vertical integration—that is, on the formulation of the concept of vertically integrated sectors and their relation to Sraffa's sub-systems;
- On the pure labour theory of value.

3.3.1 Pasinetti on Profit Determination, Income Distribution and Capital Accumulation

The first two Cambridges controversy that erupted—primarily between Pasinetti, Kaldor and Robinson, on one side, and Meade-Samuelson and Modigliani on the other—sparked off in the mid-1960s. In the frame of this controversy, Pasinetti has written the most widely known and quoted contribution in *The Review of Economic Studies* 1962, with the title 'Rate of Profit and Income Distribution in Relation to the Rate of Economic Growth'. As was originally pointed out in Baranzini and Harcourt (1993, Introduction), this paper has, over a span of 50 years, generated at least 400 papers in scholarly journals, numerous books and is a 'must' reference in a large number of textbooks on economic analysis.[10] In his seminal paper, Pasinetti starts with a critique of Kaldor's (1956) growth model; he then postulates to two different and positive saving rates—one for the workers, and one for the capitalists or entrepreneurs. He then goes on to show that the equilibrium rate of profits is totally independent of the saving behaviour of the working class; it is determined only by the saving rate of the pure capitalists (s_c) and by the rate of growth of the system (n). (The solution $P/K = n/s_c$, is known as Pasinetti's Theorem, or the New Cambridge Equation.) Such a rate of profits is, in particular, independent of the production function and of the capital/output ratio. In this way, the Cambridge (or post-Keynesian) school was in a position (a) to provide a solution to the Harrod-Domar dilemma by specifying an aggregate saving ratio determined by the exogenously given rate of

[10] For an exhaustive list, see Baranzini (1991a); Baranzini and Mari (2011); Baranzini and Mirante (2013); for an assessment of this topic, see also Harcourt (1972, Chap. 5; 2006, Chap. 7; 2012a).

growth of population, capital/output and entrepreneurs' propensity to save; (b) to determine the long-period equilibrium value of the rate of profits, the distribution of income between profits and wages, and the distribution of disposable income between the classes; and (c) to allow for the existence of an income residual (very much in line with classical and neo-Ricardian models) —namely the wages, consistent with the assumption of a relationship between the savings of that class of individuals (the capitalists or entrepreneurs) who determine the process of production and the patterns of capital accumulation. This range of results is obtained by Pasinetti within a fairly simple framework and on the basis of relatively few assumptions, much less 'hybrid, opposite and extreme' than those of the neo-classical model. It is worth noting that, in *The Review of Economic Studies* of 1966, the opening paper by Samuelson and Modigliani, written with the aim of rejecting the post-Keynesian approach, was followed by a reply by Pasinetti, and also by two papers supporting Pasinetti by Nicky Kaldor and by Joan Robinson. Stemming from the Kaldor/Pasinetti model, we find a very high number of subsequent contributions branching out in various directions and covering many aspects of the wider research programme relevant for the general topic of income distribution, profit determination and capital accumulation, from both theoretical and applied perspectives. Among the research lines grafted onto the Kaldor/Pasinetti model, we may distinguish at least the following seven.[11]

3.3.1.1 The Introduction of a Differentiated Rate of Return on Savings for the Classes

This hypothesis was first explored by Laing (1969), Harcourt (1972, 217) and Balestra and Baranzini (1971); it has inspired a large literature. It was also taken up by Pasinetti (1974, 139–41) who showed that, under general conditions, this hypothesis reinforces the validity of the Cambridge Equation. The implications of the assumption of a different rate of return for the accumulated savings are far-reaching. It directly affects the distri-

[11] In order to discuss the seven research lines, we draw again on Baranzini and Harcourt (1993, Introduction) as they were elaborated by the first author.

bution of income between classes, and it affects the overall saving ratio and the patterns of wealth accumulation. On this point, see also Maneschi (1974), Campa (1975), Pasinetti's reply (1975), Baranzini (1975b, 1976, 1991a), Fazi and Salvadori (1981), Pasinetti's reply (1983), Salvadori and Panico (1993) and Panico (1985, 1987, 1988, 1998).

3.3.1.2 The Introduction of the Monetary Sector and of Portfolio Choice

The contributions in this field were first motivated by a desire to assess the neutrality of money in these caste-models of growth and distribution. Second, it was important to determine whether the equilibrium rate of interest, in a monetary context, would maintain the same characteristics as in the real world. The introduction of the monetary factor and of the portfolio choice (where groups of individuals or classes may choose among different assets with different rates of return and different variances) has the merit of bringing together the 'objectivist' and 'subjectivist' Keynesian research programme. Additionally, stochastic models including portfolio choice, under fairly general conditions, confirm the polarization of different socio-economic classes, with a very different rate of wealth accumulation (see Baranzini 1976, 1991b, Chap. 7; Baranzini and Mari 2011; Baranzini and Mirante 2013). See also Pettenati (1993), Mastromatteo (1996, 2000), Delli Gatti (1987), Delli Gatti and Gallegati (1990), Commendatore (2002, 2003) and Seccareccia (1996).

3.3.1.3 The Stability Analysis and the Long-Term Properties of the Model

Many authors have considered the adjustment time required for the economy to return to the steady-state situations from any initial disturbance, as well as stability conditions, in general. The adjustment time which is required to arrive at the steady-state solutions (or to return to them, in the case of initial disturbances) is, in general, quite long. Taniguchi (1987) has shown that, in the specific case of the Kaldor/Pasinetti model, there exists a 'traverse' which, from one steady-state equilibrium, approaches asymptotically a new long-run equilibrium path provided that the rate of profits is constant over the long period. This is, however, quite understandable in a long-term steady-state model, where changes in the distribution of income must be matched by changes in the distribution of wealth from which capital income is earned. Above all, the Kaldor-Pasinetti model displays good local and global stability. One should also bear in mind that its chief aim was not to determine the rapidity of convergence towards the steady-state but, rather, to study the mechanisms that, under general conditions of long-term equilibrium, determine the distribution of income and wealth. Given an external shock, Mückl (1978, 1984) has shown that, as the economy converges towards long-term equilibrium, the distribution of income will still be determined by the behavioural parameters of both classes. Most analyses in this area confirm the stability of the model and its ability to adapt to external shocks.

3.3.1.4 The Introduction of a Public Sector

Another line of enquiry has been taken up by a number of authors who considered the implications of the introduction into the post-Keynesian model of a public sector with its own propensity to save, to consume and to run into deficits or surpluses. The starting point is Steedman (1972), who considers the case of a perfectly balanced government budget, and shows that the existence of government expenditure and taxes should not affect the validity of the Kaldor/Pasinetti theorem while, except for quite particular cases, it denies the possibility of the Meade-Samuelson-Modigliani's Dual Theorem. Furthermore, in the case of a government budget deficit or surplus, the Cambridge Equation maintains its relevance. Indeed, in this specific case (see Pasinetti 1989b, replying to Fleck and Domenghino 1987, 1990; Denicolò and Matteuzzi 1990) it may be proved that the equilibrium rate of profits is determined by the natural rate of growth divided by the capitalists' propensities to save, here 'modified' by the effects of both taxations on profits and of government deficit (surplus) spending. See also Mastromatteo (1989, 1994), Baranzini (1991a, b, 1992, 1995), Panico (1997, 1999) and Pasinetti (1989a).

3.3.1.5 The Introduction of the Micro-Foundations into the Model

The aim of this research line is not exclusively that of providing some micro-foundations to the post-Keynesian model of distribution and accumulation but, rather, that of providing a framework where the propensities to save of the various classes are not simply exogenously given, but are a function of economic, demographic and institutional parameters of the system. The results obtained in this framework have provided us with new insights into the micro-mechanisms of the accumulation of savings and of the inter-generational transmission of wealth. In this way, the historical aspects of savings and capital accumulation are brought to the forefront.[12]

3.3.1.6 The Distribution of Wealth and the Income Shares of the Economic Classes

Still another area of research has been concerned with the determination of the share of income and wealth (both intergenerational and life-cycle) accruing to each class of the system. This aspect is important, since the seminal works mentioned above only focused on the distribution accruing to the factors of production on the basis of the value of the equilibrium rate of profits. The contributions in this area have, in certain cases, led to the formulation of models where the level of aggregate saving of the system is determined by the type of income and not by class status. This, of course, tends to weaken the hypothesis of constant propensities to save related to the existence of homogeneous socio-economic classes, and introduces the possibility of a more flexible approach to the treatment of savings.

3.3.1.7 Other General Aspects of the Kaldor/Pasinetti Model

In particular, we should mention the inclusion of other types of socio-economic classes and the applicability of the Meade-Samuelson and Modigliani Dual Theorem. A large number of papers have considered

[12] On this point see, for instance, Britto (1969, 1972) and Baranzini (1991a).

the existence of other types of socio-economic classes, mainly stimulated by the contribution of James Tobin (in 1960) where the Kaldor/Pasinetti model is generalized to include many sub-classes of capitalists and workers. Additionally, the relevance of the Meade-Samuelson and Modigliani Dual Theorem (dubbed the 'Anti-Pasinetti' Theorem) has drawn increasing attention. (See, for instance, the April 1991 issue of the *Oxford Economic Papers* with contributions by Miyazaki and Samuelson, following Baranzini 1975a.)

A similar line of inquiry was also taken up by Augusto Schianchi (see Paragraph 2.3.8 above) in 1978 in his paper 'Growth and Distribution in a Three-Class Model: A Note', which starts by quoting Stiglitz (1975, 1328), according to whom 'the basic Cambridge equation, that the rate of return on capital is equal to the rate of growth divided by the savings propensity of capitalists, is only true if there is no land, no exhaustible natural resources, etc.'. In his paper, Schianchi verifies the validity of the Cambridge Equation. He develops a three-class model where rentiers earn an income equal to $R + P/K{\cdot}K_r$ with a propensity to save equal to s_r. In this case, Schianchi obtains two solutions for the equilibrium rate of profits: the first is equal to the Cambridge Equation $[P/K = n/s_c]$, while the second, not surprisingly, is equal to the Dual Theorem $[1/Y = s_w/I]$. Then, Schianchi (1978, 105) proceeds to differentiate the rate of savings of the classes on the basis of the type of income earned: in this way, the savings function of the system becomes $S = s_c\ P/K\ K_c + s_{ww}\ W + s_{wp}\ P/K\ K_w + s_{rr}\ R + s_{rp}.P/K\ K_r$. In this case, the first solution for the equilibrium rate of profit (equal to the rate of interest) is, again, the Cambridge Equation or the Kaldor-Pasinetti theorem $P/K = n/s_c$, while the second solution may be obtained by solving the following equation $s_{ww} + R/Y\,(s_{rr}\ s_{wp} - s_{ww}\ s_{rp})\ 1/s_{rp} = 0$. As Schianchi notes, in a three-class economy where rentiers earn a normal profit rate on their accumulated savings and, additionally, earn a rent equal to R, while the capitalists earn a normal profit rate on their capital, and workers earn their usual income from wages and from accumulated savings (with a usual P/K interest rate), the Cambridge Equation represents a general solution for which the capital stock of the three classes increases at the equilibrium rate $n = I/K$. Nevertheless, an interesting by-product of the analysis concerns the applicability of the Meade-Samuelson and Modigliani Dual Theorem: in this case, when it applies (indeed, for very unrealistic values of the propensities to save) the distribution will depend also on the propensities to save of the rentiers class.

Finally, we introduce a note on Piero Garegnani's position in this field of analysis. Garegnani has always been lukewarm, to say the least, with respect to the Kaldor/Pasinetti or Cambridge Equation $P/K = n/s_c$. This is particularly in relation to Joan Robinson's and (to a certain extent) Nicky Kaldor's early contributions; and less to do with Pasinetti's successive propositions and outcomes (of a more 'normative' nature, especially in the case of his 'natural rate of profits'). (We owe this point to Enrico Bellino.) Essentially, Garegnani—together with other scholars such as Ferdinando Vianello and, to a certain extent, also John Eatwell—is uneasy with the idea that, in order to have a higher rate of growth of the system, it is necessary to reduce the share of wages. In fact, Garegnani argues that, in the presence of under-capacity (not an unrealistic assumption), total output may be increased without increasing the profits share and so reducing the share of wages. These aspects have been considered in Garegnani (1962, 1992). In the latter case, Garegnani discusses the strategy following which it is possible to sustain a growth process without decreasing the share of wages.

3.3.2 Pasinetti on Capital Theory

In the mid-1980s, John Eatwell, Murray Milgate and Peter K. Newman, the editors of *the New Palgrave Dictionary of Economics*, first published in 1987, asked Luigi Pasinetti and Roberto Scazzieri to write the entry 'Capital Theory: Paradoxes'. Somewhat surprisingly, the same entry was also included in the 2008 version of the *New Palgrave Dictionary of Economics*, this time edited by S. N. Durlauf and L. E. Blume, who have no connections to the Cambridge school. This proves the centrality that Pasinetti has played in the controversy on capital theory. As pointed out in Baranzini and Harcourt (1993, 9), it was in the 1950s that economists first began to believe that it could no longer be taken for granted that there is a unique, unambiguous profitability ranking of production techniques in terms of physical capital intensity along the scale variation of the rate of profits. According to Pasinetti (2003, 227):

> Up to the 1966 QJE [*Quarterly Journal of Economics*, 503–83], many skirmishes had indeed taken place, especially between Joan Robinson and Bob Solow—rather harsh in tones, but hardly convincing in substance. The real point of departure of the controversy was provided by the last chapter—XII: 'Switch in methods of production'—of Piero Sraffa's (1960) book, where it was shown that the same method of production can become the most profitable one of many different levels of the wage-rate/rate-of-profit distribution curve, thus contradicting the neoclassical basic contention of a monotonic inverse relationship between capital and its 'price' (the rate of profits). For a few years nobody paid much attention to Sraffa's result. For example, Joan Robinson—who came across it by chance—called it a 'curiosum'. Indirectly, it was Samuelson (1962) who revived it. He first tried to construct a 'surrogate production function'; and then, since the conditions to be imposed were extraordinarily restrictive, he made a conjecture, which David Levhari (1965), a graduate student of Samuelson, developed into a full *non-switching theorem*. This theorem, if true, would have falsified Sraffa and would have given full generality to Samuelson's 'surrogate production function'. (Pasinetti 2003, 227)

Hence, in the early 1960s Paul Samuelson, together with a number of other fellow economists, started looking for the conditions that would ensure a strictly monotonic relation between the rate of profits and capital intensity (capita/labour ratio) even in the presence of a non-linear relation between the wage rate and the rate of profits. This was claimed, as Pasinetti points out above, to have been found by David Levhari, in an article published in 1965 in the *Quarterly Journal of Economics*. Here, Levhari claimed to have shown that while reswitching and capital-reversing could occur in an industry, they would not occur in the economy as a whole. Geoff Harcourt has often maintained (also in private conversations with the first of the present authors) that Piero Sraffa, having read Levhari's paper, asked him to disprove his findings. Harcourt replied, 'I cannot master matrix algebra', so Sraffa asked Pasinetti instead. Whether this is true or not remains to be seen. In any case, the refutation of Levhari's thesis came promptly from Pasinetti in a paper presented at the *First World Congress of the Econometric Society* held in Rome in 1965. That paper gave rise to a host of other papers (and to a discussion on both sides of the Atlantic among economists who had participated at the World

Congress) gathered together in a 'Symposium on Capital Theory' by the *Quarterly Journal of Economics*, November 1966. Paul Samuelson wrote his 'summing up' paper, as well as a note with David Levhari, in which they said that the reswitching theorem was wrong. It is worth noting that the first paper of this symposium was Luigi L. Pasinetti's paper 'Changes in the Rate of Profits and Switches of Techniques'. The remaining structure of the symposium was: David Levhari and Paul A. Samuelson, 'The Nonswitching Theorem is False'; Michio Morishima, 'Refutation of the Nonswitching Theorem'; Michael Bruno, Edwin Burmeister and Eytan Sheshinski, 'The Nature and Implications of the Reswitching of Techniques'; Piero Garegnani, 'Switching of Techniques';[13] and Paul A. Samuelson, 'A Summing Up'. In 1969, Pasinetti published a new paper in *The Economic Journal* ('Switches of Techniques and the "Rate of Return" in Capital Theory'):

> Pasinetti shares this methodological view for his next major foray in capital theory was his 1969 *Economic Journal* article on the relevance of the 'new' results for Fisherian theory. The latter itself had a principal part to play in the modern debates when Solow (1963) used it as the means to get away—he claimed—from the aggregate production function, aggregate 'capital' and 'its' marginal product, preferring to pitch the analysis in terms of intertemporal prices and, in particular, to concentrate on the social rate of return on investment. (Baranzini and Harcourt 1993, 10–11)

Pasinetti's 1969 paper was again attacked, especially by Robert Solow, Christopher Dougherty, John Craven, Christopher C. Bliss and Avinash Dixit. The main point remains, however, the disjunction between the

[13] In his second footnote, Garegnani stresses that 'Levhari's conclusions were first challenged by Dr. Pasinetti in a paper delivered at the Congress of the Econometric Society, September 1965.' He continues: 'The possibility of the "return" of a system had been stated with a view to its implications for a critique of the traditional theory of distribution—by Mr. Sraffa in his *Production of Commodities by Means of Commodities* (Cambridge: Cambridge University Press 1960), § 92 and 94. That possibility had earlier been noticed by Mrs. Robinson ('The Production Function and the Theory of Capital', *Review of Economic Studies*, XXI (1953–54), 106; also, *The Accumulation of Capital*; London: Macmillan 1956, pp. 417–18) and by Mr. Champernowne ('The Production Function and the Theory of Capital: A Comment', *The Review of Economic Studies*, XXI (1953–54), 119, 130). The contention in Levhari's article was apparently that, while the 'return' of a method is possible, the same is not true for a system (*op. cit.*, 103).' (Garegnani 1966, 554n).

'profit-wage rate' relationship and the 'technique of production-profit rate' relationship. More specifically, slight changes in the rate of profits may lead to sharp variations in the choice of techniques of production in terms of capital intensity (per man). This is a property of our economic systems, first pointed out by Pasinetti, which has never been challenged. The implications are far-reaching: for the price system, variations may be quite small but, for the choice of techniques and the distribution of income, such variations will be much greater. This is what Pasinetti maintains in his paper on the 'Cambridge Capital Controversies':

> A vast literature followed. Attempts were made to minimize the shattering effects of reswitching and capital reversing on neoclassical models, by focusing on an intertemporal general equilibrium scheme, where reswitching and capital reversing can be hidden or confused with many other difficulties and causes of instability of the solutions. Yet, even among the general equilibrium theorists, one fact remains undisputed as a result of the 1966 *QJE* symposium, namely that the relationship between capital—whatever the way in which it is measured or aggregated (Fisher 1971)—and its 'factor price' is in general a non-monopolistic relation. This characteristic is contrary to the assumptions underlying neoclassical capital theory, including the recent models on endogenous growth. (Pasinetti 2003, 228)

In addition, he concludes thus:

> Samuelson closed the 1966 *Symposium* with a few wise words (p. 583): 'If all this causes headaches for those nostalgic for the old time parables of neoclassical writing, we must remind ourselves that scholars are not born to live an easy existence. We must respect, and appraise, the facts of life.' Current neoclassical economists do not seem to like Samuelson's 'facts of life'. True, we have been told by Thomas Kuhn (1962) that 'normal science' must sometimes put up with black spots like inconsistencies and adverse evidence, ignoring them temporarily and waiting for further investigations. But the non-monotonic adverse relation between capital intensity and rate of profit seems to be more than a mere black spot. Indeed, Sraffa thought that it could swallow up the whole neoclassical theory of capital—a 'black hole', we might say, rather than a black spot. (Pasinetti 2003, 228)

3.3.3 Pasinetti on Structural Dynamics and Vertical Integration

Roberto Scazzieri and Michelle Baddeley, the conveners of the conference in honour of Luigi L. Pasinetti, sponsored by the Cambridge Political Economy Society, that took place at Gonville and Caius College, Cambridge, on 12th–13 September 2012, maintain that:

> In modern economic systems permanent and irreversible changes coexist with changes that are transitory and reversible. The economics of structural change focuses on permanent changes in the fundamental relationships among components of any given economic system, independently of whether they are brought about by *cumulative changes* negligible in the short run or by *structural breaks* leading to changes in the long-run properties of the system. There has been a revival of interest in the long-run transformations of socio-economic systems in many different fields of research, such as when considering the long-term dynamic prospects of advanced economies or the catching-up processes of less developed economies. (Baddeley and Scazzieri 2012)

Pasinetti's 'vertical integration' approach provides a way of representing the dynamics of the economic system that has been crucial for the development of economic analysis since its early application in the *Wealth of Nations* by Adam Smith

> The concept of vertical economic structure, in its dynamic applications, has been mainly associated with the analysis of technological requirements for economic expansion (Smith), or with the technological interrelatedness in its implications for the diffusion of particular impulses (Pigou). On the other hand, vertical integration has been linked with the autonomous role of effective demand on the dynamic path (Malthus and Keynes). The analytical formulation introduced by Pasinetti provides a logical framework in which technological and demand conditions may be integrated in order to give a comprehensive interpretation of the dynamics of the 'wealth of nations', concerning both its absolute level and possible changes in its composition (structural economic dynamics). (Baranzini and Scazzieri 1990, 299)

Step by step, Pasinetti's work became a 'theoretical essay on the dynamics of industrial systems'; its publication was held back by two elements, which account for the long period that elapsed since it was first written for a Ph.D. dissertation at Cambridge and submitted at the end of 1962. The first of such elements is connected with the publication of Sraffa's *Production of Commodities by Means of Commodities*, which brought attention back to the concept of 'circularity' in economic theory. Pasinetti's dynamic analysis had already the advantage of avoiding the fixity of coefficients that had forced inter-industry analysis 'into a strait-jacket'. A few years later, Pasinetti (1973) was able to establish a link with Sraffa's analysis and to work out, without any loss of generality, all analytical inter-industry connections. Pasinetti put forward a vertically integrated model explicitly derived from the elimination of inter-industry flows of intermediate commodities:

> Pasinetti introduces a vertical integration of production processes that allows a reclassification of the inter-industry commodity flow so as the intermediate input requirements for each produced commodity are reduced to the corresponding quantity of labour input and to a certain residual quantity of physical means of production. This procedure can be performed more than once so that eventually one is left with a negligible residual of physical means of production and with the quantity of labour input directly and indirectly required to produce the commodity under consideration. In the particular case in which the starting point is provided by a production technology, in which commodities are produced by means of labour and other produced commodities, one is left with an economic system of the 'pure labour type'. (Baranzini and Scazzieri 1990, 241)

In this case, the stock of each particular intermediate commodity (performing the role of capital goods) is also split into distinct components depending on the final use with which they may be associated. For example, the total quantity of steel used as an intermediate commodity in the whole economic system has to be split into as many parts as there are possible uses. As a result, the overall economic system ends up by being split into as many sub-systems as there are final uses. It is thus reduced to 'A society of individuals [who] carry out an activity of production and an activity of consumption. All consumption goods are made by labour alone; labour is therefore the only "factor of production"' (Pasinetti 1986, 421).

According to this framework of analysis, the production process is represented in its purest form: men produce commodities by means of their activity alone, and the produced commodities are used only for their personal consumption. As a result, no intermediate goods or services need to be taken into account. However, the same 'one way' picture of the overall technology may be maintained if the procedure of vertical integration, which has been outlined above, is applied to a production technology in which commodities are produced by means of labour and other commodities (labour and intermediate inputs). For, in this case, the produced commodities that may be used as inputs in each other's production are reclassified depending on the type of *final* consumption good in whose production they are indirectly used. (For example, the corn used as an input for the production of machine tools to be used in the textile sector will now appear as a quantity of corn directly used in the textile sector.) As pointed out in Baranzini and Scazzieri (1990, 241–42), this ingenious device put forward by Pasinetti allows economic analysis to 'break' the structure of the 'circular flow', and to bring forth the uni-directionality underlying the production process. Once this is achieved, only one other logical step is required to obtain an increasingly smaller residual of produced inputs by iteration of the vertical integration procedure outlined above. Pasinetti's (1973) contribution to the study of vertical integration rigorously outlines the logic of uni-directionality in the specification of economic structure. Pasinetti provides two important insights into the concept of economic structure; that is:

- A classification of the concept of uni-directionality in the analysis of the relationship between production and consumption process;
- The presentation of a method of inquiry that allows for the consideration of the aspects of uni-directionality in the framework of circular economic structure. (This means that uni-directional linkages may be focused on both in a completely circular structure and in a vertical structure including sub-systems of a circular type; see Baranzini and Scazzieri 1990, 242.)

Finally, we may say that the exclusion in Pasinetti's analysis of the intermediate commodities provides a sort of 'short-cut' for a direct link between the technological conditions determining the 'productive power' of the economic system (as influenced by technical progress) and the level and composition of effective demand. Additionally, vertical integration allows for the handling of technical progress without unsettling the relationship between changes in the productive potentiality of the economic system and the level of disposable income. The latter, in fact, determines the level and composition of effective demand, which is so crucial in Keynesian macro-economic models.

3.3.4 Pasinetti on the Pure Labour Theory of Value

Pasinetti (1986) argues that exchange-production duality may be traced back to a deeper dichotomy in the theories of value. Many precious insights are to be gained from the pre-theoretical stages of the discussions on value, where diverging principles become acceptable when being considered within a normative framework. Pasinetti then identifies in Adam Smith and William Stanley Jevons the reference points for discussing two alternative paradigms: (a) the *pure-preference model* (or pure-exchange model), which looks at all economic problems as if they were problems of optimum allocation of resources, and where prices are determined by individuals' preferences and resources endowment (Adam Smith); (b) a *pure-labour economy model*, where production and exchange are inherently linked by labour specialization and where prices emerge from the necessity of an extensive division of labour (William Stanley Jevons). In particular, Pasinetti stresses the importance for each paradigm of developing its basic structure by concentrating on one single principle. Pasinetti maintains that alternative visions of the economic system may be associated with different aims of analysis—each of them with a large degree of autonomy.

As originally expounded in Baranzini and Harcourt (1993, 19–21), starting from this analytical scheme, Pasinetti (1986, 1988) put forward a 'pure' labour theory of value and distribution. He first introduced a set of 'newly defined sub-systems', much more comprehensive than those considered in Pasinetti (1973, 1981, Chap. 7) since 'they include not only the labour and the means of production for the reproduction of each subsystem, but also the labour and the means of production necessary to its *expansion* at its particular rate of growth ($g + r_i$)' (Pasinetti 1988, 126–27). By additionally assuming that:

(a) the rate of growth of these 'newly defined sub-systems' may be different (due to a different rate of growth of technical progress and changes in the level and/or composition of demand);
(b) there will be a particular natural rate of profits for each hyper subsystem (where a natural rate of profits is defined as a rate of profits which is equal to the rate of growth of demand for the corresponding consumption good); and
(c) defining by $l^{(i)}$ the vector of the vertically hyper-integrated labour coefficient for commodity i,

Pasinetti (1988, 129) obtains the specific set of natural prices $p^{(i)} = (l^{(i)})\cdot w$, where w is the wage rate. This result is remarkable since, as Pasinetti himself points out, it is a complete generalization of the pure labour theory of value; in fact, each physical quantity of any consumption good is shown to be unambiguously related to a physical quantity of labour. What is more important 'the two [i.e. physical quantities of consumption and of labour] have, between them, a physically self-replacing, and expanding, circular process' (Pasinetti 1988, 130). Not surprisingly, Pasinetti's analysis reveals a strong intellectual sympathy with Adam Smith; first, for the representation of the productive system as a set of vertically integrated sectors, and then for the associated concept (common to both Pasinetti and Smith) that labour may be considered as the ultimate source of wealth; *A Theoretical Essay on the Dynamics of the Wealth of Nations*, the subtitle of Pasinetti's 1981 volume *Structural Change and Economic Growth*, is significant in this respect.

Finally, in the volume *Structural Economic Dynamics: A Theory of the Economic Consequences of Human Learning* (1993), Pasinetti offers a theoretical investigation of the development through time, as a consequence of human learning, of a 'pure labour economy'; that is to say, an economy in which production activity is carried out by labour alone—'labour unassisted by any intermediate commodity' (as the author himself defines it). The theory is simple; yet it is aimed at catching a number of basic features of our industrialized societies. Economists have known for a long time of two basic phenomena at the root of the long-term movements of our industrial societies: capital accumulation and technical progress. Nevertheless, according to Pasinetti, the privileged position has always been given to capital accumulation. In Pasinetti's 1993 volume, this approach is reversed and technical progress is assigned the central role. Within a multi-sector framework, he first describes (against a background of 'natural relations') the structural dynamics of prices, of production and of employment (implied by differentiated rates of productivity growth and of expansion of demand); he then discusses a whole series of problems that arise at the institutional level. According to Pasinetti, personal and social learning, know-how and diffusion of information emerge as the fundamental factors accounting for the features and fate of industrial societies: the source of their wealth, but also the source of their troubles. The 'pure labour theory of value' allows Pasinetti to shift the theory of long-term economic development from a traditional framework based on capital accumulation to new foundations based on learning, technical progress and diffusion of knowledge. Numerous other Italian economists have intervened in the above mentioned lines of inquiry, and we would refer to the reference bibliography at the end of the volume.

3.4 Other Post-Keynesian Economists

3.4.1 Introduction

According to Geoff Harcourt who, with Luigi Pasinetti, is the senior living post-Keynesian economist, post-Keynesianism is 'a *portemanteau* term which is used to contain the work of a heterogeneous group of economists who nevertheless are united not only by their dislike of mainstream of neoclassical theory and the IS/LM general equilibrium version of "Keynesian" theory; but also by their attempts to provide coherent alternative approaches to economic analysis' (Harcourt 1987, 924–25). In this section, we shall consider various Italian economists who may be considered, at least to a certain extent, to be of the post-Keynesian strand: Nino Andreatta, Paolo Leon, Fernando Vianello, Ferdinando Targetti, Joseph Halevi, Massimo Ricottilli, Anna Carabelli, Maria Cristina Marcuzzo, Claudio Sardoni, Ferruccio Marzano. All of them have or have had strong Cambridge connections; and we are well aware that this list is not exhaustive and that distinguished scholars may have been left out.

3.4.2 Nino (Beniamino) Andreatta

Nino (Beniamino) Andreatta (1928–2007) was both an economist and a politician. He graduated in law at the University of Padua in 1950, and completed his studies in economics at the Catholic University of Milan. In 1956 (at least in the Easter Term, probably longer), he was an academic visitor at Cambridge. In 1961, he went to India as a consultant to the Indian Planning Commission on behalf of the Massachusetts Institute of Technology. In India, he worked alongside a number of distinguished economists, among whom was Amartya K. Sen. In his political career in Italy, he was a Member of Parliament and of the Senate. He held several ministerial posts: 1979–80 Italian Minister of the Budget; 1980 Italian Minister for Regional Affairs; 1980–82 Italian Minister of Treasury; 1993–94 Minister of Foreign Affairs; 1996–98 Minister of Defence. In 1962, at the age of 34, he won and took up a full professorship at the University of Ancona at Urbino. The following year, he moved to the University of Bologna, where he subsequently founded the Institute of Economics and the Faculty of Political Science. There, he gathered a group of first-class economists: Romano Prodi, Carlo D'Adda, Alberto Quadrio Curzio, Angelo Tantazzi, Giorgio Basevi, Filippo Cavazzuti and, later on, Guido Gambetta, Paolo Onofri, Anna Stagni, Roberto Scazzieri and Gilberto Antonelli. He has been defined an 'eclectic post-Keynesian economist'; fundamentally because of his firm belief that distribution, growth and accumulation depend on social, behavioural and political values, and not merely on technological parameters. His main mentors were Siro Lombardini and Carlo Felice Manara at the Catholic University of Milan, and Nicholas Kaldor and Joan Robinson in Cambridge. Additionally, he was, over the years, very much influenced by

Luigi Pasinetti, with whom he had a close scientific (as well as personal) relationship. Nino Andreatta's contribution to the post-Keynesian theory spans principally from about 1955 to 1965. His volume on *Distribuzione del reddito e accumulazione del capitale* (*Income Distribution and Capital Accumulation*), published in 1958, is an original and, then, much up-to-date analysis in this framework.[14] One may recall that Andreatta was in Cambridge in the spring of 1956, at least six months before Pasinetti. Alberto Quadrio Curzio and Claudia Rotondi (2013a, b) have unearthed a letter dated 5 June 5 1956[15] (which we have translated into English) that Andreatta wrote to Francesco Vito, then Chairman of the Faculty of Economics of the Catholic University of Milan, concerning his stay at Cambridge during the Easter Term 1956:

> By now the [Easter] term is nearly over, and I may summarize my thoughts. [...] I have taken part in various classes, one of which run jointly by the Universities of Cambridge, London [probably LSE] and Oxford. It is difficult for me to summarize the distinguishing features of the [sub-]Faculty. [...] It seems to me that its core is represented by Joan Robinson, Kahn and Kaldor. [...] Joan Robinson's recent volume, *The Theory of Capital Accumulation*, of which I was able to read the proofs, attempts to integrate into Harrod's macro-dynamics the distribution and capital intensity (and vintage) as it was put forward, for instance, by Wicksell. Kaldor's paper on income distribution ['Alternative Theories of Distribution'] published in the recent issue of the *Review of Economic Studies* has much in common with Joan Robinson's research programme. [...] I have met and discussed [...] my paper on pricing and investment in public enterprises with Balogh and Little in Oxford, Kahn, Robinson, Sraffa, Dobb here, as well with younger Cambridge lecturers [...]. (Nino Andreatta to Francesco Vito, 5 June 1956)

[14] Even if, from the very start, he was always bubbling with new ideas, Nino Andreatta initially found it painstaking to write this volume, as would be the case with many of his theoretical essays. His mentor Siro Lombardini, who at that time spent part of the summer in his mountain retreat in Valle d'Aosta, summoned him there in 1957, and forced him to write one or two pages each day, strictly supervising him. Andreatta's dissatisfaction with this essay is proved by the fact that he did not deliver the manuscript within the deadline that Francesco Vito had set him. Vito eventually decided to send to press a draft of the manuscript, which was not the final version. This is why the volume contains a number of printing mistakes. This is a personal recollection that Lombardini told in the 1980s to the first author of this essay.

[15] See Quadrio Curzio and Rotondi (2013, 18–19) and Rotondi (2013a).

As has been mentioned, Alberto Quadrio Curzio and Claudia Rotondi, as well as several other economists, have defined Andreatta as an 'eclectic post-Keynesian'. He was convinced that economic dynamics is moulded by a great number of variables and parameters, making it nearly impossible to constrain them into a unique frame. The first part of Andreatta's essay (1956) contains a critical assessment and a number of extensions of Kaldor's (1956) post-Keynesian model of growth, distribution and accumulation; the very paper that was published in the *Review of Economic Studies* when Andreatta was at Cambridge. In Kaldor's essay, the class of entrepreneurs exclusively earns profits and has a positive propensity to save; while the workers' class exclusively earn labour income and have an irrelevant propensity to save. In this way, the whole capital stock and profit income accrue only to the capitalists. Andreatta's extension of Kaldor's model concerns:

(a) The case in which there is no technical progress;
(b) The case in which technical progress is exclusively due to an increase in labour productivity;
(c) The study of the implications of redistributive policies from profits to wages.

Moving on to the process of capital accumulation, Andreatta enquires into the conditions for which:

(a) The distribution between profits and wages remains constant;
(b) The rate of profits remains constant through time and with different social-economic settings;
(c) The rates of profits and distribution remain constant with modifications of the capital/output ratio and of technical progress.

We may conclude that, to a certain extent, the contribution of Nino Andreatta has, in part, been ground-breaking within the huge literature (see above on Luigi Pasinetti) stemming from Kaldor's seminal paper of 1956. It is certainly a pity that Andreatta's analysis was not widely published in English, since we are sure that it would have stirred much scientific interest.

3.4.3 Paolo Leon

Paolo Leon (1935–2016) was a post-Keynesian economist. He studied law at La Sapienza, Rome, where he was a pupil of Giorgio Fuà. From 1958 to 1961, he was (with the support of a Stringher grant from the Bank of Italy) a research student at King's College, Cambridge, where he was tutored by Richard Kahn. Between 1961 and 1968, he worked as an economist at the World Bank and left as Division Chief of the Economics Department. He taught at Bologna, Venice and Catania. Since 1992, he served as Professor of Public Economics at Rome Tre, which he contributed to set-up. Since the early 1960s, Paolo Leon has carried out research in the framework of the theories of structural dynamics. In 1967, aged 30, Leon published (with Johns Hopkins University Press) the volume *Structural Change and Growth in Capitalism*, which, inter alia, was much appreciated by Joan Robinson for its treatment of economic dynamics. In fact, in his work he maintains that the rate of return of the various sectors of the economy differ widely. Additionally, he focuses on the implications of consumer demand cumulative changes in the long run as a result of a persistent increase in per capita income (Engel's Law). Such modifications in the composition of demand are reflected, soon or later, in the composition of production in the presence of a long-run, 'fully settled' adjustment between production of commodities and use of commodities. Paolo Leon maintains that economists have failed to provide adequate theories explaining the relation between consumption, production, profits and prices. Hence, his study challenges the traditional representation of the capitalist system. The main hypotheses about long-run growth of demand and production are the following, as they have been formulated in the presentation of his 1967 volume:

> [Leon's] central theme is that the rate of profits is not uniform, but rather is permanently differentiated industry by industry and sector by sector, creating monopolist tendencies. This differentiation derives from the varying growth patterns in the consumption of commodities. His concept of a series of profit rates drastically alters the traditional theories about the long-run functioning of the system and suggests a system of prices dominated by demand. The equilibrium of the system is shown to depend on

> another hypothesis: the dominance of producers over consumers in establishing prices, based on the tendencies of producers to behave as a group in times of change and crises. The author has thus posited two separate price systems, one based on demand, the other based on supply. Reality, however, allows for only one system, and he argues that the latter tends to have the greater influence over prices.

While it is true that Pasinetti (and Kaldor, in his correspondence with him in the late 1950s and early 1960s) has been probably the first author to take into account Engel's Law in his model of structural dynamics, growth and distribution, Paolo Leon has been one of the first to consider in detail the empirical applications of this law. Then, later on, we find also, among many others, the works of Gualerzi (1991, 2002, 2012), Reati (1998a, 1998b, 2014), Reati and Raganelli (1993), Garbellini and Wirkierman (2013, 2014a, 2014b) and Notarangelo (1999). In particular, Angelo Reati (1934–2013), in his last (posthumous) publication, starts from 'a conceptualization of structural change as an uneven phenomenon punctuated by technological revolutions that give rise to long-term movements of real and monetary variables, i.e. long waves'. He suggests the following explanation of 'radical technical change':

> drawing upon Post-Keynesian theory, the neo-Schumpeterian school of techno-economic paradigms, and the work of Luigi L. Pasinetti, we suggest guidelines for economic policy to manage structural change and its consequences. While economic policy cannot by itself fully tame the dynamics of structural change, it can ameliorate its disruptive effects, firstly by helping us to manage the stagnation phase of the long wave in order to avoid a deep depression; secondly by preparing the way for a new long-wave and, thirdly, by facilitating the establishment of the institutional conditions for the diffusion of the new technological paradigm. The paper concludes by comparing these suggested policies with those pursued by the dominant western economies after the Second World War. We find that three broad factors—a misdiagnosis of the nature of the crisis that began in the 1970s; a shift in power relations that was strongly unfavourable to the working class; and the rise of neoliberal ideology—led to the adoption of policies that had disastrous social and economic consequences. (Reati 2014, 1)

Leon maintained that much of his work in applied economics was done in order to criticize the U-turn in economics brought about by the policies of Margaret Thatcher and Ronald Reagan, showing that supply-side policies in situations of deficient effective demand caused slow growth, useless government spending and increasing public debt. He has recently published a volume on *The Economics of Effective Demand* to show that it is the economy as a whole that determines agents' behaviour, rather than the other way around. According to him, firms are influenced, in the division of their functions, by changes in the macroeconomy (that he defines as 'the macrofoundations of microeconomics'). In his latest work (of 2007) on *The State, the Market and the Community*, he has tried to define the nature of the state as 'the agent of society or community'. The idea that markets can substitute the government, by limiting its activities to minimal tasks (defence, justice, police) and that economic policies are useless does not square with Leon's macrofoundations of microeconomics: no expectation is so rational as to take account of Kahn's and Leontief's multipliers, as well as of all counter-intuitive macroeconomic laws.

3.4.4 Fernando Vianello

Fernando Vianello (1939–2009) graduated in law at Bologna in 1963 with a thesis on Italian economic development written under the supervision of Paolo Sylos Labini. In 1966, he was admitted to Jesus College, Cambridge, where, in 1968, he obtained a BA in economics. At Cambridge, he attended lectures and seminars given by Joan Robinson, Nicholas Kaldor, Richard Kahn and James Meade. His early works were in the fields of the theory of value (see his much quoted entry on the 'Labour theory of value' in the *New Palgrave Dictionary of Economics*), of income and wealth distribution. He dedicated particular attention to the link between capital accumulation and the profits rate. He also dedicated attention to the major classical political economists (such as Adam Smith, David Ricardo and Karl Marx) and the post-Keynesians (Joan Robinson, Richard Kahn and Nicholas Kaldor), where he kept in the foreground the theories of distribution and profits determination. In the late 1980s and 1990s, he focused on the topic of prices, interest rates and effective demand in the Keynesian framework, before switching to the wide implications of the European Monetary System and the European single currency. As previously mentioned, together with Michele Salvati, Sebastiano Brusco, Andrea Ginzburg and Salvatore Biasco he took part in the steering committee that founded the Faculty of Economics of the University of Modena. Among his pupils we find Giovanni Bonifati, Annamaria Simonazzi, Paolo Trabucchi and Antonella Palumbo.

3.4.5 Ferdinando Targetti

Ferdinando Targetti (1945–2011) has extensively researched on Nicholas Kaldor; see Targetti (1985, 1986, 1991, 1992, 1993; Targetti and Thirlwall 1983). Targetti was a research student at Pembroke College, Cambridge from 1972 to 1974. He has widely published on the theory of value and growth, and on the Italian economy. In his volume *Nicholas Kaldor* he maintains that:

> The present volume is not a textbook on Kaldorian economics nor the intellectual biography of an economist. [...] A biography it is certainly not, nor did I ever intend it to be. Indeed, as I commenced my labours, Kaldor said to me: 'I can't see why one wants to write about my life, because there is nothing in it of any great importance. It's my ideas that are interesting.' (Targetti 1992, vii)

Targetti tried, instead, to show the way in which Kaldor 'did economics'; according to him Kaldor's strategy was the same as Keynes's. First, to incorporate the phenomena examined into an analytical framework;

> but this he constantly altered to accommodate new facts, novel situations, further problems. [...] Theory is abstraction and theory is indeed important, but raw facts should never be sacrificed on the altar of elegant abstraction. Facts change, they press for attention, and they compel new patternings of reality. This, the method of Keynes, was also the method of his great pupil [Kaldor]. (Targetti 1992, vii)

Not surprisingly Kaldor's influence on British economic policies was second only to that of Keynes himself. Targetti also explains the reasons for which Nicholas Kaldor underwent a surprising evolution from his membership of the Austrian neo-classical school to his embracing of Keynesianism. Furthermore, Targetti explains why Kaldor's groundbreaking works are part of a very coherent research programme which made him, together with Joan Robinson, Richard Kahn and Michael Kalecki, 'the leading representative of the post-Keynesian school, an outstanding critic of the neoclassical theory of equilibrium, growth and distribution, and a convinced opponent of the monetarist school'. Targetti co-edited, with Anthony Thirlwall, the posthumously published *Raffaele Mattioli Lectures* of 1984 by Kaldor (*Causes of Growth and Stagnation of the World Economy* 1996).

3.4.6 Joseph Halevi

Joseph Halevi gained a degree in philosophy (curriculum studiorum in economics) at the then *Università degli Studi*, Rome (now La Sapienza), at the beginning of 1975. Sergio Steve was his supervisor and Paolo Sylos Labini was the co-supervisor. The thesis covered Kalecki's theory, the trade cycle, market structures and the role of the public finance. During 1974, he spent several months at Cambridge under the scientific guidance of Nicholas Kaldor; Sergio Steve had sent a letter to Piero Sraffa asking him to allow Halevi to use the Marshall Library. Halevi began his academic life in the autumn of 1975, having been hired on a very temporary basis by the Department of Economics of the New School of Social Research in New York. He received a full-time appointment at Rutgers University in New Jersey when the department was headed by Paul Davidson. In New York, Halevi developed a strong association with Edward Nell and Adolph Lowe, which later led to several essays on Lowe's structural approach. He also established a deep working friendship with Harry Magdoff and Paul Sweezy, which led him, during the ensuing decades, to contribute to the journal *Monthly Review*. In the autumn of 1978, he was appointed at the University of Sydney. From the late 1980s, he combined his work there with engagements at the ISMEA in Paris and at the universities of Grenoble and Nice. From 1997 until 1999, he served as full-time Professor at the University of Grenoble and, as a result, in 1998 he was appointed by France's Ministry of Scientific Research as a member of the National Selection Committee for the recruitment of full professors. Halevi maintains[16] that 'I have never been a neo-Ricardian according to the research line of Piero Garegnani. Instead I have found myself much closer to Pasinetti. Actually, Sylos Labini, Pasinetti and Harcourt have inspired me for focusing on modern economic theories. This emerges quite clearly from the publication of four recently edited volumes (jointly with Geoff Harcourt, Peter Kriesler and John Nevile) with Palgrave-Macmillan.' According to Halevi, Pasinetti's contribution is fundamental for the comprehension of the working of the economic mechanisms quite independently from the institutional set-up. According to him, Pasinetti's approach helps us to enquire into uncommon issues. For instance, he quotes his 1996 paper on 'The Significance of the Theory of Vertically Integrated Processes for the Problem of Economic Development' (*Structural Change and Economic Dynamics*). Here, the vertically integrated approach is instrumental for the study of economic planning of the Soviet and Indian type (à la Feldman and Mahalanobis), since Pasinetti's approach overcomes the dichotomy of investment/consumption typical of these schemes.

> As a teacher, I have always considered the Sraffa-Pasinetti and Pasinetti-Kaldor Cambridge analytical schemes as a necessary condition in order to discuss any modern economic theory. In this sense I may be easily associated with this School of thought, but I do not consider myself as exclusively Cantabridgian, since the Italian School with Sylos Labini, Steve, Graziani, Caffè, Napoleoni, Saraceno and Luigi Pasinetti himself offers much more

concludes Halevi.

[16] Letter to authors, 18 October 2015.

3.4.7 Massimo Ricottilli

Massimo Ricottilli, after completing his studies in economics at Bologna, with financial support from the Ford Foundation, the Italian Research Council and the University of Naples, was a graduate student from 1972 to 1975 at Clare Hall, Cambridge. In his first year, he was supervised by Geoff Harcourt, who was spending a sabbatical year there; subsequently he was supervised by John Eatwell. At Cambridge, he read widely on capital theory and unbalanced growth. His initial research line focused on the determination of effective demand in a closed economy. The aim was to highlight how effective demand stemming from autonomous sources—in particular, public expenditure—shapes the production profile of an economy; how the employment of available manpower is distributed among industries, and how growth impulses stemming from the autonomous demand percolate through industries. In order to illustrate these effects, Ricottilli resorted to a specific analytical device: that is, by partitioning the economy into sub-sectors, each featuring, in equilibrium, the growth rate of the specific element of effective demand that takes the role of the driving force. This approach soon led to the analysis of structural transformation. From the 1990s onwards, Ricottilli focused on the long-run issues relating to transition and development. The inception for this was the recognition of the failure of prevalent theory cogently to come to grips with the process of transformation from a backward economy to a modern industrial one. It was, indeed, understood that what was left out of most theories is an analytical account of what may be defined as transitional paths: the crossover from a state of low-level of productivity and slow growth equilibrium to one of high productivity and, consequently, high income determined by technological progress. At the core of his investigation is a structural analysis of the crossover from an economy functioning at a lower productivity level as specified by a given technical and capital structure to one with a higher one, to be achieved by an investment process deeply altering the capital structure profile. The outcomes of this approach are illustrated in Ricottilli 2009 and 2013. This research line was later continued to enquire about the innovation and investment processes resulting from the complex interaction amongst technologically leading firms; the main results are provided in Andergassen et al. (2005, 2006). The outcome in terms of derived effective demand and related income distribution has further been investigated in Ricottilli (2015), where he argues that there exists an inherent structural tendency for crucial investment demand to come in waves of unpredictable scale.

3.4.8 Anna Carabelli

Anna Carabelli is one of the finest scholars of Keynes's method. She obtained a First degree in economics at the Università Bocconi of Milan, and a Ph.D. in economics at Cambridge with a thesis *On Keynes's Method* that was published by Macmillan in 1988. She is now full Professor of Economics at the Faculty of Economics of the *Università degli Studi del Piemonte Orientale* at Novara. She has specialized in macro- and monetary economics, and was a member of the *Consiglio di presidenza* of the *Società italiana degli economisti*. She has investigated Sraffa's and Keynes's methodology with lengthy research in the King's College Modern Archives and on Sraffa's papers in the Wren Library at Trinity College. Sheila Dow (1991, 132 and 139) has reviewed Carabelli's *On Keynes's Method* and Roderick M. O'Donnell's *Keynes: Philosophy, Economics and Politics*, both published by Macmillan in 1988 and 1989 respectively, by writing:

> Both [volumes] are immensely scholarly. Although an impressive literature has already built up on Keynes's philosophy, these provide the most complete accounts to date of the full corpus of Keynes's philosophical writing. [...] It is impossible to convey the full wealth of detail contained in these two books. They are both the outcome of tremendous scholarship that is all the more admirable for its pioneering quality.

3.4.9 Maria Cristina Marcuzzo

Maria Cristina Marcuzzo, Professor of Economics at La Sapienza, Rome, since 2000, was a visiting scholar in 1986/87 at King's College in Cambridge and has spent many other periods of research in Cambridge.

She has edited and published extensively on the Cambridge school of economics and on Cambridge scholars, including biographies and the works of Joan Robinson, Nicholas Kaldor, Richard Kahn, John M. Keynes, John Hicks and many others. She has edited a comprehensive volume *Economists at Cambridge. A Study through their Correspondence 1907–46*. She was elected in 2015 to the Lincei Academy in Rome. Maria Cristina Marcuzzo has written a number of papers and edited several volumes with Annalisa Rosselli, yet another outstanding scholar in this field.

3.4.10 Claudio Sardoni

Claudio Sardoni (1948) is now full Professor of Economics at the *Facoltà di Scienze Statistiche* of La Sapienza, Rome. Although Claudio Sardoni has not earned a Cambridge higher degree, his links with Cambridge and the post-Keynesian school of economics are quite strong. In fact, he has spent quite a number of a sabbatical leaves in Cambridge. His links with Cambridge have been reinforced by the fact that he married one of Geoff Harcourt's daughters, Wendy (who is Professor at the International Institute of Social Studies of the Erasmus University). After earning a degree in '*scienze statistiche e demografiche*' at La Sapienza, Rome, in 1978, Sardoni spent part of the academic year at the LSE. From 1979 to 1983, he was a graduate student in the Department of Economics of the University of Adelaide, where he obtained his Ph.D. with a dissertation on 'Economic Crises and Effective Demand in Ricardo, Marx and Keynes' under the supervision of G. H. Harcourt. Since then, he has published or edited a large number of papers and essays. In a number of his contributions, Sardoni claims that it is necessary to return to the classical and broad Keynesian tradition in order to understand the dynamics of modern economies. Sardoni puts forward a critical examination of the foundations of macro-economics as they were developed in the tradition of Ricardo, Marx, Keynes and Kalecki, which are then contrasted with the current marginalist mainstream. Inter alia, he pays particular attention to the market forms, and to the micro- and monetary foundations of the modern economic system. Geoff Harcourt, introducing Sardoni's (2011) volume *Unemployment, Recession and Effective Demand. The Contributions of Marx, Keynes and Kalecki*, maintains:

> Claudio Sardoni sets out the principal propositions of modern macroeconomics, especially those of the New Keynesians and the New Classical Macroeconomists. He compares them, often to their disadvantage, with the corresponding analyses of Marx, Keynes and Kalecki and his own synthesis of the propositions of these three authors.
>
> Claudio Sardoni is never a bigot or a zealot—he looks for the positive aspects in his writings of the authors examined. He calls for tolerance and open-mindedness, a willingness to learn from those with whom you disagree, and to examine their writings always within their own contexts in order to see what is worthwhile and helpful to take on in your own approach. Most of all, he calls for dialogue and a willingness to frame analysis and arguments in such a way that comprehension and communication are possible and new lessons may be learnt. […] His [Sardoni's] writings are a role model of proper procedure allied with cumulative persuasion through weight of evidence, sound scholarship and argument. (Harcourt 2011, vii–viii)

As mentioned, among many other topics, Sardoni (2002) has also considered the micro-foundations of the Keynesian macro-economics model:

> All strands of contemporary mainstream macroeconomics share the strong belief that macro-economic theory must be based on sound microfoundations, which is generally interpreted as macroeconomics being based on neoclassical microeconomic foundations. In other words, macroeconomic analysis must be consistent with the fundamental features of the neoclassical model of the economy. […] I argue that macroeconomics must indeed be based on rigorous microeconomic foundations, but this does not imply that the microfoundations of macro-economics must be neoclassical.
>
> […] Although I share the conviction that the behaviour of individuals is conditioned by macroeconomic factors, I believe that this should not imply that the development of macroeconomic analysis can be carried out by ignoring microeconomic issues. It cannot be ignored that aggregate outcomes derive, though in a non-simplistic way, from individual decisions and actions'. (Sardoni 2002, 4 and 11; quoted in King 2012, 153)

Taken in their entirety, Sardoni's contributions are characterized by a strong post-Keynesian imprint; his originality, scholarship and sound knowledge of the great economists of the past, as Harcourt has pointed out, are 'framed in such a way as to make it suitably useful and valuable for contemporary analysis'.

3.4.11 Ferruccio Marzano

Ferruccio Marzano (1936) earned a degree in law at Rome and, in 1963, a B.A. in economics at Cambridge. Later, he moved to Harvard. In 1968, he returned to Italy, where he was promoted to full Professor in 1976. From 1989, he was called to La Sapienza, Rome, as Professor of Economic Development, and was, on different occasions, visiting scholar at Pisa, Oxford, Lodz and Sofia. He has published extensively in the fields of capital theory, income distribution and profit determination, Keynesian economics and the history of economics analysis. He has also undertaken research and published in the field of ethics and economics, as well the non-profit sector. In 1999, jointly with Giancarlo Gandolfo, Marzano edited a volume for Palgrave Macmillan on *Economic Theory and Social Justice*. According to the editors, the book discusses 'the role that economic policy may play in tackling economic problems, including poverty and unemployment in both the developed and the developing world, and in promoting a new international economic order. The instability caused by capital accumulation and global financial markets is assessed and the links between social choices, economic policy and moral values are addressed throughout'. In 2002, Marzano edited a volume with F. Carlucci on *Poverty, Growth and Welfare in the World Economy in the 21st Century* (Lang) and, in 2003, again with Giancarlo Gandolfo, a volume on *International Economic Flows, Currency Crises, Investment and Economic Development* (Euroma). Just before going to print we note an important omission. In fact, among the (post-) Keynesian economists with Cambridge links, we should have included Giorgio Rampa, full professor of economics in the Dept. of Economics and Management of the University of Pavia, and chairman of the department since 2014. After earning a first degree in economics at the University of Pavia, in the academic year 1980–81 he obtains an M. Phil in economics at Cambridge (thanks to a scholarship of the Luigi Einaudi Foundation, and an Adam Smith Fund grant). In Cambridge he also wins the Stevenson Prize of the Faculty of Economics and Politics. Back in Italy, in 1988 he is awarded the prize for the best Ph.D. thesis in economics. Giorgio Rampa has published widely in the field of macro-economics, economic dynamics, trade, growth, input-output models as well as specific fields of micro-economics. A full list of his works is provided in his web page at the University of Pavia.

3.5 Alberto Quadrio Curzio's Contribution to the Cambridge-Italian School of Economics[17]

Alberto Quadrio Curzio was a research student at St John's College, Cambridge, from September 1962 to September 1963.[18] Since that time, he has been very closely associated with Cambridge; first, with Robin Matthews and, later on, especially, with John Eatwell. He was recently appointed Distinguished Academic Visitor at Queens' College and at the Judge Business School, and was Member of the Advisory Board of the Centre for Financial History of the University of Cambridge, directed by D'Maris Coffman at Newnham College.

Quadrio Curzio has contributed to the Oxbridge school of political economy in a dual role.[19] The first was devoted to preserving the

[17] This paragraph has been written jointly with Roberto Scazzieri.

[18] He could not stay there longer for serious personal and family problems, which arose at the beginning of 1963. Having returned to Italy, Quadrio Curzio went to work at 'Ilses', a research office for the Lombardy Region where he stayed for two years while simultaneously collaborating with Carlo Felice Manara and Luigi Pasinetti at the Catholic University of Milan.

[19] From a scientific and cultural point of view, the Oxbridge school of economics had a remarkable impact on the accomplishment of Quadrio Curzio, both in the Italian context and for his network of research, academic, social and political European institutions. At the European level, he has collaborated intensively with the President of the European Commission, Romano Prodi. He is also a member of Academia Europaea; and has a growing role in the Balzan Prize Foundation, where he is member of the board, as well as chairman of the Lincei-Swiss Academies Committee. Since 1968, he has been a leading member of the publishing house Il Mulino, which he founded in 1983, and since then has managed *Economia Politica. Journal of Analytical and Institutional Economics*. From 1977 to 1987, he was elected to represent the Italian economists to the *Consiglio Nazionale delle Ricerche* (the equivalent of the SSRC in Britain), where he was responsible for the strategy and financing of public-funded research in the field of economics. Additionally, for more than two decades he chaired the Faculty of Political Science of the Catholic University of Milan. Since 2009, he has been President of the Class of Moral Sciences of the Lincei Academy, the world's most ancient scientific academy; and since July 2015 President of the same Academy. More generally, side-by-side with his life-long personal friend and colleague Luigi Pasinetti, he has invigorated a line of the *new classical type*, by restoring the relevance of the Cambridge school outside Cambridge itself and, in particular, in Italy. He has connected political economy and economic policy along lines labelled as *social liberalism* where private and public partnerships have a fundamental role in

relevance of such an approach in Italian research and academic institutions. His aim was also to extend this approach to the political and social fields. The second of Quadrio Curzio's contributions is represented by his scientific research programme considered here below with respect to the following analytical domains: scarce resources, income and wealth in a structural perspective; the process of accumulation, multi-sectoral links and technological scarcity within structural dynamics; raw commodities, industrial markets and the long-term evolution of economics systems. He has hence followed the path traced by economists in the structural tradition such, as Thomas Robert Malthus, David Ricardo, Piero Sraffa and Wassily Leontief. Many of his academic volumes and papers have appeared with major international publishers since the 1980s. Summing up, we may say that the research programme started in the mid-1960s by Quadrio Curzio has provided an ambitious and ground-breaking analytical framework for the analysis of resource-based structural economic dynamics, as in that tradition non-produced resources play a critical role in shaping economic dynamics. The volume *Resources, Production and Structural Dynamics* (see Baranzini et al. 2015) was edited in order to provide an assessment of Quadrio Curzio's research programme, and to tackle new lines of investigation.

3.5.1 Rent and Income Distribution in Multi-sectoral Models of Economic Structure

Since the mid-1960s, Quadrio Curzio has concentrated on the *constraints* linked to the existence of any given, and relatively persistent, economic structure, and on the analysis of the *opportunities* that such constraints might embody. Additionally, he has thoroughly examined the *institutional settings* compatible with specific structural constraints; institutional settings that might generate positive, and even virtuous, processes of structural economic dynamics. Since his early works, Quadrio Curzio

setting up a worthy democracy rooted in institutions, society and the economy. This line of political thought connects Alberto Quadrio Curzio with Romano Prodi, since they both were students at the Catholic University of Milan and pupils of Siro Lombardini in the late 1950s.

has developed his analytical framework on foundations provided by the modern multi-sectoral analysis put forward by Wassily Leontief, Richard Stone, Jan von Neumann and Piero Sraffa, and by his close colleague and friend Luigi Pasinetti. This type of analysis considers in great detail the inter-dependencies among sectors of production and consumption; and it confines to the background the role of market structure and dynamics. In this way, the general framework of analysis differentiates itself from the traditional Walrasian analysis; also, it builds on concepts and tools of the classical political economy of François Quesnay, Adam Smith and David Ricardo. Within this scientific tradition, which we might label as *contemporary classical analysis*, the contribution of Quadrio Curzio takes a distinctive character for the central role assigned to what he calls the '*antagonism-coexistence*' between producibility and scarcity, a relationship he considered as a fundamental feature of the growth processes that have taken place at least since the first industrial revolution (see also Quadrio Curzio 1988, 1998; Quadrio Curzio and Scazzieri 1983, 1990). He has mainly concentrated on non-reproducible or de facto non-reproduced resources, and on the implications that the use of such resources has on income distribution and on the dynamics of economic systems.

The role of non-produced resources and rent was first addressed within the analytical framework of structural economics by Quadrio Curzio (1967) in his volume *Rendita e distribuzione in un modello economico plurisettoriale* (*Rent and Distribution in a Multi-Sector Model*). This contribution was followed by the volume *Accumulazione del capitale e rendita* (*Accumulation of Capital and Rent*) published in 1975, and by the essay 'Rent, Income Distribution and Orders of Efficiency and Rentability', published in 1980. Quadrio Curzio's research is a forceful reminder that non-produced resources and rent have been one of the main focuses of investigation within the structural economics approach since the early contributions by Thomas Robert Malthus and David Ricardo. The historical setting of Quadrio Curzio's contribution comes out clearly in his surveys, among which the entries 'Land Rent' (1987) in *The New Palgrave Dictionary of Economics*, 'Rent' (1998) in *The Elgar Companion to Classical Economics* (*ECCE*) and still others (1990, 1993b, 2011). However, in the twentieth century, with the exception of Sraffa's (1960) contribution, Chap. XI ('On Land') in *Production of Commodities by Means of*

Commodities, neglible attention has been given by theoretical models to natural resources, their scarcity, rent, non-produced and scarce means of production, and their quasi-rent. More precisely, almost all postwar economic theory considered these problems irrelevant—or, at least, secondary. This is why Quadrio Curzio set himself to bridge this gap in economic analysis, with the publication in 1967 of *Rendita e distribuzione in un modello economico plurisettoriale* and in 1975 of *Accumulazione del capitale e rendita*. In these volumes, he outlines two different models with the complementary objectives of introducing: (a) primary productive factors (different from labour), or more generally non-reproducible or non-produced scarce productive factors, into a general model of production; and (b) rent in a residual theory of income distribution. The model hence focuses on the inter-relations between the price-distribution system and the quantity system of different produced commodities. According to him:

> To give full account of all these inter-dependencies we need to build a system that, starting from those of Leontief, Sraffa, and von Neumann, develops the analysis—to our knowledge—in a yet unexplored direction. [...] Our model [...] shows [...] a brand new type of causal dependence between the price distribution system and the quantity system, a feature that is derived from the particular treatment of scarce factors and the associated rents. (Quadrio Curzio 1967, 10, our translation)

These models were later generalised in Quadrio Curzio (1980; 1st edn 1977), Quadrio Curzio et al. (1987), Quadrio Curzio (1990, 1996b) and Quadrio Curzio and Pellizzari (1996, 1999). The main results are the following. First, within this frame of analysis, rent becomes the critical factor in determining the distribution between income shares, thus significantly changing the order of priority among rents, profits and wages. As matter of fact, in the Ricardian model of distribution, first, total wages (based on the 'natural' wage-rate) were determined, then total rents; profits were considered to be a residual. In the post-Keynesian model of distribution, the first distributive variable to be determined is total profits allowing for full-employment investment, while wages are a type of residual (but this with certain upper and lower limits). For Quadrio Curzio, instead, rent is fundamentally determined by technological conditions, through the mutual influence of efficiency ranking, scale of production and structure of production. In this way, the interdependence between the scale and the structure of any given economic system takes centre stage, and overall economic dynamics is shown to be determined by a plurality of factors working along multiple causal layers. This approach allows for a close examination of 'variations of efficiency, structure, and scale of production' (Quadrio Curzio 1990; Quadrio Curzio and Pellizzari 1996, 1999) and brings in dynamic factors that may work both in the case of non-produced resources and also independently of them. The emergence of 'technological rent' is a case in point:

> while surplus rent and structural rent depend respectively on different fertility of lands, and the existence of two simultaneous processes that produce the same commodity, 'technological rent' [a concept introduced by Quadrio Curzio] takes into consideration broader dynamic aspects of technology. These latter aspects emerge as effect of some scarcities generated by either increased levels of production or changes in income distribution or movements in the order of efficiency between processes that make use of scarce resources (Quadrio Curzio and Pellizzari 1999, 32)

3.5.2 Quadrio Curzio on Horizontal and Vertical Approaches for the Analysis of Economic Structure

Quadrio Curzio's research is an important contribution to the investigation of the role that different representations of economic structure can play when considering the complementariness, both *within* any given time period, as well as *across* different time periods, that may be generated by the interdependence of productive activities, and by the existence of relatively persistent relationships between production and distributional arrangements. (These are primarily relationships between production structures and income distribution among profits, wages and rents, both *within* any given industrial sector as well as *among* different sectors.) As pointed out in Baranzini and Scazzieri (1990, 304–5; 2nd edn, 2012), Quadrio Curzio's starting point is provided by von Neumann's approach, but maintains the role of non-produced resources in the foreground. According to him:

> The *interdependence* between raw materials, primary commodities and produced goods means that the raw materials themselves act as an aspect and, indeed, a constraint on production processes. The latter constraint thus results from an interdependence in which means of production of all kinds assume a combined role with relative substitutability. (Quadrio Curzio 1986, 312)

This means that, according to this framework of analysis, means of production, including non-produced resources, play a critical role in explaining the complementarities within any given time period, and the structural constraints acting on the distribution of income once interdependencies among productive activities are considered. The circular (or horizontal) approach to economic interdependence provides a vantage point for the analysis of constraints on coordination among production processes within each single period. In particular, Quadrio Curzio's horizontal analysis of interdependence provides a new, and remarkably powerful, tool for the investigation of single-period complementarities thanks to the introduction of the 'splitting coefficients' (*coefficienti di erogazione ripartiti*, in the Italian original) that characterize what he calls the 'global technology' approach. These coefficients allow for the specification of different sources of supply for any given intermediate input when this input is delivered by a plurality of processes, and allow for the exploration of the technological, distributional and social interdependences that this plurality of sources introduces into the structure of the economic system (Quadrio Curzio 1967, 1977, 1980, 1990, 1996a; Quadrio Curzio et al. 1987). The switch to a vertical representation of production processes, which Quadrio Curzio systematically discusses for the first time in *Accumulazione del capitale e rendita* (Quadrio Curzio 1975), allows for the utilization of what he calls the 'composite technology' point of view (Quadrio Curzio 1975, 1986, 327–34). Unlike a global technology, a composite technology calls attention to the sequential dependence between successive time periods brought about by the full or partial accumulation of the net products that the economic system generates within any single time period. In Quadrio Curzio's analysis, both a global and a composite technology describe a production structure characterized by the plurality of sources of supply for some essential, non-produced means of production. However, the complementarities and constraints highlighted by the two points of view are different. A *global technology* calls attention to complementarities within any single time period; that is, to the mutual constraints acting in a set of interdependent and simultaneous production activities. Here, the need to meet interdependence conditions leads to synchronization devices that operate through the system of prices and the emergence of producers' rents. On the other hand, a *composite technology* calls attention to complementarities over time; that is, to constraints acting for a set of sequentially related configurations of an economic system. Here, alternative sources of supply for certain essential means of production lead to distinct patterns of capital accumulation for the different sub-systems (sub-economies) into which the economic system can be split depending on which supply sources are considered. This dynamic process presupposes a degree of coordination over time that is mainly achieved through structural changes working through the system of physical quantities, and the emergence of a differentiated pattern of capital accumulation for the different sub-economies. A remarkable outcome is that capital accumulation is associated with *changing proportions* between the different sub-economies and, eventually, with the *substitution* of one sub-economy for another as the overall economic system moves across time.

3.5.3 Quadrio Curzio on Accumulation of Capital, Residuals and Uneven Economic Dynamics

In Quadrio Curzio's contribution, the structural analysis of non-produced resources and rents suggests a fresh look at the dynamics of economic systems under natural or technological scarcities. This is done within medium- and long-term perspectives that highlight the role of historical context in determining the actual dynamic path followed by any given economic system. At the root of Quadrio Curzio's analysis is the utilization of the composite technology approach described above, which entails a fundamental departure from classical multisectoral analysis:

> One of the cornerstones of the production schemes *à la* von Neumann, *à la* Leontief, or *à la* Sraffa is that, with the accumulation of the entire surplus, the rate of growth of production and surplus coincide and remain constant [...] One of the cornerstones of the economic dynamics with non-produced means of production is [...] the absence of the above identities, and the change over time of the rates of growth. (Quadrio Curzio and Pellizzari 1999, 33; see also Quadrio Curzio's previous analysis in Quadrio Curzio 1975, 1986, 1990).

The composite technology approach calls attention to the configuration of any given economic system considered as a set of vertically integrated production (specific to it and essential to its operation). In Quadrio Curzio's original formulation, if the economic system makes use of a plurality of non-produced resources associated with techniques of different efficiency (say, *I*, *II*,..., *K*), as soon as non-produced resource (I) is fully utilized, sub-system *A*(*I*) may no longer be expanded and any further increase of production levels would require the activation of sub-systems requiring the utilization of the other non-produced resources *II*,...,*K*. In this way, as production levels are expanded, sub-systems *A*(*II*),..., *A*(*K*) are successively called into operation as soon as the upper utilization bounds for the corresponding non-produced resource are reached.

> The above representation of production structure highlights one important feature of the trajectory that the economic system may follow as scarcity constraints become binding one after the other: one possible effect in activating a new process is the change of structure of the technology. There is then the problem of the accumulation of net product with a technology whose structure differs from that in which the net product itself has been created. In short, changes of technology—even in the absence of technical progress—may [give rise to] the problem of residual net products which cannot be (immediately) accumulated. (Quadrio Curzio and Pellizzari 1999, 82)

The formation and utilization of residual net products is subject to complementarities and bottlenecks within the production structure, and these generate both constraints and opportunities for capital accumulation: 'because of the presence of different types of non-reproduced means of production sequentially activated, the economy may pass from situations in which the entire net product can be accumulated to situations in which residuals are created, and back again to situations of total accumulation' (Quadrio Curzio and Pellizzari 1999, 83). Under successively binding constraints due to the availability of essential non-produced resources, certain accumulation trajectories become unfeasible. On the other hand, new accumulation trajectories may become feasible due to the production complementarities generated as part of the ongoing processes of structural change. In particular, as Quadrio Curzio and Pellizzari note:

> [t]he growth rates of production and net product may either increase or decrease and frequently change behavior over time. For example, the activation of a less efficient process with NPMP [non-produced means of production], characterized however by a bundle of means of production much closer in quantity and quality with the available residuals, may bring about an increase in the growth rates rather than a dynamic slow down. (Quadrio Curzio and Pellizzari 1999, 83)

The above trajectory may be described as follows. Let $q\ (I)$ be the vector of the quantities of commodities produced by operating the production processes represented by technology matrix $A(I)$. If technology matrix $A(I)$ is subject to the availability constraint $T_i\ (I) \leq T_i^*\ (I)$ on a non-produced resource i ($i = 1,\ldots,k$), an economic system using this technology and following its maximum expansion trajectory may reach the upper activation bound for $A(I)$ at $T_i\ (I) = T_i^*\ (I)$. In this case, the quantities produced by $A(I)$ cannot increase and the net products delivered by this technology become redundant with respect to its own absorption capacity. Any further increase of the quantities produced would thus require the activation of a different technology matrix $A(II)$, in which the non-produced resource i is substituted by non-produced resource j. If $A(II)$ does not need for its expansion the net products that $A(I)$ delivers, those net products (residuals) could be 'stocked, exported, or consumed' (Quadrio Curzio and Pellizzari 1999, 86), but would not enter the accumulation process.[20]

The composite technology heuristic opens a new field of investigation into the structural dynamics of economic systems. It allows a focus on the distinct dynamic impulses that may originate in different parts (sub-systems) of the economy and that may bring about different patterns of overall dynamics depending on the way in which the distinct sources of motion react on each other over time. In particular, Quadrio Curzio's composite-technology dynamics calls attention to the existence of distinct sources of capital accumulation within the economic system, and highlights—through the dynamics of residuals—the complex, and often unexpected, complementarity relationship between the persistence of old and the introduction of new techniques of production. The global-technology approach integrates the above point of view by highlighting the interdependence between 'old' and 'new' production techniques at any given time. In this way, the structural dynamics of economic systems is seen as characterized by the systematic interaction of factors leading to the *coexistence* of techniques of different maturity and factors leading to the *substitution* of new for old techniques as capital accumulation unfolds. As Michael Landesmann pointed out, Quadrio Curzio's analysis 'provides an interesting analytical framework which integrates "traverse analysis" into a classical framework' (Landesmann 1988, 176). It is also a framework calling attention to the *plurality* of long-term trajectories open to economic systems when the internal structure of the accumulation of capital is explicitly considered. In this way, Quadrio Curzio's contribution to dynamic economic analysis highlights the role of historical context in closing off or opening up medium- and long-term opportunities. This point of view lends itself to close integration between structural analysis and structural policy, and emphasizes the critical role of institutional conditions in the activation of specific paths of structural economic dynamics (see also Quadrio Curzio 2007).

[20] However, the possibility of stocking or exporting residuals may indirectly increase productive capacity. This would require either the transfer of commodity stocks to some future date, or the immediate export of residuals in order to import the commodities needed in the accumulation process.

3.6 Richard Stone and Italian Speaking Economists

3.6.1 The Framework of Analysis

The specific role of the theoretical framework in establishing empirical bases for the application of the circular process of economic structure at Cambridge was initially studied by Richard Stone in his contribution, going back to the early 1940s, on the foundations of national and social accounting. As we shall see, Italian scholars, as well as Swiss-Italian scholars, were involved with this programme later on, which yielded Stone the Nobel Prize in 1984. The seminal contribution of Richard and Giovanna Stone-Saffi[21] (see Stone and Stone 1977) to the introduction of schemes aimed at 'a comprehensive, orderly, consistent presentation of the facts of economic life' is rooted in the circular concept of economic structure, which may be traced back 'to the Political Arithmeticians in England in the second half of the seventeenth century and in particular to the work of William Petty and Gregory King' (Stone and Stone 1977, 152–53). The logical procedure in terms of which it is possible to gain information relative to economic structure starting from data concerning overall magnitudes such as national income and 'other income totals' (Stone and Stone) is laid out by stressing the role of disaggregation as a prerequisite for structural analysis, since it is by defining 'the constituents of these totals', and by showing 'how they are related to each other to form a closed network of flows' that it is possible to gain 'some insight into the basic structure of an economic system' (Stone and Stone 1977, 31). The specifications of this approach are expounded in Baranzini and Scazzieri (1990, 311–12; 2nd edn 2012).

In 1941, (John) Richard Nicholas Stone, together with James E. Meade, another eminent Oxbridge economist, produced the first estimates of

[21] In 1941, Richard Stone married his second wife, Feodora Leontinoff, after his first marriage was dissolved in 1940. His second wife died in 1956 and, in 1960, he married Giovanna Saffi (Croft-Murray), great-grandchild of Italian patriot Aurelio Saffi, who had been his partner in many of his works since the mid-1930s. Giovanna Saffi, after Piero Sraffa who moved to Cambridge in 1927, was probably the second Italian scholar active in the field of economics in Cambridge, even if she was not trained as an economist.

British national income and expenditure. After standardizing the systems of national accounting, he moved onto the analysis of aggregate demand with systems of equations, and to the analysis of aggregate consumption and saving functions. At Cambridge, together with J. A. C. Brown (who later moved to Oxford for a chair in econometrics, becoming a friend and colleague of various young Italian scholars there), T. S. Barker and others, he launched the Cambridge Growth Project of the British Economy, where he integrated social, reproducible goods and demographic components. He received the Nobel Prize in 1984 'for having made fundamental contributions to the development of systems of national accounts and hence greatly improved the basis for empirical economic analysis'. As early as 1951, Stone was anticipating that:

> Anyone who believes in the maintenance of a social economy and the avoidance of the totalitarian direction of all aspects of economic life must be concerned at the present time with the creation of an institutional framework which will permit a social economy, with the essential features of free markets, free choice of occupations and free choice in the spending of disposable income, to function more in accordance with contemporary social ideals. In the achievement of this goal and in re-drafting the rules of the economic game in such a way that both laissez-faire and overall physical control are rejected as a basis for economic organization, national income and expenditure studies and their extension to the technique of national budgeting have, I believe, a great deal to offer. (Stone 1951; quoted in Johansen 1985, 4)

In order to do this, Richard Stone maintained that it is necessary to focus on the stabilization of economic activity, on the equity in income distribution, and on competitive mechanisms. Studies on income and national expenditure, conducted also in terms of input-output analysis, do offer a significant support. Stone had in mind a clear research program, which set out in detail in the proposal for funding made to the Nuffield Foundation in the summer 1945: 'The ultimate aim of applied economics is to increase human welfare by the investigation and analysis of economic problems of the real world.' The most popular model in the 1950s and 1960s for the study of the structure of an economic system was certainly the input-output model, developed by Wassily Leontief.

The model has as its basis a *table of intersectoral transactions*, which records the flows of goods and services between the various sectors of a production system. From this classified set of data, it is possible to build a set of *technical coefficients*, which become the coefficients of the unknowns of a linear system of equations, the input-output system. The sequence described clearly shows the close connection between data and model, and between empirical evidence and theoretical foundation, a philosophy shared by the two authors, Leontief and Stone.

The input-output analysis had some limitations, such as the assumption of fixed production coefficients and the main focus on the production side of an economic system. Richard Stone's contribution to overcoming these limitations is of fundamental importance. Very relevant is his attempt to apply input-output analysis to other not strictly productive areas of an economic system. It aims at a systematic survey and formalization of aspects related to the distribution and redistribution of income. The resulting *Social Accounting Matrix*, by including accounts for institutional sectors, 'closes' the input-output model, by 'endogenizing' some important variables. We might say that the major contribution of Richard Stone to the theory of the formation, distribution and redistribution of income lies in the definition and construction of the social accounting matrix and the consequent extension of the input-output model.

3.6.2 Luigi L. Pasinetti Building on Stone's Foundations

A number of Italian and Swiss-Italian economists have refined parts of the pioneering works of Wassily Leontief and Richard Stone. First, we would like to mention Luigi Pasinetti's contribution to the diffusion of linear models of production. In his *Lectures on the Theory of Production* (first published in Italian in 1975), the Leontief model is seen as a link in the chain leading from the *Tableau économique* of François Quesnay to the model of *Production of Commodities by Means of Commodities* by Piero Sraffa, passing through the circular model of production of David Ricardo and the scheme of simple reproduction of Karl Marx. The contributions of Sraffa and Pasinetti change the focus and objectives of production models: from 'quantity models' to 'price models' and from 'practical' to 'theoretical' objectives. In the preface to his 1981 volume on *Structural Change and Economic Growth*, Pasinetti writes, recalling his early Cambridge and Harvard days:

> Both the macro-dynamic growth models and input-output analysis impressed me at the time; but they left me profoundly dissatisfied when I tried to use them in order to understand what is going on in economic systems with a very high degree of dynamism, i.e. of technical progress. And I began to think that an attempt might be made to develop a theoretical scheme which, while retaining the analytical character of input-output analysis, could also deal with uneven increases in productivity, in the way the macro-dynamic models had begun do to, but only for the very simplified case of a one-commodity world. It was from this determination to look for new tools of analysis that the present work has come into being. (Pasinetti 1981, xi)

Nevertheless, there was an additional point of dissatisfaction for Pasinetti; that is, the underlying assumption that the elasticities of demand with respect to disposable income were unity for all goods and services. This excluded possible changes in the composition of demand due to changes in the level of disposable real income; such as those associated with Engel's Law, according to which the composition of (aggregate) demand changes through time as real income per capita increases. An important feature of Pasinetti's contribution is that the patterns of structural dynamics associated with Engel's Law may be adequately examined through a vertically integrated framework. In Pasinetti's, view the structural implications of Engel's Law lead to a type of economic analysis where attention may be focused on vertically integrated sectors, rather than on the conventional industries of circular theories (see Baranzini and Scazzieri 1990, 303; 2nd edn, 2012). It is worth noting:

> The basic theoretical scheme underlying the present work was conceived and formulated before the publication, and quite independently, of Sraffa's *Production of Commodities by Means of Commodities*. Sraffa's book brought theoretical attention back to the process of production considered as a

> circular process. This is precisely what, on purpose, I had completely eliminated from my analysis, by adopting not only a vertically integrated conception of the production process but also sharp simplifications as to the employment of labour and capital goods in each single sector. My approach had the great advantage of leading to dynamic analysis straightaway, without that fixity of coefficients which had constrained all inter-industry analysis into a static strait-jacket. (Pasinetti 1981, xii)

The vertically integrated sector, with its technical coefficients derived as a linear combination of the production coefficients of an input-output model, widens both the theoretical bases and the understanding of economic reality. Additionally, the notion of a vertically integrated sector does not depend on technical changes, and is therefore quite useful for the study of technical progress and economic dynamics. (We are grateful to GianDemetrio Marangoni for pointing this out to us.) In fact, Pasinetti adds:

> Any process reaches its completion only when the product which comes out is a final commodity (consumption or investment good). A vertically integrated sector is, therefore, from an inter-industry point of view, a very complex 'sector', as it repeatedly goes through the whole intricate pattern of inter-industry connections. However, from the point of view of the homogeneity of the inputs, it becomes a very simple one, as it eliminates all intermediate goods and resolves each final commodity into its ultimate constituent elements: a (flow) quantity of labour and a (stock) quantity of goods. It may be interesting to recall that this procedure was used by Léon Walras himself in his *Eléments*, although in a more rudimentary way. (Pasinetti 1981, 110)

In this way, it is possible to observe the mechanisms of structural dynamics, skipping the complex interrelations among different productive processes as they are described in the classical circular representations of the economy. 'This is achieved by setting into the background the role of intermediate products, which are at the centre of the circular approach' (Baranzini and Scazzieri 1990, 304; 2nd edn, 2012).

3.6.3 Paolo Costa and GianDemetrio Marangoni Building on Stone (and Leontief)

Two further Italian economists who have followed in the footsteps of Richard Stone and Wassily Leontief are Paolo Costa and GianDemetrio Marangoni. Their book *Economia delle interdipendenze produttive* (1995b) presents the input-output analysis in all its dimensions and in all its development prospects. The input-output model is expanded to take on the connotation of a general equilibrium model, no longer limited only to manufacturing processes but extended to the social and natural environment. The enlargement of the input-output model occurs through the 'closure' of the model itself; that is, the transformation of the exogenous factors in endogenous variables. So, the closure of the input-output model with respect to consumption is realized by explicitly considering the relationship between the amount of income and final consumption. The closure of the input-output model with respect to foreign trade ties national sectoral production to levels of import and export of goods and services. To close the input-output model with respect to investments means to bind investments to the levels of sectoral production, according to an adequate theory of capital accumulation. In this regard, it is worth mentioning here another work by Costa and Marangoni (1995a). The paper presents one of the first estimates of the capital stock in Italy, disaggregated by branch of origin and branch of destination. The tables of 23 rows and 23 columns are constructed using the perpetual inventory method, and consider different assumptions about depreciation and the average life of capital assets. The work of Costa and Marangoni (1995a) ends with the presentation of some applications of input-output to the study of the environmental impact of economic activity, addressing a question raised by Leontief (1970). Finally, we may note that in a short essay in 1973 'Process, Capacity and Control in an Input-output System' published in the *L'industria*, Richard Stone discusses the possible use of input-output analysis at micro-economic level for the choice of production processes. The idea was taken up and developed by Marangoni and Fezzi in their paper 'Input-Output for Management Control: The Case of Glaxo-Smithkline', *Economic Systems Research*. This is an innovative and potential new area of application of input-output analysis.[22]

3.6.4 Luigi Solari and the School of Geneva on Stone

We should also mention, in this framework, the works undertaken from the early 1960s at the University of Geneva, at the Departement d'économétrie, by a small group of economists led by the Swiss-Italian Luigi L. Solari (1932–1977), who was appointed at one of the earliest chairs of econometrics in Europe, and who had, among his younger researchers, Fabrizio Carlevaro and Erminio Baranzini, also from the Italian speaking part of Switzerland. After the premature death of Luigi Solari, another distinguished econometrician of Swiss-Italian origin, Pietro Balestra, was called to the chair of econometrics at Geneva with an exceptional 'procedure d'appel'. This is what Richard Stone says concerning Luigi Solari's volume *Théorie des choix et fonctions de consummation semi-agrégées: modèles statiques* in his 'Tribute to Luigi Solari' read at the European meeting of the Econometric Society held in Geneva in 1978:

> it is a truly econometric work in that it covers estimation problems and applications as well an economic theory. It begins with the theory of demand by an individual household and goes on to aggregation problems. It then takes up two demand systems: the linear expenditure system and the indirect addilog system. In discussing the first, Solari points out that the committed expenditures (the elements of the vector *c* in the usual notation) need not all be positive, though negative values of supernumerary income (often written as μ-p'*c*) are not admissible, and goes on to work

[22] Baranzini and Marangoni (2015) edited a volume *Richard Stone: An Annotated Bibliography*. This 'Annotated Bibliography' is part of the 'Stone Collection' at the Central Library of the University of Lugano, Switzerland. It presents brief comments on each item in the Collection, biographical notes and some more general scientific arguments. The Collection comprises Richard Stone's complete works in the field of economics and consists of approximately 200 articles and books, published between 1936 and 1991, the year of his death, as well as some posthumous works, manuscripts and secondary literature. Much of the material comes from a donation by Richard Stone's wife, Giovanna, that was made to the late Pierluigi Porta and the first author of this volume. The remaining part has been assembled and made available by the authors of this Bibliography and by the Library of the University of Lugano.

> out the consequences of this generalization. In discussing the second system he emphasises the concept of the hierarchy of goods, an idea which had always played an important part in René Roy's work on demand analysis. After dealing with economic theory Solari turns to various methods of estimating the parameters of demand systems and of carrying out the calculations. He concludes his applications of the linear expenditure system to Britain, Denmark, France, Italy and its major regions, Norway and Switzerland and of the indirect addilog system for Switzerland alone. (Stone 1978)

The last major work of Luigi Solari, written together with E. Rossier with the title *De l'économie qualitative à l'économie quantitative: pour une méthodologie de l'approche formalisée en sciences économiques*, published in 1977, is also reviewed by Richard Stone in his tribute to Solari. He summarised Solari's last thoughts as follows. 'Our aim is to understand the world we live in as exactly as possible and this requires quantitative knowledge, such as numerical values of demand and supply elasticities or of the dynamic multipliers of the system. But to obtain this quantitative knowledge we need an organizing framework and organizing principles and these are essentially qualitative, that is theoretical. Theory is therefore necessary to attain our aim but it is not sufficient.' (Stone 1978) This is why Solari, in this work, discusses in detail the concept and identification of the economic structure, comparative statics and dynamics, and the treatment of consumption and production. His pupils have, in the decades following his premature death in 1977, pursued some of these research lines; see, for instance, Fabrizio Carlevaro (1971, 1976, 1977, 1979), Erminio Baranzini (1978, 1996), Gabrielle Antille and Erminio Baranzini (1972), Antille E. Baranzini and Burle de Figuereido (1971). Pietro Balestra (1935–2005), who was called to the chair of econometrics set up by Luigi Solari, would also take up a number of research lines of his predecessor and maintain close personal contact with Stone; he also published a paper on the post-Keynesian theory of income distribution (see Balestra and Baranzini 1971) and was of much help to the first author of this essay in preparing a reply to Paul A. Samuelson in the *Oxford Economic Papers* in 1991.

We shall however briefly report a number of Italian scholars who have earned higher degrees at Cambridge in areas not contemplated by the present volume. We are well aware that this list is incomplete. The first is Sergio Destefanis, who is now Professor at the University of Salerno. After a First degree in economics at the University of Fribourg in Switzerland, in 1981 he earned an M.Phil. in economics at Cambridge. Thereafter, he wrote a Ph.D. that was awarded to him in 1992 with a thesis on 'The Macroeconomic Analysis of Wage Indexation, A Case Study for Italy 1963–1984' written under the supervision of James A. Trevithick. After leaving Cambridge, he took up the topics of wage and price determination, as well as the economic analysis of efficiency. In 1995, he was awarded the Tarantelli prize.

Stefano Fachin, now Professor of Economic Statistics at La Sapienza, Rome, received his Ph.D. from Cambridge in 1991 with a thesis on the 'Supply Side Shocks and Employment Dynamics'. He has specialized in econometric theory (the analysis of structural breaks, as well as the applications of the bootstrap) and in applied macro-economics. Three of his works were published in the *Oxford Bulletin of Economics and Statistics*, in *The Journal of Forecasting* and in *Labour*.

Giuseppe Ciccarone, now Chairman of the Faculty of Economics, La Sapienza, Rome, earned an M.Phil. in economics at Cambridge in 1984, and a Ph.D. in 1989. He has published a volume on the theoretical foundations of economic policy and is the co-author of a study on growth and distribution in Italy.

Angelo A. Rossi, a scholar of Swiss-Italian origin, holds a Ph.D. and a Habilitation of the University of Fribourg in Switzerland. From September 1967, with the support of a junior research fellowship of the Swiss Science Foundation, he was a research student at Trinity Hall, Cambridge, for a full year, where he was supervised by Richard M. Goodwin. There, he started working on an econometric model of the Swiss economy, before moving to Manchester to complete a Master's thesis with the well-known econometrician John (Jack) Johnston. On returning to Switzerland, Angelo Rossi took up, first, a research and teaching appointment at the Swiss Federal Polytechnic in Zurich, before being promoted to a full professorship at the IDHEAP (Swiss Graduate School of Public Administration) of the University of Lausanne. He has published widely on economic theory, on econometrics[23], and regional and economic planning. From 1998 to 2009, he was Director of the

[23] See Rossi (1966), Rossi and Schiltknecht (1971) and Rossi and Leighton (1971).

newly created University of Applied Sciences at Lugano. He has been an inspiration for a whole generation of young Swiss-Italian economists, one of whom is the first of the present authors. Massimo (Max) Beber in the early 1980s graduated in Political Science at the Catholic University of Milan, and then moved to Cambridge to undertake research work. From the webpages of the fellows of Sidney Sussex College, Cambridge, we gather that, between 1990 and 2000, Beber was a fellow of Selwyn College and a consultant with J. F. Chown and Company Ltd, London, advising on the interaction between prudential regulation and the corporate taxation of financial enterprises. Since 2000, he has been a Fellow and Director of Economic Studies at Sidney Sussex College, taking up the position of Senior Tutor in 2008. He has been a visiting lecturer at ASERI (the Graduate School of Economics and International Relations of the Catholic University of Milan).

3.7 Richard M. Goodwin and the Italian School of Economics

Pasinetti's (2007, 205–15) chapter on Goodwin has the title *'Richard Murphey Goodwin (1913–1996): The missed Keynes-Schumpeter connection'*. Others have also written on him; among these, Velupillai (1998a) in *The Economic Journal*; Palazzi (in Goodwin 1982b), Di Matteo (1990, 1992); Harcourt (1985, 2012b); Di Matteo et al. (2006). Goodwin is an important figure for Italian post-war economic thinking; in fact, while at Cambridge for the years 1951–80 he supervised a number of Italian research students, such as Pasinetti for instance. Subsequently, from 1980 until his death, he was a full Professor of Economics, and then Emeritus, at the University of Siena. It is worth recalling that Richard Goodwin, on 'leave' from Harvard, was a Rhodes Scholar at Oxford for three years from 1934 to 1937, at St John's College. He took a B.A. in PPE (Politics, Philosophy and Economics) and gained a B.Litt. at the end of his third year. At Oxford, he was supervised by Roy Harrod, who was his tutor in his second year. In his third year at Oxford, he wrote his B.Litt. thesis on monetary policy under the supervision of Henri Phelps Brown. He then went back to Harvard and took his Ph.D. there; he stayed at Harvard until 1951 where he came under the influence, as Pasinetti (2007, 209) points out, of Philippe Le Corbeiller, Wassily Leontief and, most significantly, Joseph Schumpeter. It was Richard Stone (born in 1913, as was Goodwin himself) who suggested that he come to Cambridge. First, with a Fulbright Fellowship (1951–52), and then with a faculty appointment (first, as a lecturer and, then, as a reader). Soon after retiring at Cambridge, in 1980, he won a professorship and was appointed at the University of Siena, where he retired at 75 (in 1988) and stayed, on and off, until his death in 1996. Pasinetti (2007, 211) notes that after 1980, at Siena, Goodwin's scientific activity 'literally exploded':

> Surrounded by young, admiring and at the same time challenging colleagues, by a host of puzzled but exacting students, who, as he said, 'made him work hard against his intentions' [...], his scientific output took off at an extraordinary rate. He did not simply rearrange his thoughts, as he would claim, but absorbed new mathematical tools and concepts that became available. Besides collecting, prefacing and publishing three books of previous essays, surprisingly he wrote two new books: one on the application of a new mathematical tool (chaos theory) to economics [1990] and the other (with a second part written with Lionello Punzo) on *The Dynamics of a Capitalist Economy* (Goodwin and Punzo 1987). Resuming original enthusiasm, he thus finally wrote the book that had been expected from him since his Harvard days. (Pasinetti 2007, 211)

Strictly connected with the works of Richard Goodwin, we first mention Kumaraswamy (Vela) Velupillai (1947). From 2001 to 2015, he was a full Professor (*professore di chiara fama*) of Economics at the University of Trento, where he founded the Algorithmic Social Sciences Research Unit. He is at present distinguished Professor of Economics at the New School of Social Research in New York. Velupillai has a long and distinguished curriculum. Born in Colombo, Sri Lanka, he took a B.E. at the University of Kyoto, a Master's at the University of Lund in Sweden, and a Ph.D. at Cambridge. He attended King's College(1973–76), first being supervised by Kaldor and then by Richard Goodwin; the title of his thesis was 'Aspects of the Structural Dynamics of Capitalist Economies'. Velupillai has written extensively in his fields of research and, among other things, in 1989 edited a volume in honour of Richard Goodwin. In 1998, two years after the death of Goodwin, he published two Goodwin biographies. His great friendship with the late Ferdinando Targetti has surely been behind his appointment '*per chiara fama*' at the University of Trento. He has devoted his recent efforts to the field of computable economics, macroeconomic theory, and the history and philosophy of economics. He has tried to mathematize both macro- and micro-economic analysis and, in particular, general equilibrium theory through the approach of 'recursion theory' and 'constructive mathematics'. Both micro- and macro-economics, for him, are intrinsically computable, in analogy with, and complementary to, recursive and experimental economics. As is usual with distinguished scholars, Velupillai has forged promising pupils, among whom are Stefano Zambelli, Shu-Heng Chen, Francesco Luna, Serena Sordi and Stephen Kinsella. Stefano Zambelli (2010) recently edited a *Festschrift* in honour of Velupillai, and a special issue of the journal *New Mathematics and Natural Computation*, edited by Shu-Heng Chen, was published in his honour in March 2012.

Another distinguished economist who started his research career with Goodwin is Terenzio Cozzi. Born in 1939, he graduated from the Catholic University of Milan and, in 1962, he entered Peterhouse, Cambridge, with a grant from the *Ministero della Pubblica Istruzione.* Apart for a term with Joan Robinson, he was supervised by Richard Goodwin, and, in 1969, he earned his Ph.D. with a thesis on 'A Disaggregated Model of Economic Growth and its Stability'. His examiners were Luigi L. Pasinetti and Michael O. L. Bacharach (then a temporary teaching fellow at Balliol College, Oxford, just before moving to Christ Church). Cozzi has written widely, inter alia, on economic growth, distribution, accumulation, Keynes and Sraffa. For decades (i.e. since 1970), he was Professor of Economics at the University of Turin. He was also chairman of the *Società Italiana degli Economisti* (2007–10).

Linked with Goodwin's and Velupillai's works, we should mention also the works of Alfredo Medio. Alfredo Medio took a Ph.D. in economics at Cambridge in 1975 with the title 'Nonlinear Models of Economic Fluctuations'. He is a life member of Clare Hall, and has widely published on non-linear models of economic fluctuations, on the theory and applications to economics of chaotic and lags dynamics, as well as mathematical models in economics. He has published two important volumes with Cambridge University Press. The first on *Nonlinear Dynamics: A Primer* and the second (jointly with Marji Lines) on *Chaotic Dynamics. Theory and Applications to Economics*. To a larger readership, Medio is known for his important entries in the *New Palgrave Dictionary* on 'Multiplier-Accelerator' and on 'cycles'.

Yet another distinguished, though often withdrawn, Italian economist who had studied at Cambridge and then went on to teach at the Catholic University of Milan, joining a strong team of former Oxbridge economists, was Luciano Boggio (1941–2012). From 1973 to 1976, Boggio undertook research at Cambridge, under the supervision of Luigi Pasinetti, Christopher C. Bliss and Domenico Mario Nuti. There, he earned a Ph.D. in economics with a thesis on 'Growth and Specialization in an Open Economy'. In the same year, he won a national competition for a full professorship; he then taught at the University of Calabria, Parma (1979–89) and, from 1989 onwards, at the Catholic University of Milan. His main research interests were, first, the role of international competitiveness on growth; second, the theoretical themes on the formation of relative prices (relative stability of production prices) and models of growth (Goodwin's model in particular); and, finally, the technological/economic catching-up by developing countries and its effects on trade and the welfare of developed countries. His textbook on growth and development, written jointly with G. Seravalli, was used in 23 Italian universities.

We should also add that at Siena was full Professor Frank O. Hahn (1925–2013). Michio Morishima (1923–2004), although without an official appointment, also spent long periods of his last two decades in Siena. The teaching and tutoring of these economists have surely had a deep and long-lasting effect on students and faculty of Siena. We should also add that Amit Bhaduri has, for many years, been a Professor at the University of Pavia; and that, since 2004, Christopher Leslie Gilbert, former fellow of Whadham College, Oxford, has been a Professor of Econometrics at Trento. We cannot, of course, report on their research plans and publications in detail, but it is clear that a number of Italian universities have attracted a number of prominent Oxbridge economists, so counterbalancing the Italy → Oxbridge flow of young Italian research students and scholars.

Richard Goodwin, during his teaching and stay in Siena (1980–96) was the leader of a group of younger economists who were attracted by his passion for dynamic economics and beyond. Goodwin acted as a catalyst in attracting young students from around the world to the Ph.D. programme, where he taught until his very last days. Thanks to its charismatic personality, Siena became a worldwide centre of discussion and elaboration on the themes of non-linear dynamics and long-term fluctuations. Among Goodwin's distinguished colleagues and friends from Siena, we quote the most prominent: Massimo Di Matteo, Lionello Punzo and Alessandro Vercelli. Of course, there are many others that we will have omitted. Massimo Di Matteo (1950) was a research student from 1974 to 1976 at Hertford College in Oxford, where he studied for a B.Phil. (now an M.Phil.) in economics with grants from Mediocredito and Fondazione Einaudi. The Oxford B.Phil. degree in those years was quite demanding. After his stay in Oxford, Di Matteo went back to the University of Siena where, in 1995, he became a full Professor. At Siena, he was a member of a research group for several years that was led by Richard Goodwin and Michio Morishima and undertook a comparative study of the economic development of Italy and Japan. Massimo Di Matteo worked closely with Goodwin; he has written numerous essays and edited volumes on Goodwin's scientific contribution (see Di Matteo 1982, 1988, 1990, 1992, 2011; with Filippi and Sordi 2006). Additionally, he became acquainted with Michio Morishima. How fruitful Michio Morishima's stay in Siena is proved by Di Matteo's (2013) paper 'Economic Dynamics as a Succession of Equilibria: The Path Travelled by Morishima' where he maintains that:

> In the paper I bring to the attention of the economists and historians of economic thought the idea of economic dynamics that one can found in the first book by Morishima published in 1950 but totally overlooked. It has a great interest not only because there it appears for the first time the application of new mathematical concepts ('structural stability') but also because he pursues a way of dynamizing general equilibrium theory that has been neglected in the postwar developments that appears to have been inspired by Samuelson. The paper has three parts. In the first and second parts I outline the development of economic dynamics and its applications to general equilibrium elaborated by Morishima; in the third part a comparison between the prevailing

idea of economic dynamics as originally put forward by Samuelson and that elaborated by Morishima is developed and discussed. (Di Matteo 2013, 123)

Lionello Franco Punzo is Professor of Economics at the University of Siena. After the laurea in economics at Siena, he took an M.Phil. in economics at the LSE. His interests have been in the theory and empirics of economic growth and complex dynamics, as well as in the fields of mathematical modelling and methodology, comparative growth and development, and, more recently, in the economics of tourism sustainability. He has, among many other publications, written or edited, with Goodwin, *The Dynamics of a Capitalist Economy* (1987); with Fabel and Farina (eds), *European Economics in Transition* (2001); and with Leskow and Puchet (eds), *New Tools of Economic Dynamics* (2005). Alessandro Vercelli is another distinguished Italian scholar with Oxbridge roots who played a central role in the growth of the Faculty of Economics of Siena in general, and in the vast research programmes of Richard Goodwin, Frank Hahn and Michio Morishima carried out while at Siena. He did this together with his colleagues Lionello Punzo, Massimo Di Matteo and others in the 1980s, 1990s and beyond. (See also Paragraph 2.3.14 above.)

3.8 From Oxford to Cambridge, and from Production Theory to Structural Change, Economic Dynamics and More: Roberto Scazzieri

After the mid-1980s Roberto Scazzieri, who lectured at the universities of Bologna and Padua before being appointed full Professor at Bologna in 1990, decided to move his research interests from Oxford to Cambridge, where he was first appointed Visiting Fellow at Clare Hall in 1992; Visiting Fellow at Gonville and Caius College in 1999; Visiting Fellow, Centre for Research in Arts, Social Sciences and Humanities (CRASSH) in 2004; Visiting Research Fellow, Centre for History and Economics, King's College; and Senior Research Associate at the Centre for Financial History, Newnham College. After devoting many years in Oxford to the theory of production (see Paragraph 2.7.2 above), at Cambridge he continued this research line while also focusing on the economics of structural change, working primarily on a comparison between 'horizontal' and 'vertical' models of economic structure, and on the micro-foundations of structural economic dynamics in a series of projects that have involved collaborative research with Alberto Quadrio Curzio, Luigi Pasinetti, Michael Landesmann, Lilia Costabile, Richard Arena, Pierluigi Porta, Harald Hagemann, Adrian Pabst, Prue Kerr and the first author of the present volume. More recently, he has undertaken research on the role of social structures in determining the patterns of economic interdependence and the characteristics of production linkages and networks. This work is partly theoretical and partly historical or empirical; the historical side of this work has been conducted in association with Carlo Poni[24] (Poni and Scazzieri 1994, 2007). On the theoretical side, recent developments of this research line are to be found in collaborative work with Adrian Pabst, formerly at Cambridge and now at the University of Kent (Pabst and Scazzieri 2012, 2016).

The comparison between 'horizontal' and 'vertical' models of economic structure is at the core of the volume *The Economic Theory of Structure and Change*, edited by Roberto Scazzieri and the present author, published in 1990 and reprinted in paperback in 2012. In this volume, attention is focused on the relationship between 'horizontal' and 'vertical' treatments of the economic structure that have characterized economic theory. The former focuses on the circular character of economic relationships, as exemplified in the Quesnay-Leontief approach; while the latter concentrates on the relationship between the 'fund' of productive resources and the production of finished goods. The nine essays of the volume provide a linkage between the two approaches and suggest a new conceptual framework combining an appreciation for the importance of the technical relationships with an assessment of the institutional setting of the economic system for processes of uneven dynamics. Linked with these issues, and with Hicksian economics, is the volume edited by Hagemann and Scazzieri, *Capital, Time and Transitional Dynamics*, published in 2009. It is not surprising that Scazzieri revisits a theme that he discussed

[24] Carlo Poni is a distinguished scholar of production networks in early modern Europe; he was a Visiting Fellow at St Antony's College, Oxford, and at Clare Hall, Cambridge.

at length with John Hicks in his Oxford years. In fact, as the editors point out, the aim of their volume is to evaluate the present state of modern 'traverse analysis' as initiated by John Hicks in his volume *Capital and Time* (1973)

> The analysis of an economy that originally has been in a growth equilibrium but which was disturbed by technical progress is one of the most challenging problems in economics. This book takes Hicks's work as the point of departure for theoretical work on the macroeconomic theory of capital dynamics along transitional non-steady state paths. The original contributions in this volume explore the manifold theoretical roots of traverse analysis in classical and post-classical literature, its features as a specific method of economic dynamics and its applications in a variety of fields from monetary economics to development and international economics. The essays thereby focus on the ways ahead from *Capital and Time* that have been suggested and actively pursued by a number of scholars in recent years. The central theme is the role of capital structures as a critical factor in determining the actual dynamics of any given economic system. This volume is inspired by the belief that this state of affairs is not a satisfactory one, and outlines a new agenda for capital theory. (Hagemann and Scazzieri 2009, i)

As we have already pointed out above (Section 2.7) the Hicksian contributions to economic theory have occupied Scazzieri in the conception and scientific structuring of the meeting 'John Hicks: One Hundredth Anniversary Workshop' held at Bologna in 2004; the papers were gathered and edited in 2008 by Roberto Scazzieri, Amartya K. Sen and Stefano Zamagni. This is without doubt the most up-to-date and thoughtful evaluation of Hicks's contribution, with the purpose of projecting it into the twenty-first century.

Ivano Cardinale is another Italian scholar who has taken up the study of the structural analysis of socio-economic systems (including their social classes and productive sectors), as well as decisions under 'structural and/or systemic uncertainty'. From 2012 to 2015, Cardinale was Mead Research Fellow in economics, college lecturer, and member of the Governing Body of Emmanuel College in Cambridge; in August 2015 he joined as lecturer in economics Goldsmiths of the University of

London. He had gained a B.A. (2005) in economics and finance at the University of Palermo, an M.Sc. (2007) in economics at Bologna (with a dissertation on 'Uncertainty, Similarity, and the Logic of Arguments: An Economic Theory of Political Decisions'), an M.Phil. (2009) at Girton College (with a dissertation on 'Black Swans, Entrepreneurship and Disruptive Technologies') and, finally, a Cambridge Ph.D. (2015) in organization theory with a dissertation on 'Making Sense of Unexpected Events'. Over the years, he has worked under the supervision of Roberto Scazzieri (at Bologna), Jochen Runde (at Cambridge) and Mark de Rond (also at Cambridge), and began collaborative research with both Runde and Scazzieri. For some time, Ivano Cardinale has been developing a structural political economy that specifies the structures within which political decisions take place. The starting point is the representation of economies as systems of interdependencies between sectors (Quesnay, Leontief, Pasinetti, Quadrio Curzio), both within and across countries. Structural political economy uses such economic representations as a tool of political-economic analysis: interdependencies are used as heuristics for the structure of economic interest of a given society, which may help to uncover the configuration of political interests and the relative positions of the groups that hold those interests. Such analysis grounds the space of political options available to a certain society, as well as those actually pursued, in its system of economic interdependencies and corresponding socio-political configuration.

This approach thus throws light on the interplay between political conflict and the exploration of the common interest that derives from belonging to the same political-economic system. Historical contexts are central in identifying the specific configurations of interests, and therefore the historically situated spaces of political options and the possibility that political confrontation leads to exploring solutions of common interest. Structural political economy assigns central importance to how structures influence the political strategies of groups and are, in turn, modified by them. To explain this mutual shaping, Cardinale is developing a theory of action in which structures influence the political strategies of groups by imprinting the cognitive schemes of actors who belong to those groups. Strategies, and decisions that derive from them, can, in turn, modify the structures, especially if actors become increasingly aware of those structures and the associated political options, and thereby become less conditioned by them. Cardinale is also exploring the implications of such theory of action for decision-making under fundamental uncertainty, and, together with Roberto Scazzieri, for the dynamics of the organization of production processes. Since his arrival in Cambridge, Cardinale was conference convener of various academic gatherings, including the international conference on 'The Political Economy of the Eurozone', held at the *Centre for Financial History* at Newnham College, Cambridge and co-convened with D'Maris Coffman and Roberto Scazzieri. His research work in political economy has led to collaboration with Coffman and Scazzieri on structural heuristics and structural theories of industrial fluctuations (Cardinale et al. 2014), as well as with Michael Landesmann on the political economy of tradable and non-tradable sectors within the Eurozone. He was also the principal convener of the Cambridge Research Seminar in Political Economy held at Emmanuel College. The seminar aimed at developing new categories of analysis that make it possible to explore the interface between the economic and political spheres of modern societies. It aimed to do so by combining structural analysis of political-economic systems and historical analysis, drawing on the conceptual tools of political economy—classical and modern, the institutional and structural analysis of economic systems, and economic history. By investigating the internal configuration of systems, understanding how causal mechanisms work differently in different socio-historical conditions, and by making relevant comparisons, the structural and historical approach makes it possible not only to explain the status quo, but also to identify alternative courses of action that are possible in a given context, although not realized. The seminar thus aimed to advance the understanding of political-economic systems and to contribute to the public debate by pointing to perspectives and solutions that overcome well-established categories and solutions, but are firmly grounded in what is possible in a given socio-economic context. Distinguished speakers have taken part in this programme, among them David Soskice, Alberto Quadrio Curzio, John Eatwell, Lilia Costabile, Michael Landesmann and Tim Wu.

3.9 Lilia Costabile: From the School of Naples to the Cambridge School of Economics

Lilia Costabile took an M.Phil. in economics at Cambridge in 1980 and a Ph.D. in 1986, having benefited from a British Council scholarship (1981–82) and a CNR scholarship. In 1997–98, she spent a year at Clare Hall, Cambridge, and became life member thereafter. Among her relevant publications, with specific reference to the Cambridge School of Economics (as G. C. Harcourt has defined it) we mention: Costabile and Rowthorn (1985) 'Malthus's Theory of Wages and Growth', *The Economic Journal*; Costabile (1997) 'Robertson and the Post-Keynesian Approach to Growth and Cycles' in *Capital Controversy, Post-Keynesian Economics and the History of Economics*; Costabile and Scazzieri (2012) '*Tendenze recenti del pensiero economico italiano*', in *Il Contributo Italiano alla Storia del Pensiero. Economia*. One of the most relevant theoretical contributions from Lilia Costabile is her paper, written jointly with Bob Rowthorn, on 'Malthus's Theory of Wages and Growth'. As the authors point out, an important aspect of this model is its explanation of unemployment as a permanent phenomenon and not merely as a transitory phase. More precisely, they consider in detail the interaction of Malthus's three fundamental principles of effective demand, population growth and diminishing returns. They conclude:

> The maximum rate of growth which the economy can sustain has been shown to depend both on the behaviour of population and on the extent to which technical progress offsets diminishing returns. However, the actual growth rate is determined by effective demand, though its influence on real wages. With a given investment function, only certain kinds of saving behaviour are consistent with full employment and growth at the maximum rate. If saving propensities are too high, demand will be inadequate, prices will be depressed, real wages will be too high, and the economy will stagnate. There is no automatic mechanism to eliminate the resulting unemployment, for the rising wages of the employed workers will be used, through the family, to sustain a permanent surplus of unemployed people. (Costabile and Rowthorn 1985, 435)

According to Rowthorn and Costabile, the Malthus model of growth differs substantially from Ricardo's approach, and especially from the post-Keynesian Kaldor-Pasinetti model; first, because in the post-Keynesian model full-employment (or nearly full-employment) is an assumption of the model, and the equality between ex-ante determined investment and ex-post savings is ensured by a redistribution of income between entrepreneurs (who have a larger propensity to save) and wage-earners (who have a smaller propensity to save). In Ricardo, full-employment is ensured by the natural wage rate, which is, in fact, allocated before rents and profits are distributed. But, according to Rowthorn and Costabile, Malthus assigns a central role to prices as the mechanism through which effective demand 'influences income distribution and hence economic growth'. Additionally, 'few have recognised variations in the price level as the mechanism by which saving and investment are brought into equality in the Malthusian system'. On the whole, we may say that Rowthorn and Costabile's mathematical model of Malthus's theory of economic growth and stagnation is important for the understanding of the classical school of thought, as is also the case with Pasinetti's (1960a) formulation of the Ricardian theory of growth.

Lilia Costabile has also written extensively on another distinguished Cambridge economist, Dennis Robertson. In her 1997 paper 'Robertson and the post-Keynesian approach to growth and cycles', she tries to re-establish the links between Robertson's theory and the post-Keynesian distribution theory. She does that by focusing on the role of Robertson 'as a precursor of the post-Keynesian approach to the theory of growth and cycles' (Costabile 1997, 310). At the end of her insightful analysis, she concludes that Robertson's equations, although 'rudimentary':

> show the extraordinary 'tension' which he imposed on the 'Cambridge equation', into whose simple symbols he initially grafted the equilibrium conditions for a stationary economy. This should not blind us to the fact that he anticipated many of the basic questions, which were later to be asked by the post-Keynesian analysis of growth, and many of their answers too. (Costabile 1997, 320)

Costabile adds that Robertson, to a certain extent, anticipated Domar's condition of equality between the actual and the warranted growth rate of the system, in the same way as he anticipated Harrod's 'natural' growth rate. However, she also points out that the equality between investment and savings by Robertson is not ensured via savings decisions but, rather, 'via changes in the price level and, consequently, in the distribution of income from wages to profits, or vice-versa (just as in Kaldor's [1955–56] model)' (Costabile 1997, 321). Finally, we should mention the volume that Costabile has edited recently, on the *Institutions for Social Well-Being* that contain several contributions by Italian scholars associated with Cambridge: Roberto Artoni, Francesca Bettìo, Alessandra Casarico, Massimo D'Antoni, Ugo Pagano and Roberto Scazzieri. The volume aims at examining the thesis according to which the imperatives of economic growth and healthy public finances are not easy to be reconciled with equity and solidarity. In other words, it would seem that social goals have to give way to economic arguments. It is surely worth noting that this issue was addressed by the editor of the volume, Lilia Costabile, and the contributors, among whom we find Tony Atkinson, well before 2008; that is, well before the financial crisis exploded with full force, precipitating the level of deficits and public debts of most industrialized countries. This is a proof that distinguished Italian scholars who were trained in Cambridge are often ahead of time in identifying economic and financial distortions that are, to say the least, in the making! As Costabile points out:

> This book explores questions concerning the efficiency and effectiveness of economic policies and their implications for social equity. The economic arguments presented support the adoption of an integrated approach to both economic and social objectives, and show how welfare states and other institutions can contribute to both equity and efficiency goals. The contributing economists, while well aware of the complex relations between efficiency and equity, do not share a common viewpoint on matters of policy. But none of them subscribes to the above-mentioned interpretation that gives priority to efficiency over social justice. (Costabile 2008, x)

A conclusion that certainly, and unfortunately, anticipates the turn of events that would precipitate most industrialized countries into a dramatic financial and public accounts situation from 2008 onwards.

3.10 Pier Luigi Porta: From the Lombard Enlightenment to the Cambridge School of Economics

Pier Luigi Porta (1945–2016) was another much distinguished associate of the Italian-Cambridge school of economics who spent much time on the Cam. Porta first arrived in Cambridge in September 1970 with a grant from the British Council. He was admitted as a research student at Christ College and, in the following year, he took a Master's in development economics. He came back to Cambridge later with the support of various grants, was an academic visitor to the Faculty of Economics and, since 1993, he had been a life member of Wolfson College. In Italy, in the early 1970s, he became involved with the Italian edition of Ricardo for the series *Classici dell'economia* (for Unione Tipografico-Editrice Torinese—UTET), which he eventually edited and published by the mid-1980s. That Italian edition was meant to be based on Sraffa's definitive edition of the *Works and Correspondence of David Ricardo*. However, according to the authors of this essay, Porta will be remembered for the editing in 1992 of David Ricardo's *Notes on Malthus's 'Measure of Value'*, for Cambridge University Press. As Porta has pointed out to us, this booklet is a companion volume to 21 previous Royal Economic Society editions of *The Works and Correspondence of David Ricardo*, edited by Piero Sraffa with the collaboration of Maurice Dobb. It completes the record on Ricardian value theory by reporting on Ricardo's response to Robert Thomas Malthus's 1833 pamphlet on *The Measure of Value Stated and Illustrated.* Ricardo's *Notes* were, in Sraffa's words, 'the only considerable item not appearing in the *Royal Economic Society* edition of his works':

> The first publication of Ricardo's *Notes* was encouraged by the late Piero Sraffa, to whom the editor [Pier Luigi Porta] showed a copy of the MS [Manuscript] in January 1978. The idea of an edition of the *Notes* as a companion volume to the *Royal Economic Society* edition of Ricardo and Malthus was first suggested in May 1987 by Roberto Scazzieri. (Porta 1992, xxi)

Not surprisingly, Porta maintains[25] that the main gist of Piero Sraffa's contribution to Political Economy lies, first, in his criticism of the neo-classical-marginalist system and, second, in his endeavour to establish an alternative approach to the discipline. Hence, according to him, for almost an entire century, there is a definite continuity within the Cambridge school of economics taken in a long-run perspective, from Alfred Marshall down to the 1970s; that is, the time span that bears the imprint of a strong profile of the Cambridge identity. Marshall, Keynes and Sraffa are the founding fathers of the school and they mark three very different ways of achieving the same objective: the criticism of the 'static' philosophy of the neo-classical-marginalist school of economic analysis and thought. Porta's interpretation and contribution is firmly based on the belief that Marshall pursued this objective by emphasizing the 'social economy' perspective. Keynes chose, instead, to lay the emphasis on the criticism of Say's Law in the context of a deeper analysis of the short-run dynamics of the system. Finally, Sraffa had the surplus theory, or the basis of Marx's *Mehrwert*, in mind. Those are three completely different ways to go beyond the purely allocative horizon. Sraffa's strategy began with an analysis of the surplus, which soon turned into research on problems of the definition and measure of the surplus itself, in order to provide a secure basis for the approach. In choosing Marx as his own starting point, Sraffa was unique in conceiving his own research programme as a clearly non-marginalist programme, designed to revert to a classical canon in Marx's sense. At the same time, Sraffa, who had commenced research with a positive and constructive aim in mind for a new approach to economics, through time felt obliged to retreat to what he referred to as a prelude

[25] The arguments that follow have been formulated by Porta himself in a correspondence dated July 2013 that he had with the first author of the present volume.

to a critique of marginalist economics. The prelude thus concentrated on the negative task of proving the marginalist approach untenable and therefore to be abandoned, losing somewhat sight of the main aim (of which Sraffa continued to be perfectly conscious at all stages) of providing an alternative—a task explicitly left to others.

Over the years, Porta gradually came to study Sraffa progressively more closely. From 1978, Porta started having access to his (Sraffa's) unpublished papers, since Sraffa allowed him to work in his college rooms in Nevile Court at Trinity College-a privilege that was granted to very few scholars indeed. Eventually, Porta came to realize that his approach to Sraffa and to the whole of Cambridge School paralleled Pasinetti's contributions in his book of 2007 (*The Cambridge Keynesians. A Revolution Still to Be Accomplished*). Porta's introduction to the Italian edition of Ricardo (1984) emphazised the novelty of the Sraffian interpretation of Ricardo. At the same time, it pointed out that Sraffa was playing down the significance of the dynamic side of Ricardo's approach and concentrated almost exclusively on value and distribution. The question of technical change in Ricardo, made prominent especially in the use of diminishing returns in agriculture, was not at centre stage, so much so that Sraffa invented a solution to the invariable measure of value, which is based on given technology. That approach then led Porta to study, in particular, those authors who had a dynamic approach within the Cambridge school—in particular, Nicholas Kaldor and, above all, Luigi Pasinetti.

From the early 1990s, Porta became increasingly conscious that Pasinetti's frame of analysis represents an important step in the critique of economic theory, of which Sraffa had laid down the prelude. Moreover, Porta came slowly to realize that Pasinetti's approach is to be read as a development of economic thought along the Italian tradition and, more particularly, it is to be understood in the light of the Italian Enlightenment (to which Quadrio Curzio and Scazzieri have also contributed). The dynamic emphasis, according to Porta, sets Pasinetti squarely within the strand of the Italian school of economic thought. In this way, the Cambridge School of Economics, within which Pasinetti occupies an important place, comes to rehabilitate the works of Adam Smith, and to set a direct thread between Scottish and Italian Enlightenment. This applies to the foundations of Pasinetti's *structural* analysis, on the one hand, together with his concern for the *dynamic nature* of the fundamental problems, on the other, as well as to the analysis of the *institutions* and the practical conditions to which the theory should apply.[26]

This led Porta to a line of inquiry which focuses on Adam Smith. The idea of the classical school in economics, from time to time, has taken inspiration from different specific contexts. In some cases, it has sometimes been common to prioritize the Smith-Ricardo-Marx line stressing value and distribution. From another angle, it is instead intended to give space to a Smith-Ricardo-Marshall/Walras-Pareto line, with emphasis on *allocation* and *equilibrium*. Of course, here, Porta uses a deliberately simplified representation, which should be carefully qualified: for example, to include debates developed over recent years on the contribution made by Marshall. However, a further relevant perspective leads him to highlight how, today, classical economics provides a way to revive concepts rooted in the economics of *growth*. In that sense, the perspective leads to conceive the classical paradigm as a child of the Enlightenment, and of the Italian Enlightenment, in particular: there is everything one needs to emphasize in terms of dynamic processes, learning, institutions and reasons for action. At the same time, structural dynamics finds its natural place as the only constructive branch of post-Keynesian Cambridge, which is set for Porta to have a future. Unfortunately his ambitious research programme came abruptly to an end with his premature death on 29 January 2016.

[26] In 2012, Richard Arena and Pier Luigi Porta edited a volume *Structural Dynamics and Economic Growth*, primarily intended to reassess Luigi Pasinetti's theory on structural dynamics, accumulation and distribution in the framework of the recent developments of the economic literature, with contributions from economists writing in both the mainstream and the Cambridge Keynesian tradition, including Luigi Pasinetti, William Baumol, G. C. Harcourt, Robert Solow and Roberto Scazzieri.

3.11 Institutions, Different Economic Settings and Gender Economics

3.11.1 Introduction

In this section, we shall gather together six Italian scholars with strong Cambridge connections who, from different angles, have formulated ground-breaking ways of economic analysis by considering original institutional settings or organizational structures that the classical literature had not yet offered. This is the situation with Ugo Pagano who, starting from the neo-institutional and radical schools, has defined *organizational equilibria* as situations where a set of rights brings about technological characteristics of the resources consistent with such a set of rights (technology). Yet another field of research of this area, connected with different economic settings and dynamics, is *gender economics*, a relatively new area for which there is yet no a specific definition. However, scholars of this field of analysis agree that gender economics combines economics, gender studies, sociology and demography. According to gender economics, the characteristics, roles and behaviour patterns that distinguish genders and define their social relations are not biologically determined but, rather, are the result of changes in society and culture; consequently, they differ in time and space. An example that is often cited in the literature concerns micro-finance—specifically, the fact that the decision to extend loans in developing countries mainly to women has guaranteed very high reimbursement rates and, therefore, the success of the entire programme. This difference in behaviour and attitude must be investigated in relation to public policies, investment, environment, innovation and health; they are all gender economics fields of research. Gender economics studies the influence of gender on the economy and on economic decisions; at the same time, gender economics attempts to measure the impact of decisions and of economic policies on gender. In recent years, studies on gender economics have grown considerably, especially in order to provide useful tools to quantify the benefits derived from the implementation of the concepts in business, policy and economic theory. The most promising field of application today is the evaluation of equity, efficiency and the transparency of public policies in relation to gender issues. Two main strategies have been developed, mainly in the last two decades: *gender mainstreaming* and *gender budget analysis*. Gender mainstreaming aims at reaching gender equality. Gender perspectives and gender equality are no longer an end per se: they become a reference for all public activities (development policies, research, legislation, resource allocation, and so on). Gender budget analysis examines public expenditure and revenue, highlighting their different impacts on gender (a topic of particular relevance concerns the different effects of taxation on the professional activities of men and women). Francesca Bettìo, Antonella Picchio del Mercato, Giuliana Campanelli-Andreopolus, Annamaria Simonazzi, Paola Villa and still other Italian scholars have produced seminal works within this framework.

3.11.2 Ugo Pagano

Ugo Pagano (1951) is professor at the University of Siena, where he graduated in 1973. One year later, he left for Cambridge; there, in 1983, he earned his Ph.D. in economics. Immediately afterwards, he was appointed Fellow of Pembroke College and university lecturer. According to his personal page, his 'fields of interest include institutional and evolutionary economics, law and economics, varieties of capitalism, innovation and IPR, bioeconomics and the economics of nationalism and globalization'. In order to endogenize the notions of 'means' and 'ends', he is convinced that it is necessary to explain that considering only leisure in a given utility function is equivalent to assuming that workers are 'physical things' like corn or iron, and not specifically 'human beings'. In 1985, he published a volume on *Work and Welfare in Economic Theory* (Blackwell) that was reviewed by David Collard in *The Economic Journal* as follows:

> Many of us have long been puzzled by an apparent lack of interest on the part of economists, whose subject 'is the study of mankind in the ordinary business of life' in the process of work. In modern analysis work is, indeed, of enormous interest and importance for two instrumental reasons; it is a means of earning money to buy goods and it uses up leisure

> time—both of these enter into individual utility functions. But work itself does not. In a purely formal sense it often turns out not to matter very much whether we talk of the disutility of work or the utility of leisure. To that extent the matter is not of great concern. And it is highly convenient to treat leisure as a commodity so that non-leisure (work) can be brought squarely within the standard optimisation exercise for households. Yet the worry persists. Ugo Pagano, in this excellent and stimulating book, has chased the problem into the open: it may no longer be concealed. Much of what Pagano has to say is summarised in a single passage. 'Since profit-maximising (or even output-maximising) behaviour requires that a given amount of manpower must be allocated by deskilling jobs, profit-maximising managers act consistently with social welfare maximisation. *When workers' preferences are taken into account*, however, deskilling no longer necessarily improves social welfare'; page 117, italics added. (Collard 1986, 224)

Summing up, we may conclude that Ugo Pagano is, above all, known for having defined *organizational equilibria* as characterized by a 'set of resources' compatible with a given 'set of rights'. In this sense, the institutional set-up turns out to be crucial for the definition and evolution of civil societies.

3.11.3 Francesca Bettìo

Francesca Bettìo is Professor of Economics at Siena. She holds a degree in political science from Bologna (1973), an M.Sc. from the LSE (1978), and a Ph.D. from the University of Cambridge (1984), where she enrolled in 1978. Her Ph.D. thesis was on the sexual division of labour in Italy. She has taught in several Italian universities and, in the academic year 2002–03, she was a Monte dei Paschi Visiting Fellow at St Antony's College, Oxford. According to her personal page at the University of Siena, her main areas of expertise are labour, gender and population economics. Her research interests range from fertility and female labour market issues—including wage differentials, discrimination, and labour market segmentation—to the economic analysis of the family, of care work and, recently, of international female migration. Her ongoing research projects address the potential conflict between care for the elderly and paid work, the impact of the economic crisis on female and male employment, and the gender gap in pension income. She has a long record of working for international organizations, primarily the European Commission, and is currently Lead Coordinator of the European Network of Experts on Gender Equality (ENEGE), a network of experts from 34 countries. She published a volume on *The Sexual Division of Labour*, with Clarendon Press in 1988.

3.11.4 Antonella Picchio del Mercato

Antonella Picchio del Mercato is full Professor at the University of Modena. She holds an M.A. in economics from the Utah State University, a degree in political science from the University of Padua, an M.Phil. from the University of York and a Ph.D. from the University of Cambridge, where she enrolled with a grant from the CNR. She has taught, inter alia, macroeconomics, gender economics and human development. According to her page at the GEM-IGW and GEM-Europe, she is Fellow of the Human Development and Capability Association and editor of the *Journal of Human Development and Capabilities*. She is the author of the volume *Social Reproduction: The Political Economy of the Labour Market* (Cambridge University Press 1992), editor of *Unpaid Work and the Economy: Standard of Living in a Gender Perspective* (Routledge 2003, 2006) and the author of seminal papers on the history of economic thought, surplus approach and gender economics. Her volume *Social Reproduction* has been presented as follows:

> An important characteristic of labour that distinguishes it from capital is that it bears the costs of its own sustenance, the extent to which it does so varying with different institutional arrangements. Economic theory has generally overlooked this, one consequence being that it has neglected the distinctive role played by women. This book traces the deepening insensitivity of post-classical economic theory to this issue, taking the 1834 *Poor Law* and the reassessment of it in 1909 as illustrations of the social implications of this theoretical inadequacy. These examples reveal the general

remoteness of housewives from market discipline, and the need for state intervention to offer them support.

Generally speaking, the aim of Picchio's more recent work has been to define the process of social reproduction from a demographic point of view, by taking into account the complexity of such a process as it is represented by individual life-cycles in different social contests. Picchio's aim is to enquire into the growing tension between the significance of producing commodities for the markets and that of reproducing human beings, brains and relations. Such a tension reflects itself on men, women and on overlapping generations—but it is a feature of the capitalistic system. Such tension is obviously to be found in the labour market. According to Antonella Picchio, mainstream economics separates the 'mercantile' sphere from the 'domestic' sphere; and women are the main victims of such an approach.

3.11.5 Giuliana Campanelli

Giuliana Campanelli (-Andreopoulos) earned a laurea in political science at Bologna in 1978. In 1981, she gained an M.Phil. in economics at Trinity College, Cambridge; followed, in 1990, by a Ph.D. on 'Growth and Structural Changes of the Italian Economy: 1960–79' written under the supervision of Prof. Brian Reddaway. She was a lecturer at the University of Bologna (1982–91), Associate Professor at the University of Catania (1992–94) and at the University of Bologna (1995–2001). In 2001, she moved to the William Paterson University (NJ, USA) where she was appointed full Professor in 2007. Her research interests cover the history of economic thought and, in particular, the early mathematical formulations of classical economists (particularly W. Whewell); the economics of development and, in particular, processes of growth, as well as changes in the production structure; and gender economics, in particular female economists in academia. Her paper, published in 2009 in the *Cambridge Journal of Economics*, entitled 'Growth and Changes in Economic Structure: A Straightforward Statistical Approach with an Application to the Italian Economy' starts as follows:

> The paper presented here, part of my PhD dissertation written under Professor Brian Reddaway's guidance, is offered as an example of his approach to applied economics as well as a tribute to his legacy. The scope of this paper is to suggest an operational approach to the analysis of growth, an approach that allows us to grasp immediately the most important changes that might occur in the structure of an economy. This procedure is applied to the Italian economy over the period of its most rapid growth (1960–79) to see whether some of the most important results established in the literature on modern economic growth are confirmed. (Campanelli-Andreopoulos 2009, 421)

As mentioned, Giuliana Campanelli's research also focuses on gender economics and, in particular, on women economists in academia. This is strongly reflected in her studies on unpaid work and consumption, and on the relationship between women and development. Specifically, her paper in the *Journal of Diversity Management* entitled 'Tariffs in Apparel and Footwear: A Gender Approach' examines whether gender plays a role in the setting of tariffs and how they affect consumption. Her policy recommendation is not only to lower tariffs, but also to eliminate gender differences and their implications.

3.11.6 Annamaria Simonazzi

Annamaria Simonazzi is Professor of Economics at La Sapienza, Rome. She earned her First degree in Modena and, in 1975, she enrolled for a Ph.D. at Cambridge. She is the director of the Master's in Economics and local coordinator of the European Ph.D. in Socio-Economic and Statistical Studies. According to her personal page at the *Institute for New Economic Thinking*, she presides over the Scientific Committee of the *Fondazione Giacomo Brodolini*, a research institute carrying out research activities, technical assistance and capacity building in the fields of labour, economics, development and culture in Europe. Her research interests range from macroeconomics, to social policy, and gender and labour economics. Her publications include the paper 'Economic Relations between Germany and Southern Europe' in the the *Cambridge Journal of Economics* (2013, co-authored) 'Change in Care Regimes and Female Migration'; 'The

"Care Drain" in the Mediterranean' in the *Journal of European Social Policy* 2006 (co-authored); 'Italy: Continuity and Change in Welfare State Retrenchment' in D. Vaughan-Whitehead (ed.) *The European Social Model in Crisis—Is Europe Losing its Soul?*, Elgar 2015. Prior to this, she has written on Keynesian economics.

3.11.7 Paola Villa

Paola Villa is full Professor of Industrial Economics in the University of Trento. In 1974, she earned a degree in political science at the Catholic University of Milan; in 1978 she earned a B.A. in economics at Cambridge, and in 1984 a Ph.D. Her main research field is labour economics, with an emphasis on gender economics. She has widely published on labour market segmentation, wage structure, the role of small firms and labour market regulation and deregulation. In the last two decades, she has focused on the issues connected with women's integration into the labour market, the dynamics of households, the role of the social state and the dynamics of fertility. In 1981, she published a paper on 'Labour Market Segmentation and the Construction Industry in Italy' in a volume edited by the Academic Press; in the 1980s, she co-authored a number of papers with Sebastiano Brusco on labour market segmentation. Since the early 1990s she has worked and published with Francesca Bettìo on trends and prospects for women's employment in Italy and elsewhere. Not surprisingly, she has also co-authored a number of scientific papers with Annamaria Simonazzi. It is also worth quoting the paper written jointly by Bettìo, Simonazzi and Villa on the 'Change in Care Regimes and Female Migration: The "Care Drain" in the Mediterranean' published in the *Journal of the European Social Policy* and which was a precursor to migration events that, at that time, were just commencing.

3.12 Oxbridge-Italian Scholars and the History of Economic Analysis

Italian economists—particularly those who were, in one way or another, linked with the University of Cambridge—have researched and published extensively on pre-classical, classical, marginalist and Keynesian economists. The list is very long, and we cannot mention them all; it is a daunting task that may be taken up by somebody else in the future. We provide below a partial list of the scholars, not necessarily in alphabetical order, who have contributed to the publication, assessment, reconstruction and formalization of the works of a restricted number of eminent political economists. The reference bibliography at the end of this volume will include a selection of the works here below; lack of space prevents us from providing all of them:

François Quesnay: Gianni Vaggi (1985, 1987, 2002); Pasinetti (1977, 1980, 1981); Quadrio Curzio and Scazzieri (1977–82, 1983); Candela and Denicolò (1982); De Vivo (2009); Garegnani (1999); Baranzini and Scazzieri (1990);

Adam Smith: Quadrio Curzio and Scazzieri (1977–82, 1983); Vivenza (1999b, 2001); Scazzieri (2006); Pasinetti (1974, 1981, 1993, 2007); Roncaglia (2005); De Vivo (2001b, 2007); Pivetti (1987b); Vianello (1999); Garegnani (1999); Baranzini and Scazzieri (1990); Baranzini and Quadrio Curzio (2012);

Anne Robert Jacques Turgot: De Vivo and Sabbagh (2015);

William Whewell: Campanelli (1982), Maneschi (2001);

David Ricardo: Piero Sraffa (1951, 1960); Pasinetti (1960a, 1974, 1977, 1981, 1982, 1989a, 1993, 2007); Quadrio Curzio and Scazzieri (1978–82, 1983); Quadrio Curzio (1967, 1975, 1988, 1998); Maneschi (1983, 1992, 1993, 1998, 2004, 2006, 2008); Casarosa (1978a, 1982a); Pier Luigi Porta (1983a, b, 1984a, 1990, 1992, 2014); Caravale (1976); Caravale and Tosato (1980); Campanelli (1982, 1996); Parrinello (2011); Arena (1992); Kurz and Salvadori (1993); Marcuzzo and Rosselli (1991); Zamagni (1984); Rossi (1966); De Vivo (1985a, 1987, 1994, 1996, 2004, 2007); Costabile and Rowthorn (1985); Pivetti (1987b); Roncaglia (1982); Roncaglia and Hollander (1982);

Robert Thomas Malthus: Porta (1992); Costabile (1983a); Costabile and Rowthorn (1985); Amendola et al. (1993); Quadrio Curzio (1975, 1980); Quadrio Curzio and Scazzieri (1978–82, 1983); De Vivo (2004, 2007, 2012);

Robert Torrens: De Vivo (1985a, 1986, 1996, 2000, 2001a, 2007);

Alfred Marshall: Becattini (2004); Raffaelli et al. (2010); Raffaelli, Becattini & Dardi (2006); Caldari (2004, 2007); Caldari and Masini (2011); Belussi and Caldari (2009); Casarosa (1978b, 1981, 1982b, 1984); Roncaglia (2000);

Arthur Cecil Pigou: Marcuzzo and Rosselli (2005); Bridel and Ingrao (2005); Caldari and Masini (2011); Baranzini and Scazzieri (1990);

John Maynard Keynes: A list here would be too long. Around 70 Italian economists with Oxbridge roots have published (or edited) volumes, essays and scientific papers on Keynes or on Keynes's economics;

Dennis Holme Robertson: Costabile (1983b, 1997); Besomi (2004); Naldi (2005);

Piero Sraffa: Our list would be incomplete. See also J. M. Keynes above;

Roy Forbes Harrod: Besomi (1995, 1996, 1999, 2000a, b, 2001, 2003, 2004, 2005a, b, c, 2006a, b, 2008); Medio (1979); Pugno (1992); Rampa et al. (1988); Varri (1996); Quadrio Curzio and Scazzieri (1978–82, 1983);

John Richard Hicks: Amendola and Gaffard (1988, 1998, 2001, 2008); Baranzini (2008); Casarosa (1978a, 1982a); Casarosa and Zamagni (1985); Cesari and D'Adda (2008); Ciocca (2008); De Cecco (2008); Ferri (1971, 2008); Fontana (2004); Marcuzzo and Sanfilippo (2008); Masera (1972, 2008); Onofri and Stagni (2008); Pasinetti and Mariutti (2008); Quadrio Curzio and Scazzieri (2008); Scazzieri et al. (2008); Scazzieri and Zamagni (2008); Velupillai (2008); Zamagni (1973, 1984);

Joan Violet Robinson: Besomi (2005c, 2006a, b); Biasco (1996); Ciccone (1984); Ciocca (1996); Garegnani (1989); Harcourt and Kerr (2009); Leon (1967); Lombardini (1996); Marcuzzo (1996a, b); Marcuzzo et al. (1996); Naldi (2005); Nardozzi (1996); Pivetti (1996); Salvadori (1996); Scazzieri (1996b); Varri (1996); Vianello (1996); Zamagni (1996);

Richard Ferdinand Kahn: Andreatta (1956); Besomi (2005b); Dardi (1993); Marcuzzo (1994, 1996a, 2002); Naldi (2005); Pasinetti (1989c, 1991, 2007); Leon (1967);

Nicholas Kaldor: Arena (1995); Baranzini (1992); Besomi (2005b, c); Boggio (1996); Fazi and Salvadori (1981, 1985); Gandolfo (1981); Maneschi (1974); Marcuzzo (1986); Marcuzzo and Rosselli (2005);

Naldi (2005); Panico (1992); Pasinetti (1962, 1979, 1983, 1985, 1989a, 2007); Salvadori (1991); Targetti (1986, 1991, 1992, 1993);
Richard Murphy Goodwin: Di Matteo (1982, 1984, 1988, 1989, 1992, 2011); Di Matteo et al. (2006); Gandolfo (1981); Harcourt (1985, 2012b); Pasinetti (1996, 2007); Ricci and Velupillai (1988); Velupillai (1989, 1998a, b);
Richard Stone: Quadrio Curzio and Scazzieri (1978–82, 1983); Quadrio Curzio (1967, 1975, 1988, 1998); (Pasinetti (1977, 1980, 2007); Solari and Rossier (1977); Baranzini (1978); Carlevaro (1976, 1979); Costa and Marangoni (1995a, b); Baranzini and Marangoni (2015); Marangoni and Fezzi (2002);
Luigi Lodovico Pasinetti: Andreoni (2013); Baddeley and Scazzieri (2012); Baranzini (1975a, 1991a, b, 2000, 2012); Baranzini and Harcourt (1993); Baranzini and Porta (2016); Baranzini and Quadrio Curzio (2012); Bini and Magliulo (1999); Bortis (2012); Campa (1975); Cardinale (2015); Commendatore (1999); Denicolò and Matteuzzi (1990); Faria (2001); Fleck and Domenghino (1987, 1990); Garbellini and Wirkierman (2013, 2014a, b); Hagemann (2012); Halevi (2016); Harcourt (2006, 2012a); La Marca (2005); Laing (1969); Lunghini (2008); Maneschi (1974); Mastromatteo (1989); Pettenati (1967, 1993); Reati (1998a, b, 2014); Reati and Raganelli (1993); Samuelson (1991); Samuelson and Modigliani (1966); Scazzieri (1983, 1996a); Solow (1959, 2012); Spaventa (2002); Steedman (1972); Stiglitz (1975); Taniguchi (1987); Teixeira (1998); Porta & Scazzieri (2008).

We shall now discuss a limited number of works in this area; naturally, we do not pretend to give a complete picture. For some economists, we have already provided an evaluation; see, for instance, Richard Stone.

Gianni Vaggi: We start with a short summary of two works of Gianni Vaggi, who is Professor of Development Economics at the University of Pavia, and holds a Ph.D. in economics from the University of Cambridge earned in the 1970s and written under the supervision of Maurice Dobb and John Eatwell. His examiners were Peter Groenewegen and Phyllis Deane. In 1997, he was Overseas Visiting Scholar at St John's College. He has written (and edited) several books and articles in learned journals, mainly in the field of the history of economic thought, particularly on classical political economy and on Quesnay. More recently, he has taken up the topic of development economics. His most widely quoted scientific paper was published in 1985 in *The Economic Journal* with the title 'A Physiocratic Model of Relative Prices'. In it, Vaggi first introduces the two previous and different interpretations of the *Tableau Économique*. According to him, the first strand of thought establishes no relationship between the process of physical growth (gross and net) of output and prices; while the second strand describes the *Tableau Économique* as a two-sector model, where prices depend on technology and distribution, and, again, are not related to the pace of economic growth. In his ground-breaking paper, Vaggi tries to bridge between the two strands and stresses that price determination in Quesnay:

> is closely related to his description of the process of development and growth of the French economy. Moreover, the price system presented in this article can show why Physiocratic policies could cause major problems in the social and economic structure of French kingdom. It is shown that the measures advocated by the Physiocrats might give rise to clashing economic interests between many classes of French society. Landowners could be opposed to their farmers; workers' wages might be depressed by a rise of the prices of agricultural products. Notwithstanding Quesnay's intentions, his analysis of the process of transformation of France into a developing country can hardly be reconciled with the welfare and prosperity of all social classes. Thus the model can help to single out the economic reasons which led many classes to oppose Physiocratic policies, hence jeopardising the process of development. (Vaggi 1985, 928–9)

Gloria Vivenza: A Professor at the University of Verona, Vivenza has spent various years in Cambridge and is a Life Fellow of Clare Hall. In 2001, she published a volume on *Adam Smith and the Classics. The Classical Heritage of Adam Smith* with Oxford University Press. As she points out in the volume, her work represents a complete survey of all Adam Smith's writings, and it follows Smiths topics: natural philosophy, jurisprudence, topics of economic interest, and literature. A chapter is dedicated to the recent consensus among a number of scholars that Smith's writings display strong elements of Stoicism. The volume proves, among other things: that the classics—Plato, Aristotle, Cicero and, as mentioned, the Stoics—had influence over Smith's thought; and how strong an impression classical thinking had on the intellectual élite of the eighteenth century. 'So much that the classics have left their mark on the scholarship and writing of the time', concludes Vivenza.

Among other Italian scholars who have dedicated attention to Adam Smith, it is worth quoting Roberto Scazzieri's (2006) 'A Smithian Theory of Choice' in the second issue of the *Adam Smith Review* and, above all, Alessandro Roncaglia's (2005) *The Wealth of Ideas. A History of Economic Thought*, published by Cambridge University Press, in which Chap. 5 on Adam Smith is brought to a close in this way: 'A substantive faith in man, though recognised as an essentially imperfect being, and in the possibility of progress in human societies, constituted the common element for Smith and for eighteenth-century Enlightenment Culture. But it also and mainly constitutes the positive message that renders the work of the Scottish thinker a central point of reference for pondering over man and society' (Roncaglia 2005, 154). The volume, first published in 2005, has the merit of tracing the history of economic analysis from its prehistory to the present day. It discusses at length the major figures of economic thinking, from William Petty to Piero Sraffa. According to the author: 'Economic Thought is seen as developing between two opposite poles: a subjective one, based on the ideas of scarcity and utility, and an objective one based on the notions of physical costs and surplus.' Not surprisingly, the Italian edition of this volume received the 2002 Jerome Blanqui Award from the European Society for the History of Economic Thought.

3.13 The (Scientific) Biographers

Several renowned Italian scholars with Oxbridge higher degrees or with strong connections with the two universities in the recent decades have systematically revisited, reconstructed and, in certain cases, refined the scientific works of many distinguished Oxbridge economists. Among the contributors, we find Maria Cristina Marcuzzo, Nerio Naldi, Annalisa Rosselli, Daniele Besomi, Bruna Ingrao, Claudio Sardoni, Anna Carabelli, Eleonora Sanfilippo, Fabio Ranchetti, Nerio Naldi, Ferdinando Meacci,

Giuliana Campanelli, Lilia Costabile, Roberto Scazzieri, Pierluigi Porta, Giancarlo De Vivo, Massimo Pivetti, and many others. We cannot be exhaustive here. This is how Maria Cristina Marcuzzo introduces the volume edited by herself and Annalisa Rosselli on the *Economists in Cambridge. A Study through their Correspondence, 1907–1946*:

> In many fields of research, the concentration of eminent scholars in Cambridge, which remained, until the Second World War, the intellectual centre of a country at the centre of the world, gave rise to a proliferation of ideas. In the field of economics, too, positive 'scientific revolutions' were set off by theoretical innovations, conditioning the way theory was conceived over the following years. J. M. Keynes, P. Sraffa, R. F. Kahn and J. Robinson were the leading figures in these theoretical revolutions, sparked off by internal debate and confrontation with their major opponents and interlocutors'. (Marcuzzo and Rosselli 2005, 1)

Maria Cristina Marcuzzo has also reported on a long interview with Nicholas Kaldor (see her *Nicholas Kaldor, Ricordi di un economista* 1986, as well as other writings). Luigi Pasinetti, among other papers on Kaldor and on Kaldor's writings, wrote a scientific biography in the *International Encyclopaedia of the Social Sciences* in 1979 and the especially long and thoughtful Chap. V 'Nicholas Kaldor, 1908–1986, Growth, Income Distribution, Technical Progress' in Pasinetti (2007). The latter volume also includes biographies of Richard F. Kahn, Joan V. Robinson, Piero Sraffa and Richard M. Goodwin. Several of these works have been listed in the reference bibliography at the end of this volume.

Bibliography

Amendola, M., & Gaffard, J.-L. (1988). *The innovative choice, an econometric analysis if the dynamics of technology*. Oxford: B. Blackwell.

Amendola, M., & Gaffard, J.-L. (1998). *Out of equilibrium*. Oxford: Clarendon Press.

Amendola, M., & Gaffard, J.-L. (2001). Out of equilibrium dynamics. In L. F. Punzo (Ed.), *Cycles, growth and structural change: Theories and empirical evidence, op. cit.*, pp. 115–127.

Amendola, M., & Gaffard, J.-L. (2008). Sequential analysis and out-of-equilibrium paths. In R. Scazzieri, A. Sen, & S. Zamagni (Eds.), *Markets, money and capital. Hicksian economics for the twenty-first century, op. cit.*, pp. 382–404.

Amendola, M., Froeschlé, C., & Gaffard, J.-L. (1993). Sustaining structural change: Malthus's heritage. *Structural Change and Economic Dynamics, 4*(1), 65–79.

Andergassen, R., Nardini, F., & Ricottilli, M. (2005). Firms' interaction and technological paradigms. In J. Leskow, M. Puchet, & L. Punzo (Eds.), *New tools of economic dynamics* (Lecture notes in economics and mathematical systems, Vol. 551, pp. 79–84). Berlin: Springer.

Andergassen, R., Nardini, F., & Ricottilli, M. (2006). Innovation, waves, self-organized critically and technological convergence. *Journal of Economic Behavior and Organization, 61*(5), 710–728.

Andreatta, N. (1956). L'ammortamento in relazione ad alcuni problemi di dinamica economica. *Rivista internazionale di scienze sociali, 64*(1), 12–31.

Andreoni, A. (2013). *Manufacturing development: Structural change and production capabilities dynamics*. PhD dissertation, University of Cambridge.

Antille, G., & Baranzini, E. (1972). *Input–output pour la Suisse: Expériences et analyses*. Geneva: Centre d'économétrie.

Arena, R. (1992). Une synthèse entre post-keynésiens et néo-ricardiens est-elle encore possible? *L'actualité Économique, 68*(4), 587–606.

Arena, R. (1995). Cycles et croissance: une approche neo-kaldorienne. *Revue Économique, 46*(6), 1433–1444.

Baddeley, M., & Scazzieri, R. (2012). *Introductory remarks*. The economics of structural change: Theory, institutions and policies: A conference in honour of Luigi Pasinetti. Cambridge, Gonville and Caius College, 12–13th September 2012.

Balestra, P., & Baranzini, M. (1971). Some optimal aspects in a two-class growth model with a differentiated interest rate. *Kyklos, 24*(2), 240–256. Reprinted in C. Panico, & N. Salvadori (Eds.). (1993). *Post Keynesian theory of growth and distribution, op. cit.*

Baranzini, M. (1975a). The Pasinetti and the anti-Pasinetti theorems: A reconciliation. *Oxford Economic Papers, 27*(3), 470–473.

Baranzini, M. (1975b). A two-class monetary growth model. *Schweizerische Zeitschrift für Volkswirtschaft und Statistik, 111*(2), 177–189.

Baranzini, M. (1976). *On the distribution of income in two-class growth models*. D. Phil. thesis, The Queen's College, Oxford.

Baranzini, E. (1978). *L'analyse des modèles d'entrées-sorties en économie: problèmes de méthodes et pratiques opératoires*. Berne/Frankfurt: Lang.

Baranzini, M. (1991a). *A theory of wealth distribution and accumulation*. Oxford: Clarendon Press.
Baranzini, M. (1991b). The Pasinetti and Anti-Pasinetti theorems: A reply to K. Miyazaki and P. A. Samuelson. *Oxford Economic Papers, 43*(2), 195–198.
Baranzini, M. (1992). The debate on Kaldor's theory of distribution. In F. Targetti (Ed.), *Nicholas Kaldor: The economics and politics of capitalism as a dynamic system* (pp. 143–59). Oxford: Clarendon Press.
Baranzini, M. (1995). Distribution, accumulation and institutions. In A. Heertje (Ed.), *The makers of modern economics* (Vol. II, pp. 1–28). Aldershot/Brookfield: E. Elgar.
Baranzini, E. (1996). *Les scénarios de l'évolution démographique en Suisse, 1995–2050*. Berne: Office Fédéral de Statistique.
Baranzini, M. (2000). Luigi Lodovico Pasinetti. In P. Arestis & M. Sawyer (Eds.), *Biographical dictionary of dissenting economists* (2nd ed., pp. 417–24). Cheltenham: E. Elgar.
Baranzini, M. (2008). Flexible saving and economic growth. In R. Scazzieri, A. Sen, & S. Zamagni (Eds.), *Markets, money and capital. Hicksian economics for the twenty-first century, op. cit.*, pp. 287–308.
Baranzini, M., & Harcourt, G. C. (Eds.). (1993). *The dynamics of the wealth of nations: Growth, distribution and structural change: Essays in honour of Luigi L. Pasinetti*. Basingstoke/New York: Macmillan/St. Martin's Press.
Baranzini, M., & Marangoni, G. (2015). *Richard Stone: An annotated bibliography*. Lugano: Università della Svizzera italiana.
Baranzini, M., & Mari, C. (2011). The Cantabrigensis-Italian school of income and wealth distribution. In *Gli economisti post-keynesiani di Cambridge e l'Italia*, Atti dei Convegni Lincei (pp. 235–340). Rome: Scienze e Lettere.
Baranzini, M., & Mirante, A. (2013). The Cambridge post-Keynesian school of income and wealth distribution. In G. C. Harcourt, & P. Kriesler (Eds.), *The Oxford handbook of post-Keynesian economics, op. cit.*, Vol. I, pp. 288–361.
Baranzini, M., & Porta, P. L. (2016). Luigi Lodovico Pasinetti. In R. A. Cord (Ed.), *The Palgrave companion to Cambridge economics*. London/New York: Palgrave Macmillan, 979–1001.
Baranzini, M., & Quadrio Curzio, A. (2012). *From Adam Smith to structural dynamics: Luigi Pasinetti's life-long contribution*. Paper presented at the conference 'the economics of structural change: Theory, institutions and policies, in honour of Luigi L. Pasinetti, Gonville and Caius College, Cambridge.
Baranzini, M., & Scazzieri, R. (Eds.). (1990; reprinted 2012). *The economic theory of structure and change*. Cambridge: Cambridge University Press; and 'Introduction', 1–20; 'Economic structure. Analytical perspectives', 227–333.

Baranzini, M., Rotondi, C., & Scazzieri, R. (Eds.). (2015). *Resources, production and structural dynamics*. Cambridge: Cambridge University Press.

Becattini, G. (2004). *Industrial districts: A new approach to industrial change*. Cheltenham/Northampton: E. Elgar.

Belussi, F., & Caldari, K. (2009). At the origin of industrial district: Alfred Marshall and the Cambridge school. *Cambridge Journal of Economics, 33*(2), 335–355.

Besomi, D. (1995). From *the trade cycle* to the "essay in dynamic theory". The Harrod-Keynes correspondence, 1937–1938. *History of Political Economy, 27*(2), 309–343.

Besomi, D. (1996). An additional note on the Harrod-Keynes correspondence. *History of Political Economy, 28*(2), 281–294.

Besomi, D. (1999). *The making of Harrod's dynamics*. London: Macmillan.

Besomi, D. (2000a). On the spread of an idea: The strange case of Mr Harrod and the multiplier. *History of Political Economy, 32*(2), 347–379.

Besomi, D. (2000b). Keynes and Harrod on the classical theory of investment. More on the origin of the only diagram in the general theory. *Journal of the History of Economic Thought, 22*(3), 367–376.

Besomi, D. (2001). Harrod's dynamics and the theory of growth: The story of a mistaken attribution. *Cambridge Journal of Economics, 25*(1), 79–96.

Besomi, D. (Ed.). (2003). *The interwar papers and correspondence of Roy Harrod* (3 vol.). Cheltenham: E. Elgar.

Besomi, D. (2004). Dynamics, trade and money in the correspondence between Roy Harrod and Dennis Robertson. *Research in the History of Economic Thought and Methodology, 22A*, 1–64.

Besomi, D. (2005a). The goodwilling outsider. The correspondence between Keynes and Harrod. In M. C. Marcuzzo & A. Rosselli (Eds.), *Economists in Cambridge. A study of their correspondence* (pp. 92–118). London: Routledge.

Besomi, D. (2005b). The Keynesian Tutor. Kahn and the correspondence with Sraffa, Harrod and Kaldor (with M. C. Marcuzzo as the main author, and F. Ranchetti). In M. C. Marcuzzo, & A. Rosselli (Eds.), *Economists in Cambridge. A study of their correspondence, op. cit.*, pp. 292–308.

Besomi, D. (2005c). The unlooked for Proselytiser. J. Robinson and the correspondence with Sraffa, Harrod and Kaldor' (with A. Rosselli as main author). In M. C. Marcuzzo, & A. Rosselli (Eds.), *Economists in Cambridge. A study of their correspondence, op. cit.*, pp. 309–327.

Besomi, D. (2006a). Roy Harrod and Joan Robinson on thriftiness and growth. An introduction to their correspondence, 1965–1970. *History of Economics Review, 44*(1), 1–15.

Besomi, D. (2006b). (Editing of) R. F. Harrod and J. V. Robinson, correspondence on growth theory, 1965–70. *History of Economics Review, 44*(1), 16–31.
Besomi, D. (2008). Harrod discontent with Harrodian growth theory. In R. Leeson (Ed.), *The Keynesian tradition. Archival insight into the evolution of the economics* (pp. 65–98). London: Palgrave Macmillan.
Biasco, S. (1996). Degree of mechanization of techniques and scale of mechanization of the economy. In M. C. Marcuzzo, L. L. Pasinetti, & A. Roncaglia (Eds.), *The economics of Joan Robinson, op. cit.*, pp. 148–173.
Bini, P., & Magliulo, A. (1999). Keynesianism in Italy: Before and after the general theory. In L. L. Pasinetti, & B. Schefold (Eds.), *The impact of Keynes on economics in the 20th century, op. cit.*, pp. 131–152.
Boggio, L. (1996). Growth and international competitiveness in a "Kaldorian" perspective. *Structural Change and Economic Dynamics, 7*(3), 299–320.
Bortis, H. (2012). Towards a synthesis in post-Keynesian economics in Luigi Pasinetti's contribution. In R. Arena, & P. L. Porta (Eds.), *Structural dynamics and economic growth, op. cit.*, pp. 145–180.
Bridel, P., & Ingrao, B. (2005). Managing Cambridge economics: The correspondence between Keynes and Pigou. In M. C. Marcuzzo, & A. Rosselli (Eds.), *Economics in Cambridge: A study through their correspondence, 1907–1946, op. cit.*, pp. 149–166.
Britto, R. (1969). *The life-cycle savings in a two-class growth model.* Paper presented at the December meeting of the Econometric Society, New York.
Britto, R. (1972). On differential savings propensities in two-class growth models. *Review of Economic Studies, 39*(4), 491–494.
Caldari, K. (2004). Alfred Marshall's idea of progress and sustainable development. *Journal of the History of Economic Thought, 26*(4), 519–536.
Caldari, K. (2007). Alfred Marshall's critical analysis of scientific management. *European Journal of the History of Economic Thought, 14*(1), 55–78.
Caldari, K., & Masini, F. (2011). Pigouvian *vs* Marshallian Tax. Market failure, public intervention and the problem of externalities. *European Journal of the History of Economic Thought, 18*(5), 715–732.
Campa, G. (1975). Indeterminatezza del saggio di profitto e rilevanza della propensione a risparmiare dei lavoratori e della tecnologia nel paradosso di Pasinetti. *Giornale degli Economisti e Annali di Economia, 1*(2), 16–55.
Campanelli, G. (1982). W. Whewell's contribution to economic analysis: The first mathematical formulation of fixed capital in Ricardo's system. *Manchester School, 50*(3), 248–265.
Campanelli, G. (1996). Ricardo's "curious effect": A mathematical formulation. *History of Political Economy, 28*(4), 641–662.

Campanelli-Andreopoulos, G. (2009). Growth and changes in economic structure: A straightforward statistical approach with an application to the Italian economy. *Cambridge Journal of Economics, 33*(3), 421–432.

Candela, G., & Denicolò, V. (1982). Coerenza static e incoerenza dinamica dei "Tableau Economique"'. *Giornale degli economisti e Annali di Economia, 41*(9/10), 605–637.

Caravale, G. A., & Tosato, D. A. (Eds.). (1980). *Ricardo and the theory of value, distribution and growth*. London/Boston: Routledge & Kegan Paul.

Cardinale, I. (2015). Towards a structural political economy of resources. In M. L. Baranzini, C. Rotondi, & R. Scazzieri (Eds.) *Resources, production and structural dynamics, op. cit.,* 198–210.

Cardinale, I., & Scazzieri, R. (2016). Austerity, expansion and financial policy: sectoral interdependence, time-structure of production, and medium term analysis. *Revue d'économie industrielle,* forthcoming.

Cardinale, I., & Scazzieri, R. (2017). *The Palgrave handbook of political economy,* London/New York, forthcoming.

Cardinale, I., Coffman, D'M., & Scazzieri, R. (2014). Towards a political economy of industrial fluctuations, introductory essay. In A. Aftalion (Ed.), *Periodic overproduction crises.* London: Anthem Books (English edition of A. Aftalion, *Les crises périodiques de surproduction,* Paris: Rivière, 1913).

Carlevaro, F. (1971). Formulation et estimation de consommation semi-agrégées. *The Canadian Journal of Economics, 4*(4), 441–470.

Carlevaro, F. (1976). A generalization of the linear expenditure system. In L. Solari & J.-N. Du Pasquier (Eds.), *Private and enlarged consumption: Essays in methodology and empirical analysis* (pp. 73–92). Amsterdam: North-Holland.

Carlevaro, F. (1977). Note sur les fonctions de consommation en prix et revenu réels de Fourgeaud et Natal'. *Econometrica, 45*(7), 1639–1650.

Carlevaro, F. (1979). *Luigi Solari: Essai de méthode et analyses économétriques.* Geneva: Librairie Droz.

Casarosa, C. (1978a). A new formulation of the Ricardian system. *Oxford Economic Papers, 30,* 38–63.

Casarosa, C. (1978b). Un contributo all'analisi dei fondamenti microeconomici della teoria keynesiana della domanda effettiva. *Rivista di politica economica, 68*(11), 1371–1409.

Casarosa, C. (1981). The microfoundations of Keynes's aggregate supply and expected demand analysis. *Economic Journal, 91*(361), 188–194.

Casarosa, C. (1982a). The new view of the Ricardian theory of distribution and economic growth. In M. Baranzini (Ed.), *Advances in economic theory, op. cit.,* pp. 227–239.

Casarosa, C. (1982b). Aggregate supply and expected demand analysis in Keynes's general theory: An essay on the microfoundations. In M. Baranzini (Ed.), *Advances in economic theory, op. cit.*, pp. 67–79.

Casarosa, C. (1984). The microfoundations of Keynes's aggregate supply and expected demand analysis: A reply. *Economic Journal, 94*(376), 941–945.

Casarosa, C. (2004). Gli studi nel Regno Unito della seconda generazione. In G. Garofalo, & A. Graziani (Eds.), *La formazione degli economisti in Italia (1950–1975), op. cit.*, pp. 535–554.

Casarosa, C., & Zamagni, S. (1985). Sir John Hicks: il pensiero e l'opera. *Studi Economici, 27*, 3–75.

Cesari, R., & D'Adda, C. (2008). A suggestion for simplifying the theory of asset prices. In R. Scazzieri, A. Sen, & S. Zamagni (Eds.), *Markets, money and capital. Hicksian economics for the twenty-first century, op. cit.*, pp. 252–274.

Ciccone, R. (1984). La teoria della distribuzione nell'analisi di Joan Robinson. *Note Economiche, 2*, 99–124.

Ciocca, P. (1996). "The golden age" and Joan Robinson's critique.In M. C. Marcuzzo, L. L. Pasinetti, & A. Roncaglia (Eds.), *The economics of Joan Robinson, op. cit.*, pp. 195–199.

Ciocca, P. (2008). Hicks versus Marx? On the theory of economic history. In R. Scazzieri, A. Sen, & S. Zamagni (Eds.), *Markets, money and capital. Hicksian economics for the twenty-first century, op. cit.*, pp. 146–156.

Collard, D. A. (1986). Review of work and welfare in economic theory, by Ugo Pagano (Oxford: B. Blackwell, 1985). *The Economic Journal, 96*(381), 224–225.

Commendatore, P. (1999). Pasinetti and dual equilibria in a post Keynesian model of growth and institutional distribution. *Oxford Economic Papers, 51*(1), 223–236.

Commendatore, P. (2002). Inside debt, aggregate demand and the Cambridge theory of distribution: A note. *Cambridge Journal of Economics, 26*(2), 269–274.

Commendatore, P. (2003). On the post Keynesian theory of growth and "institutional" distribution. *Review of Political Economy, 15*(2), 193–209.

Costa, P., & Marangoni, G. D. (1995a). *Economia delle interdipendenze produttive*. Padua: Cedam.

Costa, P., & Marangoni, G. D. (1995b). Productive capital in Italy: A disaggregated estimate by sectors of origin and destination: 1985-88. *Review of Income and Wealth, 41*, 439–458.

Costabile, L. (1983a). Natural prices, market prices and effective demand in Malthus. *Australian Economic Papers, 22*, 144–170.

Costabile, L. (1983b). Note sulla relazione tra credito, accumulazione e risparmio in *Banking Policy and the Price Level* di D. H. Robertson. *Studi Economici, 21*, 115–135.
Costabile, L. (1997). Robertson and the post-Keynesian approach to growth and cycles. In P. Arestis, G. Palma, & M. Sawyer (Eds.), *Essays in honour of Geoff Harcourt, op. cit.*, Vol. I, pp. 310–325.
Costabile, L. (Ed.). (2008). *Institutions for social well-being. Alternatives for Europe*. London: Palgrave-Macmillan.
Costabile, L., & Rowthorn, B. (1985). Malthus's theory of wages and growth. *Economic Journal, 95*(378), 418–437.
Costabile, L., & Scazzieri, R. (2012). Il pensiero economico nei decenni successivi al secondo dopoguerra. In V. Negri Zamagni, P. L. Porta, L. Costabile, R. Faucci, C. Perrotta, R. Scazzieri, & G. Todeschini (Eds.), *Il contributo italiano alla storia del pensiero. Economia* (pp. 739–765). Rome: Enciclopedia Italiana di Scienze, Lettere ed Arti.
Dardi, M. (1993). Lord Kahn's "the economics of the short period". In L. L. Pasinetti (Ed.), *Italian economic papers* (Vol. II, pp. 189–206). Bologna/Oxford/New York: Il Mulino/Oxford University Press.
De Cecco, M. (2008). Hick's notion and use of the concepts of fix-price and flex-price. In R. Scazzieri, A. Sen, & S. Zamagni (Eds.), *Markets, money and capital. Hicksian economics for the twenty-first century, op. cit.*, pp. 157–163.
De Vivo, G. (1985a). Robert Torrens and Ricardo's "Corn-Ratio" theory of profits. *Cambridge Journal of Economics, 9*(1), 89–92.
De Vivo, G. (1986). Torrens on value and distribution. *Contributions to Political Economy, 5*(1), 23–36.
De Vivo, G. (1987). David Ricardo. In *The new Palgrave: A dictionary of economics, op. cit., The new Palgrave: A dictionary of economics* (Vol. 4, pp. 183–198). London: Macmillan.
De Vivo, G. (1994). (Mis)interpreting Ricardo. *Contributions to Political Economy, 13*(1), 14–29.
De Vivo, G. (1996). Ricardo, Torrens, and Sraffa. A summing up. *Cambridge Journal of Economics, 20*(3), 387–391.
De Vivo, G. (Ed.). (2000). *Collected works of Robert Torrens*, 8 Vols. Bristol: Thoemmes Press.
De Vivo, G. (2001a). On Torrens's theory of profits. *Cambridge Journal of Economics, 25*(5), 697–703.
De Vivo, G. (2001b). Adam Smith and his books. *Contributions to Political Economy, 20*(1), 87–97.
De Vivo, G. (2004). Da Ricardo e Marx a Produzione di merci a mezzo di merci. Relazione al convegno 'Piero Sraffa' dell'Accademia Nazionale dei Lincei, feb-

braio 2003, Accademia Nazionale dei Lincei, *Atti dei Convegni Lincei, Convegno internazionale Piero Sraffa.* Rome: Accademia Nazionale dei Lincei.

De Vivo, G. (2007). Anglo Saxon cv continental scholarship: On critical editions of economic classics. *Contributions to Political Economy, 26*(1), 93–102.

De Vivo, G. (Ed.). (2009). *Il* Tableau Economique *di François Quesnay.* Riproduzione fotografica della copia conservata nella biblioteca della Fondazione Raffaele Mattioli. Milan: Fondazione Mattioli; and 'Introduzione', 7–12.

De Vivo, G. (2012). Malthus's theory of the "constant value of labour". *Contributions to Political Economy, 31*(1), 103–120.

De Vivo, G. (Ed.). (2014a). *Catalogue of the library of Piero Sraffa.* Milan/Turin: Mattioli/Einaudi Foundations.

De Vivo, G. (2014b). Samuel Bailey and the subversion of the classical theory of value. A note. *Contributions to Political Economy, 33*(1), 55–60.

De Vivo, G., & Sabbagh, G. (2015). The first translator in English of Turgot's reflexions *Sur la formation et la distribution des richesses*: Benjamin Vaughan. *History of Political Economy, 47*(1), 185–199.

Delli Gatti, D. (1987). *Il pensiero di Keynes (1923–1936) e l'interpretazione dei post-Keynesiani "soggettivisti".* Ph.D. Diss., Catholic University, Milan.

Delli Gatti, D., & Gallegati, M. (1990). Financial instability, income distribution and the stock market. *Journal of Post Keynesian Economics, 12*(3), 356–374.

Denicolò, V., & Matteuzzi, M. (1990). Public debt and the Pasinetti Paradox. *Cambridge Journal of Economics, 14*(3), 339–344.

Di Matteo, M. (1982). Two variations on a theme by Goodwin. *Economic Notes, 9*, 165–171.

Di Matteo, M. (1984). Alternative monetary policies in a classical growth cycle. In R. M. Goodwin, M. Krüger, & A. Vercelli (Eds.), *Nonlinear models of fluctuating growth, op. cit.*, pp. 14–24.

Di Matteo, M. (1988). Richard Goodwin and the evolution of a capitalistic economy. In G. Ricci, & K. V. Velupillai (Eds.), *Growth cycles and multisectoral economics: The Goodwin tradition, op. cit.*, pp. 93–101.

Di Matteo, M. (1989). Early discussions on long waves. In M. Di Matteo, R. M. Goodwin, & A. Vercelli (Eds.), *Social and technological factors in long term fluctuations, op. cit.*, pp. 403–418.

Di Matteo, M. (1990). Celebrating Richard Goodwin's 75th birthday. Quaderni del Dipartimento di Economia Politica, Università di Siena, 100, p. 89.

Di Matteo, M. (1992). Richard M. Goodwin. In P. Arestis & M. Sawyer (Eds.), *Biographical dictionary of dissenting economists.* Aldershot: E. Elgar.

Di Matteo, M. (2011). Towards a social philosophy for the twenty first century: Critical reflections on an unpublished essay by Richard Goodwin. *Journal of Public Finance and Public Choice, 29*(1), 33–49.

Di Matteo, M. (2013). Economic dynamics as a succession of equilibria: The path travelled by Morishima. *Structural Change and Economic Dynamics, 24*(1), 123–129.

Di Matteo, M., Filippi, F., & Sordi, S. (2006). The confessions of an unrepentant model builder: Rummaging in Goodwin's archive. *Structural Change and Economic Dynamics, 17*(4), 400–414.

Dow, S. C. (1991). Carabelli's *on Keynes's method* and O'Donnell's *Keynes: Philosophy, economics and politics. Economics and Philosophy, 7*(1), 132–139.

Faria, J. R. (2001). The Pasinetti Paradox in an intertemporal dynamic model. *Political economy* (Working Paper 13/01). University of Texas, Dallas.

Fazi, E., & Salvadori, N. (1981). The existence of a two-class economy in the Kaldor model of growth and distribution. *Kyklos, 34*(4), 582–592.

Fazi, E., & Salvadori, N. (1985). The existence of a two-class economy in a general Cambridge model of growth and distribution. *Cambridge Journal of Economics, 9*(1), 155–164.

Ferri, P. (1971). *La disoccupazione in un processo di sviluppo economico.* Milan: Giuffré.

Ferri, P. (2008). The economics of non-linear cycles. In R. Scazzieri, A. Sen, & S. Zamagni (Eds.), *Markets, money and capital. Hicksian economics for the twenty-first century, op. cit.*, pp. 309–327.

Fleck, F. H., & Domenghino, C.-M. (1987). Cambridge (U.K.) *versus* Cambridge (Mass.): A Keynesian solution of "Pasinetti's Paradox". *Journal of Post Keynesian Economics, 10*(1), 22–36.

Fleck, F. H., & Domenghino, C.-M. (1990). Government activity *does* invalidate the "Cambridge theorem of the rate of profit". *Journal of Post Keynesian Economics, 12*(3), 487–497.

Fontana, G. (2004). Hicks on monetary theory and history: Money as "endogenous money". *Cambridge Journal of Economics, 28*(1), 73–88.

Gandolfo, G. (1981). Kaldor, Goodwin, Marrama, Palomba e la teoria non lineare del ciclo economico. In *Gli economisti post-keynesiani di Cambridge e l'Italia* (pp. 115–124), Atti dei Convegni Lincei. Rome: Scienze e Lettere.

Garbellini, N., & Wirkierman, A. L. (2013). Productivity accounting in vertically (hyper-) integrated terms: Bridging the gap between theory and empirics. *Metroeconomica, 65*(1), 154–190.

Garbellini, N., & Wirkierman, A. L. (2014a). Pasinetti's structural change and economic gorwth: A conceptual excursus. *Review of Political Economy, 26*(2), 234–257.

Garbellini, N., & Wirkierman, A. L. (2014b). Blocks and circularity in labour requirements: An interplay between clusters and subsystems in the UE. *Structural Change and Economic Dynamics, 28*, 60–74.

Garegnami, P. (1966). Switching of techniques. *Quarterly Journal of Economics, 80*(4), 554–567.

Garegnani, P. (1962). *Il problema della domanda effettiva nello sviluppo economico italiano*. Rome: SVIMET.

Garegnani, P. (1970). Heterogeneous capital, the production function and the theory of distribution. *Review of Economic Studies, 37*(3), 407–436.

Garegnani, P. (1978–9). Notes on consumption, investment and effective demand. *Cambridge Journal of Economics, 2*(4), 335–353; *3*(1), 63–82.

Garegnani, P. (1984). Value and distribution in the classical economists and Marx. *Oxford Economic Papers, 36*(2), 63–82.

Garegnani, P. (1989). Some notes on capital, expectations and the analysis of changes. In G. R. Feiwel (Ed.), *Joan Robinson and modern economic theory* (pp. 344–367). London: Macmillan.

Garegnani, P. (1992). Some notes for the analysis of accumulation. In E. J. Nell, D. Laibman, & J. Halevi (Eds.), *Beyond the steady-state* (pp. 47–71). London/Basingstoke: Macmillan.

Garegnani, P. (1999). Entry: Pierangelo Garegnani. in M. Blaug (Ed.) *Who's Who in economics* (third edition), Cheltenham: Edward Elgar, 415.

Goodwin, R. M. (1982b). In M. Palazzi (Ed.), *Intervista a un economista: Richard M. Goodwin*. Bologna: Clueb.

Goodwin, R. M., & Punzo, L. F. (1987). *The dynamics of a capitalist economy: A multi-sectoral approach*. Oxford: Polity Press in association with B. Blackwell.

Gualerzi, D. (1991). *Social environment of consumption and growth: The recovery of the 1980s in the U.S. Economy.* Ph.D. Diss., New School for Social Research, New York.

Gualerzi, D. (2002). *Consumption and growth: Recovery and structural change in the US Economy*. Cheltenham: E. Elgar.

Gualerzi, D. (2012). Growth theory, structural dynamics and the analysis of consumption. In R. Arena, & P. L. Porta (Eds.), *Structural dynamics and economic growth, op. cit.*, pp. 181–203.

Guarini, R. (2013). Il cammino di Luigi Spaventa alla Sapienza: da studente a professore emerito. *Moneta e Credito, 66*(263), 249–259.

Hagemann, H. (2012). Luigi Pasinetti's structural economic dynamics and the employment consequences of new technologies. In R. Arena, & P. L. Porta (Eds.), *Structural dynamics and economic growth, op. cit.*, pp. 204–217.

Hagemann, H., & Scazzieri, R. (2009). Capital structures and economic transitions: An introductory essay. In H. Hagemann & R. Scazzieri (Eds.), *Capital, time and transitional dynamics* (pp. 1–39). Abingdon/New York: Routledge.

Halevi, J. (2016). Luigi Pasinetti and the political economy of growth and distribution. In J. Halevi, et al. (Eds.), *Post Keynesian essays from down under* (Vol. IV), *op. cit.*, pp. 310–326.

Harcourt, G. C. (1972). *Some Cambridge controversies in the theory of capital.* Cambridge: Cambridge University Press.

Harcourt, G. C. (1985). A twentieth century eclectic: Richard Goodwin. *Journal of Post Keynesian Economics, 7*, 379–387.

Harcourt, G. C. (1987). Post-Keynesian economics. In *The new Palgragve dictionary of economics*, *op. cit.*, vol. 3, pp. 924–928.

Harcourt, G. C. (2006). *The structure of post-Keynesian economics.* Cambridge: Cambridge University Press.

Harcourt, G. C. (2011). Foreword. In C. Sardoni (Ed.), *Unemployment, recession and effective demand: The contributions of Marx, Keynes and Kalecki, op. cit.*, pp. vii–viii.

Harcourt, G. C. (2012a). Luigi Pasinetti: The senior living heir of the Cambridge school of economics and the last of the great system-builders. In R. Arena, & P. L. Porta (Eds.), *Structural dynamics and economic growth, op. cit.*, pp. 137–144.

Harcourt, G. C. (2012b). Fusing indissolubly the cycle and the trend: Richard Goodwin's profound insight. Australian School of Business Research Paper No. 2012 ECON 30.

Harcourt, G. C., & Kerr, P. (2009). *Joan Robinson*. London: Palgrave Macmillan.

Johansen, L. (1985). Richard Stone's contributions to economics. *Scandinavian Journal of Economics, 87*(1), 4–32.

Kaldor, N. (1956). Alternative theories of distribution. *The Review of Economic Studies, 23*(2), 83–100.

King, J. E. (2012). *The microfoundations delusion. Metaphor and Dogma in the history of macroeconomics.* Cheltenham/Northamption: E. Elgar.

Kurz, H. D. (2002). Professor Roncaglia's Piero Sraffa. His life, thought and cultural heirtage. *History of Economic Ideas, 10*(1), 119–126.

Kurz, H. D., & Salvadori, N. (1993). The "standard commodity" and Ricardo's search for an "invariable measure of value". In M. Baranzini, & G. C. Harcourt (Eds.), *The dynamics of the wealth of nations: Growth, distribution and structural change, op. cit.*, pp. 95–123.

La Marca, M. (2005). The public sector in a model of growth and distribution à la Pasinetti: Existence of one- or two-class economies. *Metroeconomica, 56*(2), 157–181.

Laing, N. F. (1969). Two notes on Pasinetti's theorem. *Economic Record, 45*(111), 373–385.

Landesmann, M. (1988). Where do we go from here? Technical change and dynamics. *Cambridge Journal of Economics, 12*(1), 169–177.

Leon, P. (1967). *Structural change and growth in capitalism.* Baltimore: Johns Hopkins University Press.

Leontief, W. W. (1970). Environmental repercussions and the economic strucure: an input-output approach. *Review of economic and statistics, 52*(3), 262–71.

Levhari, D. (1965). A nonsubstitution theorem and switching of techniques. *Quarterly Journal of Economics, 79*(1), 98–105.

Lombardini, S. (1996). Joan Robinson's contribution to economic development. In M. C. Marcuzzo, L. L. Pasinetti, & A. Roncaglia (Eds.), *The economics of Joan Robinson, op. cit.*, pp. 135–147.

Lunghini, G. (2008). Una rivoluzione incompiuta e un programma di ricerca. Pasinetti su Keynes (e Sraffa)'. *Rivista di storia economica, 24*(1), 103–118.

Maneschi, A. (1974). The existence of a two-class economy in the Kaldor and Pasinetti models of growth and distribution. *Review of Economic Studies, 41*(1), 149–150.

Maneschi, A. (1983). Dynamic aspects of Ricardo's international trade theory. *Oxford Economic Papers, 35*(1), 67–80.

Maneschi, A. (1992). Ricardo's international trade theory: Beyond comparative cost example. *Cambridge Journal of Economics, 16*(4), 421–437.

Maneschi, A. (1993). Ricardian comparative advantage and the perils of the stationary state. In M. Baranzini, & G. C. Harcourt (Eds.), *The dynamics of the wealth of nations: Growth, distribution and structural change. Essays in honour of Luigi L. Pasinetti, op. cit.*, pp. 124–146.

Maneschi, A. (1998). *Comparative advantage in international trade: A historical perspective.* Cheltenham/Northampton: E. Elgar.

Maneschi, A. (2001). John Stuart Mill's equilibrium terms of trade: A special case of William Whewell's 1850 formula. *History of Political Economy, 33*(3), 609–625.

Maneschi, A. (2004). The true meaning of David Ricardo's four magic numbers. *Journal of International Economics, 62*(2), 433–443.

Maneschi, A. (2006). Ricardo, machinery and comparative advantage. In G. Stathakis, & G. Vaggi (Eds.), *Economic development and social change. Historical roots and modern perspectives, op. cit.*, pp. 290–301.

Maneschi, A. (2008). How would David Ricardo have taught the principle of comparative advantage? *Southern Economic Journal, 74*(4), 1167–1176.

Marangoni, G., & Fezzi, G. (2002). Input–output for management control: The case of Glaxo-SmithKline. *Economic Systems Research, 14*, 245–256.

Marcuzzo, M. C. (Ed.). (1986). *Nicholas Kaldor: Ricordi di un economista*. Milan: Garzanti.
Marcuzzo, M. C. (1994). R. F. Kahn and imperfect competition. *Cambridge Journal of Economics, 18*(1), 25–39.
Marcuzzo, M. C. (1996a). Joan Robinson and Richard Kahn: The origin of short-period analysis. In M. C. Marcuzzo, L. L. Pasinetti, & A. Roncaglia (Eds.), *The economics of Joan Robinson, op. cit.*, pp. 11–28.
Marcuzzo, M. C. (1996b). The writings of Joan Robinson. In M. C. Marcuzzo, L. L. Pasinetti, & A. Roncaglia (Eds.), *The economics of Joan Robinson, op. cit.*, pp. 330–363.
Marcuzzo, M. C. (2002). The collaboration between J. M. Keynes and R. F. Kahn from the *Treatise* to the *general theory. History of Political Economy, 34*(2), 421–447.
Marcuzzo, M. C., & Rosselli, A. (1991). *Ricardo and the gold standard: The foundations of the international monetary order*. Basingstoke: Macmillan.
Marcuzzo, M. C., & Rosselli, A. (Eds.). (2005). *Economists in Cambridge. A study through their correspondence, 1907–1946*. London: Routledge.
Marcuzzo, M. C., & Sanfilippo, E. (2008). Dear John, Dear Ursula (Cambridge and LSE, 1935): Eighty-Eight Letters Unearthed. In R. Scazzieri, A. Sen, & S. Zamagni (Eds.), *Markets, money and capital. Hicksian economics for the twenty-first century, op. cit.*, pp. 72–91.
Marcuzzo, M. C., Pasinetti, L. L., & Roncaglia, A. (Eds.). (1996). *The economics of Joan Robinson*. London/New York: Routledge.
Masera, R. S. (1972). *The term structure of interest rates: An expectations model tested on post-war Italian data*. Oxford: Clarendon Press.
Masera, R. S. (2008). Core, mantle, and industry: A monetary perspective of banks' capital standards. In R. Scazzieri, A. Sen, & S. Zamagni (Eds.), *Markets, money and capital. Hicksian economics for the twenty-first century, op. cit.*, pp. 225–251.
Mastromatteo, G. (1989). *Government intervention, self-financing by private companies and the Pasinetti process: A few reflections*. Milan: Catholic University/Mimeo.
Mastromatteo, G. (1994). Tassazione e distribuzione del reddito in un modello post-Keynesiano. *Economia Internazionale, 47*(4), 383–391.
Mastromatteo, G. (1996). Economia monetaria post-Keynesiana e rigidità dei tassi bancari. *Rivista Internazionale di Scienze Sociali, 104*(4), 555–569.
Mastromatteo, G. (2000). Microfoundations of the post-Keynesian monetary theory. *Studi Economici, 55*(71), 47–64.
Medio, A. (1979). *Harrod e il problema della dinamica economica*. Milan: Etas Libri.

Mückl, W. J. (1978). On the existence of a two-class economy in the Cambridge models of growth and distribution. *Jahrbücher für National Ökonomie und Statistik, 193*(6), 508–517.

Mückl, W. J. (1984). Über den Einfluss von parametrischen Änderungen der Sparneigung auf die Gewinnquote und den Kapitalkeoffizienten. *Jahrbücher für Nationalökonomie und Statistik, 199*(1), 76–87.

Naldi, N. (2005). Robertson and the great divide: The correspondence between Kahn, Kaldor, J. Robinson and Sraffa. In M. C. Marcuzzo, & A. Rosselli (Eds.), *Economists in Cambridge: A study through their correspondence, 1907–1946, op. cit.*, pp. 371–387.

Nardozzi, G. (1996). Joan Robinson and the rate of interest these days. In M. C. Marcuzzo, L. L. Pasinetti, & A. Roncaglia (Eds.), *The economics of Joan Robinson, op. cit.*, pp. 81–87.

Notarangelo, M. (1999). Unbalanced growth: A case of structural dynamics. *Structural Change and Economic Dynamics, 10*(2), 209–223.

Nuti, D. M. (2000). Domenico Mario Nuti, born 1937. In P. Arestis & M. Sawyer (Eds.), *A biographical dictionary of dissenting economists* (pp. 462–9). Cheltenham/Northhampton: E. Elgar.

Onofri, P., & Stagni, A. (2008). On the Hicksian definition of income in applied economic analysis. In R. Scazzieri, A. K. Sen, & S. Zamagni (Eds.), *Markets, money and capital. Hicksian economics for the twenty-first century, op. cit.*, pp. 164–181.

Pabst, A., & Scazzieri, R. (2012). The political economy of civil society. *Constitutional Political Economy, 23*(4), 337–356.

Pabst, A., & Scazzieri, R. (2016). The political economy of constitution. *Constitutional Political Economy*, forthcoming.

Panico, C. (1985). Market forces and the relationship between the rate of interest and the rate of profits. *Contributions to Political Economy, 4*(1), 37–60.

Panico, C. (1987). Interest and profit. In *The new Palgrave: A dictionary of economics, op. cit.*, Vol. 2, London: Macmillan, pp. 877–879.

Panico, C. (1988). *Interest and profit in the theories of value and distribution.* Basingstoke/New York: Macmillan/St. Martin's Press.

Panico, C. (1992). Un confronto tra i modelli macroeconomici finanziari di Tobin e quelli di derivazione Kaldoriana. In B. Jossa & A. Nardi (Eds.), *Lezioni di Macroeconomia* (pp. 329–380). Bologna: Il Mulino.

Panico, C. (1997). Government deficits in post Keynesian theories of growth and distribution. *Contribution to Political Economy, 16*(1), 61–86.

Panico, C. (1998). Interest and profit. In H. D. Kurz & N. Salvadori (Eds.), *The Elgar companion to classical economics* (Vol. I, pp. 425–430). Cheltenham/Northampton: E. Elgar.

Panico, C. (1999). The government sector in the post-Keynesian theory of growth and personal distribution. In G. Mongiovi, & F. Petri (Eds.), *Value, distribution and capital, essays in honour of P. Garegnani, op. cit.*, pp. 339–353.

Parrinello, S. (2011). Un'infondata portata attribuita alla teoria Ricardiana dei vantaggi comparati: un punto di vista post-Keynesiano. In *Gli economisti post-keynesiani di Cambridge e l'Italia* (pp. 103–110), Atti dei Convegni Lincei. Rome: Scienze e Lettere.

Pasinetti, L. L. (1960a). A mathematical formulation of the Ricardian system. *Review of Economic Studies, 27*(2), 78–98.

Pasinetti, L. L. (1960b). Cyclical fluctuations and economic growth. *Oxford Economic Papers, 12*(2), 215–241.

Pasinetti, L. L. (1962). Rate of profit and income distribution in relation to the rate of economic growth. *Review of Economic Studies, 29*(4), 267–279.

Pasinetti, L. L. (1969). Switches of techniques and the "rate of return" in capital theory. *Economic Journal, 79*(315), 508–531.

Pasinetti, L. L. (1973). The notion of vertical integration in economic analysis. *Metroeconomica, 25*, 1–29; Reprinted in L. L. Pasinetti (Ed.), *Essays on the theory of joint production, op. cit.*, pp. 16–43.

Pasinetti, L. L. (1974). *Growth and income distribution: Essays in economic theory.* Cambridge: Cambridge University Press.

Pasinetti, L. L. (1975). Determinatezza del saggio di profitto nella teoria Post-Keynesiana: Risposta al Professor Campa. *Giornale degli Economisti e Annali di Economia, 34*, 639–647.

Pasinetti, L. L. (1977). *Lectures on the theory of production.* London: Macmillan (Italian original 1975, Bologna: Il Mulino).

Pasinetti, L. L. (1979). Kaldor, Nicholas. In *International encyclopaedia of the social sciences, biographical supplement* (Vol. 18, pp. 366–369). London/New York: Collier Macmillan/The Free Press.

Pasinetti, L. L. (Ed.). (1980). *Essays in the theory of joint production.* London: Macmillan (Italian original, 1977, Bologna: Il Mulino).

Pasinetti, L. L. (1981). *Structural change and economic growth: A theoretical essay on the dynamics of the wealth of nations.* Cambridge: Cambridge University Press.

Pasinetti, L. L. (1982). A comment on the "new view" of the Ricardian theory. In M. Baranzini (Ed.), *Advances in economic theory, op. cit.*, pp. 240–242.

Pasinetti, L. L. (1983). Conditions of existence of a two class economy in the Kaldor and more general models of growth and income distribution. *Kyklos, 36*(1), 91–102.

Pasinetti, L. L. (1985). 'Nicholas Kaldor', introduction to N. Kaldor. *Economia senza equillibrio* (pp. 9–21, Italian version of Kaldor's Yale Lectures). Bologna: Il Mulino.
Pasinetti, L. L. (1986). Theory of value – A source of alternative paradigms in economic analysis. In M. Baranzini, & R. Scazzieri (Eds.), *Foundations of economics., op. cit.*, pp. 409–431.
Pasinetti, L. L. (1988). Growing subsystems, vertically hyper-integrated sectors and the labour theory of value. *Cambridge Journal of Economics, 12*(2), 125–134.
Pasinetti, L. L. (1989a). Ricardian debt/taxation equivalence in the Kaldor theory of profits and income distribution. *Cambridge Journal of Economics, 13*(1), 25–36.
Pasinetti, L. L. (1989b). Government deficit spending is not incompatible with the Cambridge theorem of the rate of profit: A reply to Fleck and Domenghino. *Journal of Post Keynesian Economics, 11*(4), 641–647.
Pasinetti, L. L. (1989c). *'Address', at the King's College Chapel R. F. Kahn Memorial Service* (pp. 6–11). Cambridge: King's College.
Pasinetti, L. L. (1991). Richard Ferdinand Kahn: 1905–1989. *Proceedings of the British Academy, 76*, 423–443.
Pasinetti, L. L. (1993). *Structural economic dynamics: A theory of the economic consequences of human learning*. Cambridge: Cambridge University Press.
Pasinetti, L. L. (1996). Richard Murphey Goodwin (1913–1996): A pupil's tribute to a great teacher. *Cambridge Journal of Economics, 20*(6), 645–649.
Pasinetti, L. L. (2003). 'Letter to the editor', in 'Comments – Cambridge Capital Controversies'. *Journal of Economic Perspectives, 17*(4), 227–228. (A Comment on A. J. Cohen and G. C. Harcourt's 'Cambridge Capital Theory Controversies') same *Journal, 17*(1), 199–214.
Pasinetti, L. L. (2007). *Keynes and the Cambridge Keynesians: A 'revolution in economics' to be accomplished*. Cambridge: Cambridge University Press.
Pasinetti, L. L., & Mariutti, G. (2008). Hick's "conversion" – From J. R. to John. In R. Scazzieri, A. Sen, & S. Zamagni (Eds.), *Markets, money and capital. Hicksian economics for the twenty-first century, op. cit.*, pp. 52–71.
Pettenati, P. (1967). Il teorema di Pasinetti in un diverso quadro di riferimento. *Studi economici, 22*(6), 581–588.
Pettenati, P. (1993). Pasinetti's theorem in a modern institutional framework. In C. Panico, & N. Salvadori (Eds.), *Post Keynesian theory of growth and distribution, op. cit.*, pp. 229–237.
Pivetti, M. (1987b). Interest and profit in Smith, Ricardo and Marx. *Political Economy, 3*(1), 63–74.

Pivetti, M. (1996). Joan Robinson and the rate of interest: An important change of view on a topical issue. In M. C. Marcuzzo, L. L. Pasinetti, & A. Roncaglia (Eds.), *The economics of Joan Robinson, op. cit.*, pp. 75–80.

Poni, C., & Scazzieri, R. (Eds.). (1994). *Production networks: Market rules and social norms.* Eleventh international economic history congress, Milan: Bocconi University, 12th–16th September 1994, Session C.11.

Poni, C., & Scazzieri, R. (2007). Environmental crisis and property rights: Historical contexts and theoretical frameworks. In A. Prinz, A. E. Steenge, & J. Schmidt (Eds.), *The rules of the game: Institutions, law and economics* (pp. 81–101). Berlin: LIT Verlag.

Porta, P. L. (Ed.). (1983a). *Opere di David Ricardo, Vol. I Princìpi di economia politica e dell'imposta.* Turin: Utet.

Porta, P. L. (1983b). Introduzione. In P. L. Porta (Ed.) *Opere di David Ricardo*, Vol. I *Princìpi di economia politica e dell'imposta, op. cit.*, pp. 9–102.

Porta, P. L. (1984a). *Scuola classica e teoria economica.* Milan: Giuffrè.

Porta, P. L. (1984b). Piero Sraffa. *Rivista Internazionale di Scienze Economiche e Commerciali, 31*(1), 14–20.

Porta, P. L. (1990). David Ricardo. La sistemazione teorica della concorrenza e del mercato. In G. Becattini (Ed.), *Il pensiero economico: temi, problemi, correnti, scuole* (pp. 101–147). Turin: UTET.

Porta, P. L. (Ed.). (1992). *David Ricardo: Notes on Malthus's 'measure of value'.* Cambridge: Cambridge University Press.

Porta, P. L., & Scazzieri, R. (2008). A revolution to be accomplished. Keynes and the Cambridge Keynesians. *Economia politica, 25*(3), 455–80.

Potier, J.-P. (1987). *Piero Sraffa, Unorthodox Economist (1898–1983). A biographical essay.* London: Routledge.

Pugno, M. (1992). *Roy F. Harrod: dall'equilibriodinamico all'instabilità ciclica.* Bologna: Il Mulino.

Quadrio Curzio, A. (1967). *Rendita e distribuzione in un modello economico plurisettoriale* (Rent and distribution in a multi-sectoral economic model). Milan: Giuffrè.

Quadrio Curzio, A. (1975). *Accumulazione del capitale e rendita* (Accumulation of Capital and Rent). Bologna: Il Mulino.

Quadrio Curzio, A. (1977). Rendita, distribuzione del reddito, ordine di efficienza e di redditività. In L. L. Pasinetti (Ed.), *Contributi alla teoria della produzione congiunta* (pp. 301–327). Bologna: Il Mulino.

Quadrio Curzio, A. (1980). Rent, income distribution and orders of efficiency and rentability. In L. L. Pasinetti (Ed.), *Essays on the theory of joint production, op. cit.*, pp. 219–40. Reprinted in H. D. Kurz, & N. Salvadori (Eds.). (2003). *The legacy of Piero Sraffa* (Vol. II, pp. 311–41). Cheltenham: E. Elgar.

Quadrio Curzio, A. (1986). Technological scarcity: An essay on production and structural change. In M. Baranzini, & R. Scazzieri (Eds.), *Foundations of economics – Structure of inquiry and economic theory, op. cit.*, pp. 311–338.
Quadrio Curzio, A. (1987). Land rent. In *The new Palgrave: A dictionary of economics, op. cit.*, London: Macmillan, Vol. 3, pp. 118–121.
Quadrio Curzio, A. (1988). Le «scarsità relative» nella storia della teoria economica e rilevanza attuale. In C. M. Guerci & G. Zanetti (Eds.), *Sviluppo economico e vincolo energetico* (pp. 39–53). Bologna: Il Mulino.
Quadrio Curzio, A. (1990). *Rent, distribution and economic structure: A collection of essays* (Quaderni IDSE, 1). Milan: CNR.
Quadrio Curzio, A. (1993b). Distribuzione della ricchezza e del reddito. In *Enciclopedia delle Scienze Sociali* (pp. 194–207). Rome: Istituto della Enciclopedia italiana Treccani.
Quadrio Curzio, A. (1996a). Production and efficiency with global technologies. In M. A. Landesmann, & R. Scazzieri (Eds.), *Production and economic dynamics, op. cit.*, pp. 105–126.
Quadrio Curzio, A. (1996b). Distribuzione dinamica del reddito e risorse scarse. In T. Cozzi, et al. (Eds.), *Benessere, equilibrio e sviluppo. Studi in onore di Siro Lombardini* (Vol. III, pp. 203–254). Milan: Vita e Pensiero.
Quadrio Curzio, A. (1998). Rent. In H. D. Kurz & N. Salvadori (Eds.), *The Elgar Companion to Classical Economics (ECCE)* (pp. 189–193). Cheltenham: E. Elgar.
Quadrio Curzio, A. (2007) *Economisti ed economia. Per un'Italia europea: paradigmi tra il XVIII e il XX secolo*. Bologna: Il Mulino.
Quadrio Curzio, A. (2011). *Resources and economic dynamics, technology and rents*. Milan: Cranec/Vita e Pensiero.
Quadrio Curzio, A., & Pellizzari, F. (1996). *Risorse, tecnologie, rendita*. Bologna: Il Mulino.
Quadrio Curzio, A., & Pellizzari, F. (1999). *Rent, resources, tecnologies*. Berlin: Springer.
Quadrio Curzio, A., & Rotondi, C. (2013b). Premessa. In A. Q. Curzio, & C. Rotondi (Eds.), *Un economista eclettico. Distribuzione, tecnologie e sviluppo nel pensiero di Nino Andreatta, op. cit.*, pp. 15–108.
Quadrio Curzio, A., & Scazzieri, R. (Eds.), (1977–1982). *Protagonisti del pensiero economico*, 4 Vols. Bologna: Il Mulino.
Quadrio Curzio, A., & Scazzieri, R. (1983). *Sui momenti costitutivi dell'economia politica*, vol. II of *Protagonisti del Pensiero Economico*. Bologna: Il Mulino.
Quadrio Curzio, A., & Scazzieri, R. (1990). Profili di dinamica economica strutturale: introduzione. In A. Quadrio Curzio & R. Scazzieri (Eds.), *Dinamica economica strutturale* (pp. 11–51). Bologna: Il Mulino.

Quadrio-Curzio, A., & Scazzieri, R. (2008). Historical stylizations and monetary theory. In R. Scazzieri, A. Sen, & S. Zamagni (Eds.), *Markets, money and capital: Hicksian economics for the twenty-first century, op. cit.*, pp. 185–203.

Quadrio Curzio, A., Manara, C. F., & Faliva, M. (1987). Produzione ed efficienza con tecnologie globali. *Economia Politica, 4*(1), 11–47.

Raffaelli, T., Becattini, G., & Dardi, M. (Eds.). (2006). *The Elgar companion to Alfred Marshall.* Cheltenham/Northampton: E. Elgar.

Raffaelli, T., et al. (Eds.). (2010). *The impact of Alfred Marshall's ideas. The global diffusion of his works.* Cheltenham/Northampton: E. Elgar.

Rampa, G., Stella, L., & Thirlwall, A. (Eds.). (1988). *Economic dynamics, trade and growth: Essays on Harrodian themes.* London/New York: Macmillan/St. Martin's Press.

Reati, A. (1998a). Technological revolutions in Pasinetti's model of structural change. *Structural Change and Economic Dynamics, 9*(3), 245–262.

Reati, A. (1998b). A long-wave pattern for output and employment in Pasinetti's model of structural change. *Economie Appliquee, 51*(2), 29–77.

Reati, A. (2014). Economic policy for structural change. *Review of Political Economy, 26*(1), 1–22.

Reati, A., & Raganelli, V. (1993). Introducing long waves into Pasinetti's model of structural change: The price movements. *Economie Appliquee, 46*(1), 5–29.

Ricci, G., & Velupillai, K. V. (Eds.). (1988). *Growth cycles and multisectoral economics: The Goodwin tradition.* Berlin: Springer.

Ricottilli, M. (2015). Innovation through local interaction, imitation and investment waves. *Structural Change and Economic Dynamics, 33*(2), 58–70.

Roncaglia, A. (1975). *Sraffa e la teoria dei prezzi.* Rome/Bari: Laterza.

Roncaglia, A. (1982). Hollander's Ricardo. *Journal of Post Keynesian Economics, 4*(4), 339–359. Reprinted in G. Caravale (Ed.). (1985). *The legacy of Ricardo* (pp. 105–123). Oxford: B. Blackwell.

Roncaglia, A. (2005). *The wealth of ideas: A history of economic thought.* Cambridge/New York: Cambridge University Press.

Roncaglia, A. (2009). *Piero Sraffa.* London: Palgrave Macmillan.

Roncaglia, A. (2013). Luigi Spaventa. *PSL Quarterly Review, 66*(266), 171–199.

Roncaglia, A., & Hollander, S. (1982). Hollander's Ricardo. *Journal of Post Keynesian Economics, 4*(3), 339–375.

Roncaglia, A., & Tonveronachi, M. (2014). Post-Keynesian, post-Sraffian economics: An outline. In D. B. Papadimitiou (Ed.), *Contributions to economic theory, policy, development and finance, essays in honor of Jan A. Kregel* (pp. 40–64). New York/London: Palgrave Macmillan.

Rossi, A. A. (1966). *La dinamica Ricardiana*. Lugano: Buona Stampa.

Rossi, A. A., & Leighton, T. (1971). Inflation in the Post-War Swiss Economy. An Econometric Study of the Interaction between Immigration and the Labour Market. Schweizerische Zeitscrift für Volkswirtschaft und Statistik, 107.4, 761–90.

Rossi, A. A., & Schiltknecht, K. (1971). Uebernachfrage und Lohnentwicklung in der Schweiz – Eine neue Hypothese. *Kyklos*, 25.2, 239–54.

Rotondi, C. (2014). Un giovane economista tra crescita e sviluppo. In A. Quadrio Curzio, & C. Rotondi (Eds.), *Gli allievi ricordano Andreatta*, *op. cit.*, pp. 27–35.

Russo, M., & Natali, A. (2008). *Sebastiano Brusco e la scuola Italiana di sviluppo locale, 605*. Modena: Dipartimento di Economia Politica.

Salvadori, N. (1991). Post-Keynesian theory of distribution in the long-run. In E. J. Nell, & W. Semmler (Eds.), *Nicholas Kaldor and mainstream economics: Confrontation or convergence?, op. cit.*, pp. 164–189.

Salvadori, N. (1996). "Productivity curves" in the accumulation of capital. In M. C. Marcuzzo, L. L. Pasinetti, & A. Roncaglia (Eds.), *The economics of Joan Robinson, op. cit.*, pp. 232–248.

Salvadori, N., & Panico, C. (Eds.). (1993). *Post Keynesian theory of growth and distribution*. Aldershot: E. Elgar, and 'Introduction', pp. xiii–xxxi.

Samuelson, P. A. (1962). Parable and realism in capital theory. The surrogate production function. *Review of Economic Studies, 29*(3), 193–206.

Samuelson, P. A. (1991). Extirpating error contamination concerning the post-Keynesian anti-Pasinetti equilibrium. *Oxford Economic Papers, 43*(2), 177–186.

Samuelson, P. A., & Modigliani, F. (1966). The Pasinetti paradox in neoclassical and more general models. *Review of Economic Studies, 33*(4), 269–301.

Sardoni, C. (2002). On the microeconomic foundations of macroeconomics: A Keynesian perspective. In P. Arestis, M. Desai, & S. Dow (Eds.), *Methodology, microeconomics and Keynes. Essays in honour ro victoria chick* (pp. 4–14). London/New York: Routledge.

Sardoni, C. (2011). *Unemployment, recession and effective demand: The contributions of Marx, Keynes and Kalecki*. Cheltemham/Northampton: E. Elgar.

Scazzieri, R. (1983). Economic dynamics and structural change: A comment on Pasinetti. *Rivista Internazionale di Scienze Economiche e Commerciali, 30*(1), 73–90.

Scazzieri, R. (1996a). Introduction to Pasinetti's structural economic dynamics: A symposium. *Structural Change and Economic Dynamics, 7*(2), 123–125.

Scazzieri, R. (1996b). The accumulation of capital and structural economic dynamics. In M. C. Marcuzzo, L. L. Pasinetti, & A. Roncaglia (Eds.), *The economics of Joan Robinson, op. cit.*, pp. 174–187.

Scazzieri, R. (2006). A Smithian theory of choice. *Adam Smith Review, 2*, 1–54.

Scazzieri, R., & Zamagni, S. (2008). Between theory and history: On the identity of hicks's economics. In R. Scazzieri, A. Sen, & S. Zamagni (Eds.), *Markets, money and capital. Hicksian economics for the twenty-first century, op. cit.*, pp. 1–37.

Scazzieri, R., Sen, A. K., & Zamagni, S. (Eds.). (2008). *Markets, money and capital. Hicksian economics for the twenty-first century*. Cambridge: Cambridge University Press.

Schianchi, A. (1978). Crescita e distribuzione in un modello a tre classi. *Ricerche Economiche, 1*, 103–106.

Seccareccia, M. (1996). Post Keynesian fundism and monetary circulation. In G. Delaplace & E. J. Nell (Eds.), *Money in motion: The post Keynesian and circulation approaches* (pp. 400–416). London: Macmillan.

Solari, L. F., & Rossier, E. (1977). *De l'économie qualitative à l'économie quantitative. Pour une méthodologie de l'approche formalisée en sciences économiques.* Paris: Masson.

Solow, R. M. (1959). Comment on Pasinetti. *Review of Economics and Statistics, 41*(3), 282–285.

Solow, R. M. (1963). Substitution and fixed proportions in the theory of capital. *The Review of Economic Studies, 29*(3), 207–18.

Solow, R. M. (2012). 'On Pasinetti and the unfinished Keynesian revolution', and 'first afterword: Pasinetti on structural dynamics. In R. Arena, & P. L. Porta (Eds.), *Structural dynamics and economic growth, op. cit.*, pp. 267–273, and pp. 274–275.

Spaventa, L. (2002). Economics and institutions: Some reflections on Pasinetti and Caravale. In D. Tosato (Ed.), *Essays in memory of Giovanni Caravale* (pp. 354–356). London/New York: Routledge.

Sraffa, P. (1922a). The bank crises in Italy. *Economic Journal, 32*(1), 178–197.

Sraffa, P. (1951). Introduction. In P. Sraffa with the collaboration of M. H. Dobb (Eds.), *The works and correspondence of David Ricardo* (Vol. I, pp. xiii–lxii), Cambridge: Cambridge University Press.

Sraffa, P. (1960). *Production of commodities by means of commodities: Prelude to a critique of economic theory*. Cambridge: Cambridge University Press.

Steedman, I. (1972). The state and the outcome of the Pasinetti process. *Economic Journal, 82*(328), 1387–1395.

Stiglitz, J. E. (1975). Review of *growth and income distribution: Essays in economic theory*, by L. L. Pasinetti. *Journal of Economic Literature, 13*(4), 1327–1328.

Stone, J. R. N. (1951). The use and development and national income and expenditure estimates. In D. N. Chester (Ed.), *Lessons of the British war economy* (pp. 83–87). Cambridge: Cambridge University Press.

Stone, J. R. N. (1978). *Tribute to Luigi Solari*. Paper presented at the European Meeting of the Econometric Society, Geneva.

Stone, J. R. N., & Stone, G. (1977). *National income and expenditure* (1st ed.). London: Bowes & Bowes (1971).

Taniguchi, K. (1987). *The existence of traverse in Pasinetti's model of growth and distribution* (Discussion Paper No. 11). University of Osaka Prefecture.

Targetti, F. (1985). Growth and the terms of trade: A Kaldorian two sector model. *Metroeconomica, 37*(1), 79–96.

Targetti, F. (1986). Kaldor. *Studi Economici, 41*, 3–70.

Targetti, F. (1991). Change and continuity in Kaldor's thought on growth and distribution. In E. J. Nell, & W. Semmler (Eds.), *Nicholas Kaldor and mainstream economics. Confrontation or convergence?, op. cit.*, pp. 411–420.

Targetti, F. (1992). *Nicholas Kaldor*. Oxford/New York: Oxford University Press.

Targetti, F. (1993). Vecchie e nuove teorie della crescita: una rassegna. *Economia Politica, 10*(2), 261–349.

Targetti, F., & Thirlwall, A. P. (Eds.). (1983). *Further essays on economic theory and policy*. London: Duckworth.

Teixeira, J. R. (1998). Luigi L. Pasinetti. In F. Meacci (Ed.), *Italian economists of the 20th century, op. cit.*, pp. 272–294.

Tonveronachi, M. (1983). *J. M. Keynes. Dall'instabilità ciclica all'equilibrio di sottooccupazione*. Rome: NIS.

Vaggi, G. (1985). A physiocratic model of relative prices and income distribution. *Economic Journal, 95*(380), 928–947.

Vaggi, G. (1987). *The economics of François Quesnay*. London/Durham: Macmillan/Duke University Press.

Vaggi, G. (2002). Quesnay and the road to modernity: Technology, markets, and polity. *Journal of the History of Economic Thought, 24*(1), 73–89.

Varri, P. (1996). Harrod's dynamic economics and Joan Robinson's generalization of the general theory. In M. C. Marcuzzo, L. L. Pasinetti, & A. Roncaglia (Eds.), *The economics of Joan Robinson, op. cit.*, pp. 188–194.

Velupillai, K. V. (Ed.). (1989). *Nonlinear and multisectoral macrodynamics. Essays in honour of Richard Goodwin*. London: Macmillan.

Velupillai, K. V. (1998a). Richard Goodwin: 1913-1996. *Economic Journal, 108*(448), 1436–1449.

Velupillai, K. V. (1998b). The vintage economist. *Journal of Economic Behaviour and Organisation, 37*(1), 1–31.

Velupillai, K. V. (2008). A perspective on a Hicksian non-linear theory of the trade cycle. In R. Scazzieri, A. Sen, & S. Zamagni (Eds.), *Markets, money and capital. Hicksian economics for the twenty-first century, op. cit.*, pp. 328–345.

Vianello, F. (1996). Joan Robinson on normal prices (and the normal rate of profits). In M. C. Marcuzzo, L. L. Pasinetti, & A. Roncaglia (Eds.), *The economics of Joan Robinson, op. cit.*, pp. 112–120.

Vianello, F. (1999). Social accounting in Adam Smith. In G. Mongiovi, & F. Petri (Eds.), *Value, distribution and capital. Essays in honour of Pierangelo Garegnani, op. cit.*, pp. 165–180.

Vianello, F. (2004). La Facoltà di Economia e Commercio di Modena. In G. Garofalo, & A. Graziani (Eds.), *La formazione degli economisti in Italia (1950–1975), op. cit.*, pp. 481–534.

Vivenza, G. (1999a). The division of land and the division of labour. Analogies and differences between ancient and modern times in Adam Smith's thought. In P. L. Porta, R. Scazzieri, & A. Skinner (Eds.), *Knowledge, social institutions and the division of labour, op. cit.*, pp. 331–350.

Vivenza, G. (1999b). Translating aristotle: At the origin of the terminology and ontent of economic value. In R. Rossini Favretti, G. Sandri, & R. Scazzieri (Eds.), *Incommensurability and translation, op. cit.*, pp. 131–156.

Vivenza, G. (2001). *Adam Smith and the classics. The classical heritage of Adam Smith's thought.* Oxford: Oxford University Press.

Zamagni, S. (1973). Struttura del capitale e crescita non uniforme, Appendix to J. R. Hicks. *Capitale e tempo. Una teoria neo-austriaca* (pp. 247–286). Milan: Etas Libri.

Zamagni, S. (1984). On Ricardo and Hayek effects in a Fixwage model of traverse. In D. A. Collier et al. (Eds.), *Economic theory and Hicksian themes* (pp. 135–151). Oxford: Clarendon Press.

Zamagni, S. (1996). Joan Robinson and reswitching. An interpretative note. In M. C. Marcuzzo, L. L. Pasinetti, & A. Roncaglia (Eds.), *The economics of Joan Robinson, op. cit.*, pp. 218–222.

Zambelli, S. (Ed.). (2010). *Computable, constructive and behavioural economic dynamics. Essays in honour of Kumaraswamy (Vela) Velupillai.* London: Routledge.

4

The Celebration of Oxbridge Scientists by Italian Economists and Institutions

Italian economists and institutions have been particularly active in organizing special activities; conferences; and talks both in honour of Oxbridge economists, or in commemoration of special events. As far as we know, no other group of national economists has done the same. We list a few, well aware that the list is incomplete:

1. *John and Ursula Hicks*: As Vera and Stefano Zamagni (2002) point out, 'During their many visits to Italy, on the invitation of someone from the first group of young Italians (who remained on the friendliest of terms with them for the rest of their lives), it was a real pleasure to accompany the Hickses to some special place in Italy they had not yet visited, and which they selected with the utmost care'. This is confirmed also by Hamouda who writes that, 'Italy, he [Sir John] loved to say, was his second home' (Hamouda 1993, 37). In 1984, the *Oxford Economic Papers* published a special volume to mark the 80th birthday of John Hicks, with contributions, among others, from Bob M. Solow, Amartya K. Sen (then still at All Souls), Robin C. O. Matthews and Stefano Zamagni. Thereafter, it was left to the Hicks-Italian school to

M. Baranzini, A. Mirante, *A Compendium of Italian Economists at Oxbridge*, DOI 10.1007/978-3-319-32219-3_4

organize two further events in honour of John Hicks: these took place in Bologna in 1989 and 2004. According to Hamouda:

> The International Economic Society, helped by the remarkable organizational skill of Stefano Zamagni, a former student of Hicks, hosted in 1989 in honour of the fiftieth anniversary of the publication of *Value and Capital* [...] Hicks was, none the less, very pleased, moved and honoured by the presence there of many distinguished participants and especially of Arrow, Hahn, Malinvaud and Sen for whom he had always had great respect. When asked some months later by his sister Mary what he might like by way of a memorial when he died, Hicks said with great joy that he felt the conference in Bologna had been his memorial.' (Hamouda 1993, 40)

The second conference in honour of John Hicks took place in Bologna on 10–11 October 2004, with the title 'John Hicks: One Hundredth Anniversary Workshop'. Roberto Scazzieri, Amartya Sen and Stefano Zamagni edited a volume with the papers presented there (Cambridge University Press, 2008). It was the 'result of interaction within the invisible college of former colleagues and pupils to John Hicks' (Scazzieri et al. 2008, xiii).

2. *Roy F. Harrod*: The Italian scientific community has demonstrated receptiveness second to none in the case of Harrod. In 1970, Oxford University Press published a volume in his honour; this was edited by Eltis et al. (1970). However, as far as Daniele Besomi recalls, the only international Harrod conference was convened in Genoa in 1996 (for the 60th anniversary of the publication of his *Trade Cycle*). The papers given at that conference were edited by G. Rampa, L. Stella and A. Thirlwall with the title *Economic Dynamics, Trade and Growth: Essays on Harrodian Themes.*
3. *Raffaele Mattioli Lectures*: These lectures represent another important instrument of international cooperation set up by the Italian scientific community. They were established in 1976 by the *Banca Commerciale Italiana* in association with University Bocconi of Milan as a memorial to the cultural legacy left by Raffaele Mattioli who, for many years, was the chairman of the bank, as well as a close friend of Piero Sraffa. The aim of the series of lectures was 'to create an opportunity for

reflection and debate on topics of particular current interest, thus providing stimuli and ideas for the increasing challenges of a continually changing worldwide economic scenario'. The proceedings of the lectures were published by Cambridge University Press. Among the Oxbridge economists who were invited, we should mention Richard F. Kahn (*The Making of Keynes's General Theory*, Cambridge University Press, 1984); Nicholas Kaldor (*Causes of Growth and Stagnation of the World Economy*, Cambridge University Press, 1996); Richard Stone (*Some British Empiricists in the Social Sciences*, Cambridge University Press, 1997); and Joseph Stiglitz and Bruce Greenwald (*Towards a New Paradigm in Monetary Economics*, Cambridge University Press, 2003). (We should add that, from 1973 to 1976, Joseph Stiglitz was Drummond Professor of Political Economy at All Souls, Oxford, where he supervised several Italian research students.)

4. *Italian Economic Papers*: We should also mention the three volumes of the *Italian Economic Papers* edited by Luigi Pasinetti (in 1992, 1994, 1998) and published by Il Mulino and Oxford University Press on behalf of the *Società Italiana degli Economisti*. The intention of the series was primarily to provide translations into English of notable articles and papers originally published in Italian language. The first volume includes classic and contemporary works, often introducing neglected works. Authors include Barone, Pareto and Pantaleoni, as well as Amoroso, Egidi and Sraffa. They discuss topics such as taxation, defining consumer behaviour, and consumption/growth rate relations. The second volume includes writings by Vilfredo Pareto (originally presented in 1895), Siro Lombardini (1953), Federico Caffé (1986), Pier Carlo Nicola (1978), Aldo Montesano (1984), Marco Dardi (1983) and Stefano Zamagni (1986). The third volume gathers the work of lesser-known economists who were active in Italy primarily between the two World Wars.
5. *Structural Change and Economic Dynamics (SCED)*: This journal represents further evidence of Italian scientific ingenuity. The journal, initially published by Oxford University Press (now published by Elsevier), was launched in 1990. *SCED* has mainly published articles about theoretical, applied and methodological aspects of structural change in economic systems, and has provided a 'forum for the cross

fertilization of applied and theoretical research on structural change and dynamics in actual economies'. A number of Italian scholars with Oxbridge connections have contributed since 1992. Among others, managing editors have been (or are) Roberto Scazzieri, Alessandro Vercelli, Luigi Marengo and Michael Landesmann (the latter has worked intensively with Scazzieri); patrons have been Luigi Pasinetti and Richard Goodwin; and associated editors have been (or are) Alberto Quadrio Curzio, Giovanni Dosi and Marco Lippi.

6. A number of Oxbridge dons moved to Italy to teach, undertake research and/or settle down; among these we should cite Richard M. Goodwin (Siena), Frank O. Hahn (Siena); Michio Morishima (Siena, but without official appointment); Amit Bhaduri (Pavia), Vela Velupillai (Trento), Christopher Gilbert (Trento); Ian Kregel (Johns Hopkins, Bologna); and Brian Francis Mc Guinness (philosopher, scholar of Wittgenstein and Sraffa).
7. A significant number of Italian-educated scholars are now teaching or undertaking research in Oxford and Cambridge. Some of them are quite distinguished, and some of them are not related to the period under consideration (1950–1990) and/or to the research lines considered in this volume. We shall, however, briefly mention Guido Ascari, Professor of Economics, Oxford; Andrea Ferrero and Francesco Zanetti, Associate Professors of Economics, Oxford; Ilaria Piatti, Associate Professor of Finance, Oxford; Francesco Billari, Diego Gambetta and Federico Varese, Professors in the Oxford Department of Sociology; Luciano Floridi, Professor of Philosophy and Ethics of Information, Oxford; Pietro Corsi, Emeritus Professor of the History of Science, Oxford; Giancarlo Corsetti, Professor of Macro-economics, Cambridge; Elisa Faraglia, Fellow of King's College, Cambridge and A lecturer at the University. As we have pointed out, this is just a partial list.
8. *Centre for Financial History*: We should also recall the Centre in this context, which was based at Newnham College, Cambridge, and directed by Dr D'Maris Coffman from 2008 to 2015. Dr Coffman was a Leverhulme/Newton Trust Early Career Fellow in the History Faculty of the University of Cambridge, before moving to the Bartlett School of University College London as senior lecturer in 2015. From

October 2008 until September 2013, Dr Coffman was the Mary Bateson Research Fellow at Newnham College. Most of her research focuses on the role of state finance in the development of capital markets in eighteenth- and nineteenth-century Europe, and the consequences of the growth of the fiscal state for agricultural commodity markets (see Coffman 2013a, b, 2015; Coffman et al. 2013; Cardinale et al. 2014). A number of Italian economists were associated with the Centre which, at the beginning of 2015, moved to Darwin College under the direction of Dr Duncan Needham. Roberto Scazzieri was, and is still, a senior research associate to the Centre, while Ivano Cardinale is an associate researcher. Apart from major research projects, the Centre organized conferences and debates; and Dr Coffman participated in a series of scientific conferences in Italy, organized, inter alia, by the Lincei Academy, the *Fondazione Centesimus Annus-Pro Pontefice*, Vatican City, and the Balzan Foundation.

9. In September 2012, Roberto Scazzieri and Michelle Baddeley were the convenors of a conference in honour of Luigi L. Pasinetti on 'The Economics of Structural Change: Theory, Institutions and Policies'; sponsored by the Cambridge Political Economy Society. At that time, Michelle Baddeley was Fellow and Director of Economic Studies at Gonville and Caius, Cambridge, and is now Professor of the Economics and Finance of the Built Environment at University College London. (We should recall Pasinetti's patronage, with Amartya K. Sen, of the *Cambridge Journal of Economics* since its foundation in the late 1970s, Richard Goodwin having died in 1996.) The conference took place at Luigi's Cambridge alma mater, Gonville and Caius College, on 12–13 September 2012. Its title—'The Economics of Structural Change: Theory, Institutions and Policy'—was very fitting. The aim of the conference was 'to provide a critical assessment of current research in the economics of structural change from a theoretical, institutional and policy perspective'. According to the two convenors of the conference:

> The lifetime work of Luigi Pasinetti, who has co-founded the Cambridge analytical tradition through a unique combination of the Classical and Keynesian lines, has highlighted structural change as the most important

> feature of modern economies since the first industrial revolution and has addressed the relationship between macroeconomic aggregates and changes in sectoral proportions as the most distinctive feature of long-term dynamics. His *Structural Change and Economic Growth* (Cambridge, Cambridge University Press, 1981) and *Structural Economic Dynamics* (Cambridge, Cambridge University Press, 1993) are path breaking constructive contributions to the theory of a multisectoral economy evolving through time under the influence of technical progress and changes in final demand composition. In Pasinetti's scheme the structural change of a multisectoral economy is conceived in terms of changing relationships between vertically integrated sectors leading to the production of different final consumption goods. In a dynamic representation of the economy, full employment and full capacity utilization presuppose structural change as change in sectoral proportions. This is expressed in terms of a fundamental macroeconomic condition that is compatible with manifold sectoral compositions of aggregates and thus highlights the importance of structural change as a means to achieve macroeconomic objectives. (Baddeley and Scazzieri 2012)

Twenty-eight scholars from all over the world contributed. Among them, we find the following Italian economists: Alberto Quadrio Curzio and Mauro Baranzini ('From Adam Smith to Structural Dynamics: Luigi Pasinetti's Life-Long Contribution'); Nadia Garbellini and Ariel L. Wirkierman ('On Concepts and Measures of Changes in Productivity'); Pier Luigi Porta ('The Cambridge School and Structural Dynamics: Luigi Pasinetti's Approach in the Light of the Italian Tradition of Economic Thought'); Giovanni Dosi, Marco Grazzi, Luigi Marengo and Simona Settepanella ('Heterogeneity, Industries and Technological Change'); Ivano Cardinale ('The Political Economy of Circular Interdependence and Vertical Integration: Opening the Black Box of "National Interest"'); Antonio Andreoni ('Industrial Policies for Manufacturing Development: Structural Dynamics and Institutional Changes'); Massimo Cingolani ('Structural Change and Its Implications for EU Policy Coordination'); Angelo Reati (1939–2013) ('The Economic Policy for Structural Change—An Outline and the Missed Opportunities'); and Roberto Scazzieri and Alberto Quadrio Curzio ('Summing Up').

Bibliography

Baddeley, M., & Scazzieri, R. (2012). *Introductory remarks*. The economics of structural change: Theory, institutions and policies: A conference in honour of Luigi Pasinetti. Cambridge, Gonville and Caius College, 12–13th September 2012.

Cardinale, I., Coffman, D'M., & Scazzieri, R. (2014). Towards a political economy of industrial fluctuations, introductory essay. In A. Aftalion (Ed.), *Periodic overproduction crises*. London: Anthem Books (English edition of A. Aftalion, *Les crises périodiques de surproduction*, Paris: Rivière, 1913).

Coffman, D'M. (2013a). Towards a New Jurusalem: The committee for regulating the excise, 1649–1653. *English Historical Review, 128*(535), 1418–1450.

Coffman, D'M. (2013b). *Excise taxation and the origins of public debt* (Palgrave studies in the history of finance). Basingstoke/New York: Palgrave Macmillan.

Coffman, D'M. (2015). The political economy of corn markets. In M. Baranzini, C. Rotondi, & R. Scazzieri (Eds.), *Resources, production and structural dynamics, op. cit.*, pp. 53–71.

Coffman, D'M., Leonard, A., & Neal, L. (Eds.). (2013). *Questioning credible commitment. Perspectives on the rise of financial capitalism*. Cambridge: Cambridge University Press.

Eltis, W. A., Scott, M. F., & Wolfe, J. N. (Eds.). (1970). *Induction, growth and trade: Essays in honour of Sir Roy Harrod*. Oxford: Clarendon Press.

Hamouda, O. F. (1993). *John R. Hicks. The economist's economist*. Oxford: B. Blackwell.

Scazzieri, R., Sen, A. K., & Zamagni, S. (Eds.). (2008). *Markets, money and capital. Hicksian economics for the twenty-first century*. Cambridge: Cambridge University Press.

Zamagni, V., & Zamagni, S. (2002). Italian economists and Linacre College. *The Linacre Journal, 6*, 25–38.

5

The Influential Role of Oxbridge Italian Economists in Science and Civil Society

Italian economists belonging to the tradition presented in this volume have also been influential in many other fields where the relationships between science and civil society are fundamental for promoting a line of thought in academia, in foundations, in scientific journals and in public opinion. As it is not possible to deal with all these initiatives, we refer to their role in the *Società Italiana degli Economisti* and in the *Accademia Nazionale dei Lincei*.

5.1 Società Italiana degli Economisti (SIE)

Numerous presidents of the *Società Italiana degli Economisti* were connected with Oxbridge. Innocenzo Gasparini (chairman 1974–7) in the early 1950s was associated at the Institute of Agricultural Economics, Oxford; Luigi Pasinetti (chair 1986–9) was at Oxbridge from 1956 to 1976; during his tenure he started editing, on behalf of the SIE, the *Italian Economic Papers* published by *Il Mulino* and *Oxford University Press* (see above); Siro Lombardini (chair 1989–92) was visiting professor at Cambridge; Alberto Quadrio Curzio (chair 1995–8) was a research student at Cambridge 1962–3 and later on associated with Queens's, the Judge Institute and the

M. Baranzini, A. Mirante, *A Compendium of Italian Economists at Oxbridge*, DOI 10.1007/978-3-319-32219-3_5

Centre for Financial History of Newnham College; during his tenure as chairman he wrote the history of the SIE, founded in 1950, later published by *Il Mulino* in 2000. Since 2001 there has been a stream of presidents of the SIE strictly connected with Cambridge economics, as Carlo D'Adda (chair 2001–4); Giorgio Lunghini (chair 2004–7); Terenzio Cozzi (chair 2007–10, see above); Alessandro Roncaglia (chair 2010–3). We may say that for decades the majority of Italian economists have often privileged 'non-mainstream' lines of thought, as proved by the election of many other chairmen of the SIE like Giacomo Becattini, Giorgio Fuà, Siro Lombardini, Sergio Steve and Augusto Graziani. Issues connected with Oxbridge economics have been at the centre of numerous Annual Meetings of the SIE. We shall report on some of them for the period 1975–2000. In 1975 T. Cozzi and G. Lunghini on 'Economic decisions', in 1976 V. Del Punta, G. Di Nardi, I. Musu and P. Savona on 'Keynes's theory after forty years'; in 1979 I. Gasparini, G. Mazzocchi and L. Pasinetti on 'Inflation today: distribution and growth'; in 1984 L. Pasinetti, F. Momigliano and D. Siniscalco on 'Structural changes of the productive system'; in 1986 T. Cozzi and S. Lombardini on 'Economic development'; in 1987 L. Pasinetti, P. Garegnani, S. Ricossa and C. Napoleoni on 'The theory of value'; in 1988 A. Quadrio Curzio and R. Scazzieri on 'Structural economic dynamics'; in 1989 J. Kregel and A. Graziani on 'Keynes's monetary analysis'; in 1995 A. Vercelli, F. Hahn and A. Rustichini on 'New trends in economic analysis'; in 1996 R. Scazzieri, C. Poni, P. L. Porta, B. Schefold and S. Zamagni on 'Economists at Bologna, 17th–20th centuries'. Within SIE took origin also the ASE (*Archivio Storico Economisti*) to which Lilia Costabile, who for many years was its scientific coordinator, gave an important contribution.

5.2 Lincei Academy (*Accademia Nazionale dei Lincei, Roma*)

The alignment of the Academy in the social sciences along Oxbridge research lines in economics is confirmed by the election of the following Foreign Fellows:

- Alfred Marshall (26.7.1842–13.7.1924; appointed Foreign Fellow 26.8.1896)

- Francis Edgeworth (8.2.1945–13.2.1926; appointed Foreign Fellow 30.1.1919)
- Arthur Cecil Pigou (17.11.1877–7.3.1959; appointed Foreign Fellow 16.6.1932)
- Dennis Holme Robertson (23.5.1890–21.4.1963; appointed Foreign Fellow 1.10.1951)
- Piero Sraffa (5.8.1898–3.9.1983; *socio corrispondente* 5.8.1953; *socio nazionale* 29.8.1965)
- John Richard Hicks (9.4.1904–20.5.1989; appointed Foreign Fellow 24.9.1952)
- Richard Stone (30.8.1913–6.12.1991; appointed Foreign Fellow 28.9.1987)
- Amartya K. Sen (3.11.1933–; appointed Foreign Fellow 22.10.1996)
- Anthony B. Atkinson (4.9.1944–; appointed Foreign Fellow 11.10.2007)
- John Eatwell (2.2.1945–; appointed Foreign Fellow 17.10.2003)
- Jan Kregel (19.4.1944–; appointed Foreign Fellow 11.11.2011)
- Mauro L. Baranzini (31.08.1944–; appointed Foreign Fellow 11.11.2011)
- Michael A. H. Dempster (10.4.1938–; appointed Foreign Fellow 8.11.2013)
- Michael A. Landesmann (appointed Foreign Fellow November 2015)

Most of these Oxbridge scholars took part in numerous conferences, workshops and other events organised by the Academy, contributing in this way to the strengthening of scientific and personal ties. Due to lack of space, it is not possible to deal here with all Italian economists elected to the Lincei Academy belonging to the classical (or Oxbridge) tradition. Luigi Pasinetti, born in 1930, may be considered the link between those born before 1930 (in particular, Piero Sraffa, Federico Caffè, Sergio Steve, Giorgio Fuà, Paolo Sylos Labini and Siro Lombardini) and those born after 1930. As to the latter group, a central role has been played by Alberto Quadrio Curzio who first was *socio corrispondente* (1996), *socio nazionale* (2002), *Segretario Accademico* (from 2003), President of the *Classe di scienze morali, storiche e filologiche* (from 2009) and President since July 2015. He had an important role in invigorating the classical Oxbridge tradition with distinguished scholars such as Alessandro

Roncaglia, Terenzio Cozzi, Giorgio Lunghini, Antonio Pedone, Pierluigi Ciocca, Roberto Scazzieri, Michele Salvati, Maria Cristina Marcuzzo, and the first author of the present essay. The Academy has also organized and sponsored numerous conferences on lines of research of the Oxbridge-Italian school of economic thought. (A similar strategy has also been brought forward by Quadrio Curzio at the *Istituto Lombardo, Accademia di Scienze e Lettere*, Milan.)

5.3 Three Generations

We review here the bearing of the research programmes of Luigi L. Pasinetti, Alberto Quadrio Curzio and Roberto Scazzieri, since they represent three successive generations of economists, with whom the first of the present authors has worked intensively. From a scientific point of view, the Italian economists of the Oxbridge school of economics of the second half of the twentieth century and beyond have certainly been pivotal in the evolution of economic thinking.

1. *Luigi Pasinetti*: Without his contribution (a) there may not have been the first controversy on the definition and measurement of technical progress stirred up by his 1959 paper in *The Review of Economics and Statistics*, with a reply by Bob Solow. Further, there may not have been the first 'two Cambridges controversy' on profit determination and income distribution, sparked off by his 1962 paper in *The Review of Economic Studies* (as confirmed by Paul Samuelson in a long letter to the first author of this volume). Moreover, the second two Cambridges controversy on capital theory would have been considerably different. Also, the Summers-Kotlikoff thesis—according to which the intergenerational transmission of wealth is higher than the 15–20 % postulated by Franco Modigliani—would not have been given the theoretical and empirical support of a number of works elaborated by Oxbridge-Italian scholars. Finally, the theory of production, structural change and technological scarcity would not have been enriched by the contribution provided by the Oxbridge-Italian school.

2. *Alberto Quadrio Curzio*: From a scientific and cultural point of view, the Oxbridge school of economics had a strong impact on the contribution of Quadrio Curzio, both in the Italian context and for his network with research, academic, social and political European institutions. At the European level, he has worked intensively with the President of the European Commission, Romano Prodi. He is also a member of *Academia Europaea* and has a growing role in the Balzan Prize Foundation of Zurich and Milan, as well as chairman of the Balzan-Lincei-Swiss Academies Committee. In due course, Quadrio Curzio has acquired a widely recognized public profile. Since 1968, he has been a leading member of the publishing house Il Mulino, for which he founded in 1983, and has managed since then, *Economia Politica. Journal of Analytical and Institutional Economics*. From 1977 to 1987, he was elected to represent the Italian economists to the *Consiglio Nazionale delle Ricerche* (*CNR*) (the equivalent of the SSRC in Britain), where he was responsible for the strategy and financing of public-funded research in the field of economics. Additionally, he chaired the Faculty of Political Science of the Catholic University of Milan and the *Istituto Lombardo, Accademia di scienze e Lettere*. More generally, he has invigorated a line of the *new classical type*, by restoring the relevance of the Cambridge school outside Cambridge itself and, in particular, in Italy.
3. *Roberto Scazzieri*: Scazzieri was among the founders and a managing editor of *Structural Change and Economic Dynamics*, launched in 1990 and initially published by Oxford University Press. Issue 7.2 of this journal was dedicated to Pasinetti's Structural Dynamics with an introduction by Roberto Scazzieri, and contributions by Izumi Hishiyama, Heinrich Bortis, Davide Gualerzi and Joseph Halevi. Scazzieri has written and edited a number of volumes jointly with Harald Hagemann, Michael Landesmann and the first author of this essay; these are centred on the Oxbridge-Italian research programme. In Cambridge during the last few years (about 2005–2016), Roberto Scazzieri, jointly with other Italian economists working in Cambridge, has set up three seminars worth recalling. First, the Cambridge Seminar in the History of Economic Analysis at Clare Hall

(CAMHIST). A group of scholars at Clare Hall, including Antonio Andreoni, Francesco Boldizzoni, Harald Hagemann, Geoffrey Harcourt, Prue Kerr, Roberto Scazzieri and Albert Steenge, have been running a seminar in the history of economic analysis for several years. What characterizes the seminar's approach is the conception of political economy as a social discipline steeped in analytical inquiry and in the specific conditions of historical context. Following John Hicks's view, that economists should know the history of their concepts in order to know what they are doing, the seminar addresses theories of the past and present in terms of their analytical content and historical significance. It is open to the wider community of economists, historians and philosophers at Cambridge. The speakers have been leading figures in the field, as well as younger academics from around the world. The second seminar initiative was 'Market Square: The Polity, Economy and Society Cambridge Research Group'. Market Square has been supported by the Centre for Research in the Arts, Social Sciences and Humanities (CRASSH) and, among its conveners, we find Antonio Andreoni (Institute for Manufacturing, now SOAS, University of London), Ivano Cardinale (Emmanuel College, now Goldsmiths, University of London) and Gian Paolo Faella (CRASSH, Cambridge, and *Scuola Normale Superiore*, Pisa). Roberto Scazzieri has been one of its Faculty Advisors. Finally, Ivano Cardinale was the principal convener of the Cambridge Research Seminar in Political Economy (co-conveners D'M. Coffman and R. Scazzieri), which was held at Emmanuel College, Cambridge for a number of years (about 2012–16).

6

Conclusions

To sum up, we would stress that:

(a) The contribution of Italian economists to the Oxbridge school of economics of the second half of the twentieth century, and beyond, has been: pivotal in the evolution of economic thinking; more insightful and decisive than that of French or German economists (just to mention the largest continental countries) and surely not inferior to those of Canada or Australia. The only exception to this, in a certain sense, relates to the contribution of the USA. Also, Italian economists have contributed to the instigation and promotion of at least four theoretical controversies (on the measurement of technical progress, on capital theory, on income distribution and profit determination, and on the inter-generational transmission of wealth).

(b) The Italian scientific community has strongly promoted in Italy the economic theories elaborated in Oxford and Cambridge from 1950 to 2000 and beyond, clearly at the forefront of economic research. Italian economists have also organized trips, sabbatical leaves and series of lectures of distinguished Oxbridge economists from that period. Oxbridge economists were often celebrated in Italy more

M. Baranzini, A. Mirante, *A Compendium of Italian Economists at Oxbridge*, DOI 10.1007/978-3-319-32219-3_6

than they were celebrated in the United Kingdom or by other communities. Trips by John Hicks, lectures at the Bocconi University (Richard Kahn, Nicholas Kaldor, Richard Stone and Joseph Stiglitz), and celebrations of Roy Harrod (Genoa 1996), John Hicks (2004), Joan Robinson (1993), Sraffa and the post-Keynesian economists at the Lincei Academy, and so forth, are proof of the drive of the Italian school of economic thought.

(c) Since the late 1970s, there has been not only been a steady flow of returning Italian economists teaching at Oxbridge, but also an important flow of non-Italian Oxbridge dons who moved permanently to Italian universities. Among the latter are Richard Goodwin, Frank Hahn, Michio Morishima, Amit Bhaduri, Vela Velupillai, Christopher Gilbert, Brian Francis McGuinness (a philosopher) and, to a certain extent, Ian Kregel. Their arrival in Italy has further enriched the research and teaching strength of Italian universities.

(d) A significant number of Italian scholars—we could say 'of the third generation'—are now teaching and researching in Oxford and Cambridge. At the same time, some of them have set up seminars and roundtables worthy of mention. We are sure there are many others that keep alive the Anglo-Italian tradition in the field of economics.

It is to be hoped that this extremely fruitful example of scientific and academic cross-fertilization will continue in the future, since the results obtained have been outstanding, to say the least.

Bibliography

Agliardi, E. (1990a). Learning-by-doing and the emergence of monopoly: A note. *Economic Letters, 32*(4), 353–357.
Agliardi, E. (1990b). On the robustness of constestability theory. *International Journal of Industrial Organization, 8*(3), 485–490.
Agliardi, E. (2001). Taxation and investment decisions: A real options approach. *Australian Economic Papers, 40*(1), 44–55.
Agliardi, E. (2004). À propos de "L'axiomatisation et les theories économiques" de Philippe Mongin'. *Revue économique, 55*(1), 123–142.
Agliardi, E. (2011). Sustainability in uncertain economics. *Environmental and Resource Economics, 48*(1), 71–82.
Agliardi, E., & Agliardi, R. (2008). Progressive taxation and corporate liquidation policy. *Economic Modelling, 25*(3), 532–541.
Agliardi, E., & Bebbington, M. (1994). Self-reinforcing mechanisms and interactive behaviour. *Economic Letters, 46*(3), 281–287.
Agliardi, E., & Bebbington, M. (1997). Self-reinforcing mechanisms and market information. *European Journal of Operational Research, 96*(3), 444–454.
Amendola, M., & Gaffard, J.-L. (1988). *The innovative choice, an econometric analysis if the dynamics of technology*. Oxford: B. Blackwell.
Amendola, M., & Gaffard, J.-L. (1998). *Out of equilibrium*. Oxford: Clarendon Press.

M. Baranzini, A. Mirante, *A Compendium of Italian Economists at Oxbridge*, DOI 10.1007/978-3-319-32219-3

Amendola, M., & Gaffard, J.-L. (2001). Out of equilibrium dynamics. In L. F. Punzo (Ed.), *Cycles, growth and structural change: Theories and empirical evidence, op. cit.*, pp. 115–127.

Amendola, M., & Gaffard, J.-L. (2008). Sequential analysis and out-of-equilibrium paths. In R. Scazzieri, A. Sen, & S. Zamagni (Eds.), *Markets, money and capital. Hicksian economics for the twenty-first century, op. cit.*, pp. 382–404.

Amendola, M., & Gaffard, J.-L. (2014). Time to build and out-of-equilibrium growth process. *Structural Change and Economic Dynamics, 29*, 19–27.

Amendola, M., Froeschlé, C., & Gaffard, J.-L. (1993). Sustaining structural change: Malthus's heritage. *Structural Change and Economic Dynamics, 4*(1), 65–79.

Andergassen, R., Nardini, F., & Ricottilli, M. (2005). Firms' interaction and technological paradigms. In J. Leskow, M. Puchet, & L. Punzo (Eds.), *New tools of economic dynamics* (Lecture notes in economics and mathematical systems, Vol. 551, pp. 79–84). Berlin: Springer.

Andergassen, R., Nardini, F., & Ricottilli, M. (2006). Innovation, waves, self-organized critically and technological convergence. *Journal of Economic Behavior and Organization, 61*(5), 710–728.

Andreatta, N. (1956). L'ammortamento in relazione ad alcuni problemi di dinamica economica. *Rivista internazionale di scienze sociali, 64*(1), 12–31.

Andreatta, N. (1957). Inflazione salariale e distribuzione del reddito in una economia di oligopoli. *Rivista internazionale di scienze sociali, 28*(4), 514–540.

Andreatta, N. (1958). *Distribuzione del Reddito e Accumulazione del Capitale.* Milan: Giuffrè.

Andreatta, N. (1961). *Calcolo economico e programmi di sviluppo.* Milan: Giuffrè.

Andreatta, N., & Harberger, A. C. (1964). A note on the economic principles of electricity pricing. In P. N. Rosenstein-Rodan (Ed.), *Pricing and fiscal policies. A study in method* (pp. 147–64). Cambridge: The MIT Press.

Andrejevic, U., Andreopoulos, G. C., & Panayides, A. (2008). Tariffs in apparel and footwear: A gender approach. *Journal of Diversity Management, 3*(3), 1–6.

Andreoni, A. (2013). *Manufacturing development: Structural change and production capabilities dynamics.* PhD dissertation, University of Cambridge.

Andreoni, A. (2014). Structural learning: Embedding discoveries and the dynamics of production. *Structural Change and Economic Dynamics, 29*(2), 58–74.

Andreoni, A. (2015). On manufacturing development under resource constraints. In M. Baranzini, C. Rotondi, & R. Scazzieri (Eds.), *Resources, production and structural dynamics, op. cit.*, pp. 407–423.

Andreoni, A., & Scazzieri, R. (2013). Triggers of change: Structural trajectories and production dynamics. *Cambridge Journal of Economics, 38*(6), 1391–1408.

Antille, G., & Baranzini, E. (1972). *Input–output pour la Suisse: Expériences et analyses*. Geneva: Centre d'économétrie.

Antille, G., Baranzini, E., & Burle de Figuereido, J. (1971). *Expériences en vue de la construction d'un tableau input–output pour la Suisse*. Geneva: Département d'économie appliquée, and Institut Battelle.

Antonelli, et al. (Eds.). (2012). *Economia come scienza sociale. Teoria, istituzioni e storia. Essays in honour of Alberto Quadrio Curzio*. Bologna: Il Mulino.

Araujo, J. T. (1992). The government sector in Kaldor-Pasinetti models of growth and income distribution. *Journal of Post Keynesian Economics, 15*(2), 211–228.

Arena, R. (1992). Une synthèse entre post-keynésiens et néo-ricardiens est-elle encore possible? *L'actualité Économique, 68*(4), 587–606.

Arena, R. (1995). Cycles et croissance: une approche neo-kaldorienne. *Revue Économique, 46*(6), 1433–1444.

Arena, R., & Porta, P. L. (Eds.). (2012a). *Structural dynamics and economic growth*. Cambridge: Cambridge University Press.

Arena, R., & Porta, P. L. (2012b). Introduction: Structural dynamics and contemporary growth theory. In R. Arena, & P. L. Porta (Eds.), *Structural dynamics and economic growth, op. cit.*, pp. 1–33.

Arestis, P., Palma, G., & Sawyer, M. (Eds.). (1997). *Capital controversy, post-Keynesian economics and the history of economics. Essays in honour of Geoff Harcourt*. London: Routledge.

Atkinson, A. B. (1971). The distribution of wealth and the individual life-cycle. *Oxford Economic Papers, 23*(2), 239–254.

Atkinson, A. B. (1974). *A model of the distribution of wealth*. University of Essex and MIT, Mimeo.

Bacharach, M. O. L., & Bernasconi, M. (1997). The variable frame theory of focal points: An experimental study. *Games and Economic Behavior, 19*(1), 1–45.

Bacharach, M., Guerra, G., & Zizzo, D. J. (2007). The self-fulfilling property of trust: An experimental study. *Theory and Decision, 63*(4), 349–388.

Baddeley, M., & Scazzieri, R. (2012). *Introductory remarks*. The economics of structural change: Theory, institutions and policies: A conference in honour of Luigi Pasinetti. Cambridge, Gonville and Caius College, 12–13th September 2012.

Baldassarri, M., & Ciocca, P. L. (2001). *Roots of the Italian school of economics and finance. From Ferrara (1857) to Einaudi (1944)*. Basingstoke: Palgrave Macmillan.

Baldone, S. (1995). Durable capital inputs: Conditions for prices ratios to be invariant to profit-rate changes: A comment on professor Samuelson. In J. C. Wood (Ed.), *Piero Sraffa: Critical assessments* (Vol. II, pp. 325–335). London/New York: Routledge.

Baldone, S. (1996). Vertical integration, the temporal structure of production processes and transition between techniques. In M. A. Landesmann, & R. Scazzieri (Eds.), *Production and economic dynamics, op. cit.*, pp. 81–104.

Balestra, P., & Baranzini, M. (1971). Some optimal aspects in a two-class growth model with a differentiated interest rate. *Kyklos, 24*(2), 240–256. Reprinted in C. Panico, & N. Salvadori (Eds.). (1993). *Post Keynesian theory of growth and distribution, op. cit.*

Baranzini, M. (1975a). The Pasinetti and the anti-Pasinetti theorems: A reconciliation. *Oxford Economic Papers, 27*(3), 470–473.

Baranzini, M. (1975b). A two-class monetary growth model. *Schweizerische Zeitschrift für Volkswirtschaft und Statistik, 111*(2), 177–189.

Baranzini, M. (1976). *On the distribution of income in two-class growth models*. D. Phil. thesis, The Queen's College, Oxford.

Baranzini, E. (1978). *L'analyse des modèles d'entrées-sorties en économie: problèmes de méthodes et pratiques opératoires*. Berne/Frankfurt: Lang.

Baranzini, M. (1979). Review of *Protagonisti del pensiero economico,* Vol. I: *Nascita e affermazione del marginalismo* (1871–1890); Vol. II: *Tradizione e rivoluzione in economia politica* (1890–1936). In A. Quadrio Curzio, & R. Scazzieri (Eds.), *Economic Journal, 89*(3), 480–482.

Baranzini, M. (Ed.). (1982). *Advances in economic theory*. Oxford/New York: Basil Blackwell/St. Martin's Press.

Baranzini, M. (1991a). *A theory of wealth distribution and accumulation*. Oxford: Clarendon Press.

Baranzini, M. (1991b). The Pasinetti and Anti-Pasinetti theorems: A reply to K. Miyazaki and P. A. Samuelson. *Oxford Economic Papers, 43*(2), 195–198.

Baranzini, M. (1992). The debate on Kaldor's theory of distribution. In F. Targetti (Ed.), *Nicholas Kaldor: The economics and politics of capitalism as a dynamic system* (pp. 143–59). Oxford: Clarendon Press.

Baranzini, M. (1995). Distribution, accumulation and institutions. In A. Heertje (Ed.), *The makers of modern economics* (Vol. II, pp. 1–28). Aldershot/ Brookfield: E. Elgar.

Baranzini, E. (1996). *Les scénarios de l'évolution démographique en Suisse, 1995–2050.* Berne: Office Fédéral de Statistique.

Baranzini, M. (2000). Luigi Lodovico Pasinetti. In P. Arestis & M. Sawyer (Eds.), *Biographical dictionary of dissenting economists* (2nd ed., pp. 417–24). Cheltenham: E. Elgar.

Baranzini, M. (2008). Flexible saving and economic growth. In R. Scazzieri, A. Sen, & S. Zamagni (Eds.), *Markets, money and capital. Hicksian economics for the twenty-first century, op. cit.*, pp. 287–308.

Baranzini, M., & Harcourt, G. C. (Eds.). (1993). *The dynamics of the wealth of nations: Growth, distribution and structural change: Essays in honour of Luigi L. Pasinetti.* Basingstoke/New York: Macmillan/St. Martin's Press.

Baranzini, M., & Marangoni, G. (2015). *Richard stone: An annotated bibliography.* Lugano: Università della Svizzera italiana.

Baranzini, M., & Mari, C. (2011). The Cantabrigensis-Italian school of income and wealth distribution. In *Gli economisti post-keynesiani di Cambridge e l'Italia*, Atti dei Convegni Lincei (pp. 235–340). Rome: Scienze e Lettere.

Baranzini, M., & Mirante, A. (2013). The Cambridge post-Keynesian school of income and wealth distribution. In G. C. Harcourt, & P. Kriesler (Eds.), *The oxford handbook of post-Keynesian economics, op. cit.*, Vol. I, pp. 288–361.

Baranzini, M., & Porta, P. L. (2016). Luigi Lodovico Pasinetti. In R. Cord (Ed.), *The Palgrave companion to Cambridge economics.* London/New York: Palgrave Macmillan, 979–1001.

Baranzini, M., & Quadrio Curzio, A. (2012). *From Adam Smith to structural dynamics: Luigi Pasinetti's life-long contribution.* Paper presented at the conference 'the economics of structural change: Theory, institutions and policies, in honour of Luigi L. Pasinetti, Gonville and Caius College, Cambridge.

Baranzini, M., & Scazzieri, R. (Eds.). (1986). *Foundations of economics. Structure of inquiry and economic theory.* Oxford/New York: Basil Blackwell; and 'Knowledge in economics: A framework', 1–87.

Baranzini, M., & Scazzieri, R. (Eds.). (1990; reprinted 2012). *The economic theory of structure and change.* Cambridge: Cambridge University Press; and 'Introduction', 1–20; 'Economic structure. Analytical perspectives', 227–333.

Baranzini, M., Rotondi, C., & Scazzieri, R. (Eds.). (2015). *Resources, production and structural dynamics.* Cambridge: Cambridge University Press.

Barba, A., & De Vivo, G. (2012). An «unproductive labour» view of finance. *Cambridge Journal of Economics, 36*(6), 1479–1496.

Barba, A., & Pivetti, M. (2008). Rising household debt: Its causes and macroeconomic implications – A long period analysis. *Cambridge Journal of Economics, 33*(1), 113–137.

Bartoli, H. (2003). *Histoire de la pensée économique en Italie*. Paris: Publications de la Sorbonne.

Barucci, P., Costabile, L., & Di Matteo, M. (Eds.). (2008). *Gli archivi e la storia del pensiero economico*. Bologna: Il Mulino.

Basevi, G., et al. (Eds.). (2014). *Gli allievi ricordano Andreatta*. Bologna: Il Mulino-AREL.

Bateman, B. W., Toshiaki, H., & Marcuzzo, M. C. (2010). *The return to Keynes*. London: Belknap Press.

Becattini, G. (2004). *Industrial districts: A new approach to industrial change*. Cheltenham/Northampton: E. Elgar.

Bellino, E. (1993). Continuous switching of techniques in linear production models. *The Manchester School, 61*(2), 185–201.

Bellino, E. (1997). Full-cost pricing in the classical competitive process. *Zeitschrift für Nationalökonomie - Journal of Economics, 65*(1), 41–54.

Bellino, E. (1999). Convergence to long-run equilibrium – On some recent variations of the "pure" cross-dual model of gravitation. *Structural Change and Economic Dyanamics, 10*(2), 225–237.

Bellino, E. (2004). On Sraffa's standard commodity. *Cambridge Journal of Economics, 28*(1), 121–132.

Bellino, E. (2006). Unemployment and growth: A critical survey. In C. Panico, & N. Salvadori (Eds.), *Classical, neoclassical and Keynesian views on growth and distribution, op. cit.* pp. 191–226.

Bellino, E. (2008). Book reviews on production of commodities by means of commodities. In G. Chiodi & L. Ditta (Eds.), *Sraffa or an alternative economics* (pp. 23–41). Basingstoke: Palgrave-Macmillan.

Bellino, E., & Femminis, G. (1991). A consumption-growth linear relation. *Cambridge Journal of Economics, 15*(4), 475–479.

Bellofiore, R. (2012). The "tiresome objector" and old moor: A renewal of the debate on Marx after Sraffa based on the unpublished material at the Wren library. *Cambridge Journal of Economics, 36*(6), 1385–1400.

Bellofiore, R., & Halevi, J. (2011). "Could be raining": The European crisis after the great recession. *International Journal of Political Economy, 39*(4), 5–30.

Belussi, F., & Caldari, K. (2009). At the origin of industrial district: Alfred Marshall and the Cambridge school. *Cambridge Journal of Economics, 33*(2), 335–355.

Berloffa, G., Modena, F., & Villa, P. (2014). Changing labour market opportunities for young people in Italy and the role of the family of origin. *Rivista italiana degli economisti, XIX*(2), 227–51.

Bernasconi, M. (2006). Redistributive taxation in democracies: Evidence on people satisfaction. *European Journal of Political Economy, 22*(4), 809–837.

Bernasconi, M., & Loomes, G. (1992). Violations of the reduction principle in an Ellsberg-type problem. *Theory and Decision, 32*, 77–100.

Besomi, D. (1995). From *the trade cycle* to the "essay in dynamic theory". The Harrod-Keynes correspondence, 1937–1938. *History of Political Economy, 27*(2), 309–343.

Besomi, D. (1996). An additional note on the Harrod-Keynes correspondence. *History of Political Economy, 28*(2), 281–294.

Besomi, D. (1999). *The making of Harrod's dynamics*. London: Macmillan.

Besomi, D. (2000a). On the spread of an idea: The strange case of Mr Harrod and the multiplier. *History of Political Economy, 32*(2), 347–379.

Besomi, D. (2000b). Keynes and Harrod on the classical theory of investment. More on the origin of the only diagram in the general theory. *Journal of the History of Economic Thought, 22*(3), 367–376.

Besomi, D. (2001). Harrod's dynamics and the theory of growth: The story of a mistaken attribution. *Cambridge Journal of Economics, 25*(1), 79–96.

Besomi, D. (Ed.). (2003). *The interwar papers and correspondence of Roy Harrod* (3 vol.). Cheltenham: E. Elgar.

Besomi, D. (2004). Dynamics, trade and money in the correspondence between Roy Harrod and Dennis Robertson. *Research in the History of Economic Thought and Methodology, 22A*, 1–64.

Besomi, D. (2005a). The goodwilling outsider. The correspondence between Keynes and Harrod. In M. C. Marcuzzo & A. Rosselli (Eds.), *Economists in Cambridge. A study of their correspondence* (pp. 92–118). London: Routledge.

Besomi, D. (2005b). The Keynesian Tutor. Kahn and the correspondence with Sraffa, Harrod and Kaldor (with M. C. Marcuzzo as the main author, and F. Ranchetti). In M. C. Marcuzzo, & A. Rosselli (Eds.), *Economists in Cambridge. A study of their correspondence, op. cit.*, pp. 292–308.

Besomi, D. (2005c). The unlooked for Proselytiser. J. Robinson and the correspondence with Sraffa, Harrod and Kaldor' (with A. Rosselli as main author). In M. C. Marcuzzo, & A. Rosselli (Eds.), *Economists in Cambridge. A study of their correspondence, op. cit.*, pp. 309–327.

Besomi, D. (2006a). Roy Harrod and Joan Robinson on thriftiness and growth. An introduction to their correspondence, 1965–1970. *History of Economics Review, 44*(1), 1–15.

Besomi, D. (2006b). (Editing of) R. F. Harrod and J. V. Robinson, correspondence on growth theory, 1965–70. *History of Economics Review, 44*(1), 16–31.

Besomi, D. (2008). Harrod discontent with Harrodian growth theory. In R. Leeson (Ed.), *The Keynesian tradition. Archival insight into the evolution of the economics* (pp. 65–98). London: Palgrave Macmillan.

Besomi, D. (2010a). The periodicity of crises. A survey of the literature before 1850. *Journal of the History of Economic Thought, 32*(1), 85–132.

Besomi, D. (2010b). "Periodic crises": Clément Juglar between theories of crises and theories of business cycles. *Research in the History of Economic Thought and Methodology, 28A*, 169–283.

Besomi, D. (2011a). Disease of the body politick. A metaphor for crises in the history of the nineteenth century economics. *Journal of the History of Economic Thought, 33*(1), 67–118.

Besomi, D. (Ed.). (2011b). *Crises and cycles in economic dictionaries and enciclopedias*. London: Routledge.

Besomi, D. (2014). Tempests of the business world: Weather metaphors for crises in the 19th century. In R. Baranzini & F. Allison (Eds.), *Economics and other branches – In the shade of the oak tree, essays in honour of pascal bridel* (pp. 291–308). London: Pickering & Chatto.

Bettio, F. (1988). *The sexual division of labour*. Oxford: Clarendon Press.

Bettio, F. (2008). Occupational segregation and gender wage disparities in developed economies: Should we still worry? In F. Bettio, & A. Verashchegina (Eds.), *Frontiers in the economics of gender, op. cit.*, pp. 167–191.

Bettio, F., & Nandi, T. K. (2010). Evidence on women trafficked for sexual exploitations. *European Journal of Law and Economics, 29*(1), 15–42.

Bettio, F., & Verashchagina, A. (Eds.). (2008). *Frontiers in the economics of gender*. London/New York: Routledge.

Bettio, F., & Villa, P. (1998). A Mediterranean perspective of the break down of the relationship between participation and fertility. *Cambridge Journal of Economics, 22*(2), 137–171.

Bettio, F., & Villa, P. (2014). Salario minimo, pro e contro. *Italianieuropei, 3*(2014), 48–56.

Bettio, F., Simonazzi, A., & Villa, P. (2006). Change in care regimes and female migration: The "care drain" in the Mediterranean. *Journal of European Social Policy, 16*(3), 271–285.

Bhaduri, A. (1981). Class relations and the patterns of accumulation in an Agrarian economy. *Cambridge Journal of Economics, 5*(4), 233–246.

Bhaduri, A. (1993). The method of the pure ratio in economic analysis. In M. Baranzini, & G. C. Harcourt (Eds.), *The dynamics of the wealth of nations: Growth, distribution and structural change, op. cit.*, pp. 175–180.

Bhaduri, A. (2006). The role of income distribution in long run endogenous growth. In N. Salvadori (Ed.), *Economic growth and distribution: On the nature and causes of the wealth of nations* (pp. 40–57). Cheltenham/Northampton: E. Elgar.

Biagioli, M. (1982). A monetary model of exchange-rate determination applied to the Italian experience with flexible exchange rates. In M. Baranzini (Ed.), *Advances in economic theory, op. cit.*, pp. 207–224.

Biagioli, M. (1995). The results of the decentralization of wage-bargaining. In D. Vaughan-Whitehead (Ed.), *Workers' financial participation: East–west experiences* (pp. 85–104). Geneva: ILO.

Biagioli, M. (2014). Can the European monetary union get out of the Labyrinth? *Boletim de Ciencias Economicas, 57*(1), 653–690.

Biagioli, M., & Curatolo, S. (1999). Microeconomic determinants and effects of financial participation agreements: An empirical analysis of the large Italian firms of the engineering sector in the eighties and early nineties. *Economic Analysis, 2*(2), 99–130.

Bianchi, P., & Lambertini, L. (2003). *Technology, information and market dynamics: Topics in advanced industrial organisation.* Cheltenham: E. Elgar.

Biasco, S. (1968). *Problemi di dinamica comparata: un'indagine sulle relazioni tra la teoria neo-Keynesiana della distribuzione e dello sviluppo e gli schemi di Sraffa.* Rome: Edizioni dell'Ateneo.

Biasco, S. (1974). Consumo e saggio di rendimento sociale. *Rivista Internazionale di Scienze Economiche e Commerciali, 21*(11), 1041–1064.

Biasco, S. (1987). Currency cycles and the international economy. *BNL Quarterly Review, 40*(160), 31–60.

Biasco, S. (1996). Degree of mechanization of techniques and scale of mechanization of the economy. In M. C. Marcuzzo, L. L. Pasinetti, & A. Roncaglia (Eds.), *The economics of Joan Robinson, op. cit.*, pp. 148–173.

Biasco, S. (2002). Una valutazione d'insieme dei nuovi scenari di tassazione d'impresa. *Politica Economica, 18*(3), 403–439.

Biasco, S. (2013). *Ripensando il capitalismo.* Rome: Luiss University Press.

Biasco, S., Roncaglia, A., & Salvati, M. (Eds.). (1993). *Market and institutions in economic development. Essays in honour of Paolo Sylos Labini.* London: Macmillan.

Bini, P., & Magliulo, A. (1999). Keynesianism in Italy: Before and after the general theory. In L. L. Pasinetti, & B. Schefold (Eds.), *The impact of Keynes on economics in the 20th century, op. cit.*, pp. 131–152.

Birolo, A. (2010). *The Italian economic research between pluralism and monism: The young economists in the last thirty years*. Munich: Munich Personal RePEc Archive.

Birolo, A., & Rosselli, A. (2010). Research standards for the Italian young academics: What has changed over the last thirty years. In A. Birolo, D. K. Foley, H. D. Kurz, B. Schefold, & I. Steedman (Eds.), *Production, distribution and trade: Essays in honour of Sergio Parrinello* (pp. 349–372). Abingdon/Oxon: Routledge.

Bliss, C. J. (2010). The Cambridge post-Keynesians: An outsider's insider view. *History of Political Economy, 42*(4), 631–652.

Bliss, C. J., & Cippà, R. (1982). Temporary equilibrium with rationed borrowing and consistent plans. In M. Baranzini (Ed.), *Advances in economic theory, op. cit.*, pp. 45–66.

Boggio, L. (1980). Full cost and "Sraffa prices": Equilibrium and stability in a system with fixed capital. *Economic Notes, 9*(1), 3–33.

Boggio, L. (1985). On the stability of production prices. *Metroeconomica, 37*(3), 241–267.

Boggio, L. (1992). Production prices and dynamic stability: Results and open questions. *Manchester School, 60*(3), 264–294.

Boggio, L. (1995). On relative stability and the coordination problem in market economies. *Revue Economique, 46*(6), 1445–1459.

Boggio, L. (1996). Growth and international competitiveness in a "Kaldorian" perspective. *Structural Change and Economic Dynamics, 7*(3), 299–320.

Boggio, L. (2006). Growth unemployment and wages: Disequilibrium models with increasing returns. In N. Salvadori, & C. Panico (Eds.), *Classical, neo classical and Keynesian views on growth and distribution, op. cit.*, pp. 227–242.

Böhm, B., & Punzo, L. F. (2001). Productivity-investment fluctuations and structural change. In L. F. Punzo (Ed.), *Cycles, growth and structural change: Theories and empirical evidence, op. cit.*, pp. 47–85.

Borghesi, S., & Vercelli, A. (2003). Sustainable globalisation. *Ecological Economics, 44*(1), 77–89.

Borghesi, S., & Vercelli, A. (2008). *Global sustainability. Social and environmental conditions*. Basingstoke/New York: Palgrave Macmillan.

Borghesi, S., & Vercelli, A. (2012). Happiness and health: Two paradoxes. *Journal of Economic Surveys, 26*(2), 203–233.

Bortis, H. (1997). *Institutions, behaviour and economic theory: A contribution to classical-Keynesian political economy*. Cambridge: Cambridge University Press.

Bortis, H. (2012). Towards a synthesis in post-Keynesian economics in Luigi Pasinetti's contribution. In R. Arena, & P. L. Porta (Eds.), *Structural dynamics and economic growth, op. cit.*, pp. 145–180.

Bridel, P., & Ingrao, B. (2005). Managing Cambridge economics: The correspondence between Keynes and Pigou. In M. C. Marcuzzo, & A. Rosselli (Eds.), *Economics in Cambridge: A study through their correspondence, 1907–1946, op. cit.*, pp. 149–166.

Britto, R. (1969). *The life-cycle savings in a two-class growth model*. Paper presented at the December meeting of the Econometric Society, New York.

Britto, R. (1972). On differential savings propensities in two-class growth models. *Review of Economic Studies, 39*(4), 491–494.

Brusco, S. (1982). The Emilian model: Production, decentralisation and social integration. *Cambridge Journal of Economics, 6*(2), 167–184.

Brusco, S. (1986). Small firms and industrial districts: The experience of Italy. In D. Keeble & E. Wever (Eds.), *New firms and regional development in Europe* (pp. 184–202). London: Croom Helm.

Brusco, S. (1989). *Piccole imprese e distretti industriali*. Turin: Resenberg & Sellier.

Brusco, S. (1992). Small firms and the provision of real services. In F. Pyke & W. Sengenberger (Eds.), *Industrial districts and local eonomic regeneration* (pp. 177–196). Geneva: International Institute for Labour Studies.

Brusco, S. (1999). The rules of the game in industrial districts. In A. Grandoni (Ed.), *Interfirm networks: Organization and industrial competitiveness* (pp. 17–40). London: Routledge.

Brusco, S., & Campus, A. (1971). Le strutture produttive e commerciali dell'industria casaria sarda. *Note Economiche, 1*(2), 3–58.

Brusco, S., & Sabel, C. (1981). Artisan production and economic growth. In F. Wilkinson (Ed.), *The dynamics of labour market segmentation* (pp. 99–113). London: Academic Press.

Caldari, K. (2004). Alfred Marshall's idea of progress and sustainable development. *Journal of the History of Economic Thought, 26*(4), 519–536.

Caldari, K. (2007). Alfred Marshall's critical analysis of scientific management. *European Journal of the History of Economic Thought, 14*(1), 55–78.

Caldari, K., & Masini, F. (2011). Pigouvian *vs* Marshallian Tax. Market failure, public intervention and the problem of externalities. *European Journal of the History of Economic Thought, 18*(5), 715–732.

Campa, G. (1975). Indeterminatezza del saggio di profitto e rilevanza della propensione a risparmiare dei lavoratori e della tecnologia nel paradosso di Pasinetti. *Giornale degli Economisti e Annali di Economia, 1*(2), 16–55.

Campanelli, G. (1982). W. Whewell's contribution to economic analysis: The first mathematical formulation of fixed capital in Ricardo's system. *Manchester School, 50*(3), 248–265.

Campanelli, G. (1996). Ricardo's "curious effect": A mathematical formulation. *History of Political Economy, 28*(4), 641–662.

Campanelli-Andreopoulos, G. (2009). Growth and changes in economic structure: A straightforward statistical approach with an application to the Italian economy. *Cambridge Journal of Economics, 33*(3), 421–432.

Campus, A. (1987a). Marginalist economics. In J. Eatwell, M. Milgate, & P. Newman (Eds.), *The new Palgrave: A dictionary of economics, op. cit.*, Vol. 3, pp. 320–322.

Campus, A. (1987b). Notes on cost and price: Malthus and the marginal theory. *Political Economy. Studies in the Surplus Approach, 3*(1), 3–17.

Candela, G., & Denicolò, V. (1982). Coerenza static e incoerenza dinamica dei "Tableau Economique"'. *Giornale degli economisti e Annali di Economia, 41*(9/10), 605–637.

Carabelli, A. M. (1988). *On Keynes's method.* London: Macmillan.

Carabelli, A. M. (2012). A new methodological approach to economic theory: What I have learnt from 30 years of research on Keynes. In J. Jespersen & M. O. Madsen (Eds.), *Keynes's general theory for today* (pp. 79–97). Cheltenham: E. Elgar.

Carabelli, A. M., & Cedrini, M. A. (2014). Chapter 18 of the general theory "further analysed": Economics as a way of thinking. *Cambridge Journal of Economics, 38*(1), 23–47.

Carabelli, A. M., & De Vecchi, N. (1999). Where to draw the Line? Keynes vs Hayek on knowledge, ethics and economics. *The European Journal of the History of Economics Thought, 6*(2), 271–296.

Caravale, G. A. (Ed.). (1976). *The Cambridge debate on the theory of capital and distribution.* Perugia: Università degli Studi/Mimeo.

Caravale, G. A., & Tosato, D. A. (Eds.). (1980). *Ricardo and the theory of value, distribution and growth.* London/Boston: Routledge & Kegan Paul.

Cardinale, I. (2015). Towards a structural political economy of resources. In M. Baranzini, C. Rotondi, & R. Scazzieri (Eds.), *Resources, production and structural dynamics, op. cit.*, pp. 198–210.

Cardinale, I., & Coffman, D'M. (2014). Economic interdependencies and political conflict: The political economy of taxation in eighteenth century Britain. *Economia Politica. Journal of Analytical and Institutional Economics, 31*(3), 277–300.

Cardinale, I., & Scazzieri, R. (2016). Austerity, expansion and financial policy: Sectoral interdependence, time-structure of production, and medium term analysis. *Revue d'Economie Industrielle*, forthcoming.

Cardinale, I., & Scazzieri, R. (Eds). (2017). *The Palgrave handbook of political economy.* London: Palgrave Macmillan, forthcoming.

Cardinale, I., Coffman, D'M., & Scazzieri, R. (2014). Towards a political economy of industrial fluctuations, introductory essay. In A. Aftalion (Ed.), *Periodic overproduction crises.* London: Anthem Books (English edition of A. Aftalion, *Les crises périodiques de surproduction*, Paris: Rivière, 1913).

Cardinale, I., Coffman, D.'. M., & Scazzieri, R. (Eds.). (2016). *The political economy of the Eurozone.* Cambridge: Cambridge University Press.

Carlevaro, F. (1971). Formulation et estimation de consommation semi-agrégées. *The Canadian Journal of Economics, 4*(4), 441–470.

Carlevaro, F. (1976). A generalization of the linear expenditure system. In L. Solari & J.-N. Du Pasquier (Eds.), *Private and enlarged consumption: Essays in methodology and empirical analysis* (pp. 73–92). Amsterdam: North-Holland.

Carlevaro, F. (1977). Note sur les fonctions de consommation en prix et revenu réels de Fourgeaud et Natal'. *Econometrica, 45*(7), 1639–1650.

Carlevaro, F. (1979). *Luigi Solari: Essai de méthode et analyses économétriques.* Geneva: Librairie Droz.

Carlucci, F., & Marzano, F. (2003). *Poverty, growth and welfare in the world economy in the 21st century.* Berne: Peter Lang.

Casarosa, C. (1978a). A new formulation of the Ricardian system. *Oxford Economic Papers, 30*, 38–63.

Casarosa, C. (1978b). Un contributo all'analisi dei fondamenti microeconomici della teoria keynesiana della domanda effettiva. *Rivista di politica economica, 68*(11), 1371–1409.

Casarosa, C. (1981). The microfoundations of Keynes's aggregate supply and expected demand analysis. *Economic Journal, 91*(361), 188–194.

Casarosa, C. (1982a). The new view of the Ricardian theory of distribution and economic growth. In M. Baranzini (Ed.), *Advances in economic theory, op. cit.*, pp. 227–239.

Casarosa, C. (1982b). Aggregate supply and expected demand analysis in Keynes's general theory: An essay on the microfoundations. In M. Baranzini (Ed.), *Advances in economic theory, op. cit.*, pp. 67–79.

Casarosa, C. (1984). The microfoundations of Keynes's aggregate supply and expected demand analysis: A reply. *Economic Journal, 94*(376), 941–945.

Casarosa, C. (2004). Gli studi nel Regno Unito della seconda generazione. In G. Garofalo, & A. Graziani (Eds.), *La formazione degli economisti in Italia (1950–1975), op. cit.*, pp. 535–554.

Casarosa, C., & Zamagni, S. (1985). Sir John Hicks: il pensiero e l'opera. *Studi Economici, 27*, 3–75.

Cesari, R., & D'Adda, C. (2008). A suggestion for simplifying the theory of asset prices. In R. Scazzieri, A. Sen, & S. Zamagni (Eds.), *Markets, money and capital. Hicksian economics for the twenty-first century, op. cit.*, pp. 252–274.

Chichilnisky, G., Heal, G., & Vercelli, A. (Eds.). (2012). *Sustainability: Dynamics and uncertainty* (Vol. 9). Dordrecht: Springer Science & Business Media.

Ciccarone, G. (2004). Finance and the Cambridge equation. *Review of Political Economy, 16*(2), 163–177.

Ciccarone, G. (2008). Finance and the Cambridge equation: Again on the rate of profits of financial intermediaries. *Review of Political Economy, 20*(3), 433–441.

Ciccone, R. (1984). La teoria della distribuzione nell'analisi di Joan Robinson. *Note Economiche, 2*, 99–124.

Ciccone, R. (1991). Review of A. K. Dutt's growth, distribution and uneven development. *Contributions to Political Economy, 10*(1), 94–102.

Ciccone, R. (1994). Surplus approach. In P. Arestis & M. Sawyer (Eds.), *The Elgar companion to radical political economy* (pp. 389–393). Aldershot: E. Elgar.

Ciccone, R. (1999). Classical and neoclassical short-run prices. In G. Mongiovi, & F. Petri (Eds.), *Value, distribution and capital. Essays in honour of P. Garegnani*, op. cit., pp. 69–92.

Ciccone, R. (2013). Public debt and aggregate demand. In E. S. Levrero, A. Palumbo, & A. Stirati (Eds.), *Sraffa and the reconstruction of economic theory* (pp. 15–43). London: Palgrave Macmillan.

Cingolani, M. (2012). *Structural change and its implications for EU policy coordination.* Paper presented at the conference 'The Economics of Structural Change: Theory, Institutions and Policies, in honour of Luigi L. Pasinetti. Cambridge: Gonville and Caius College.

Ciocca, P. (1996). "The golden age" and Joan Robinson's critique.In M. C. Marcuzzo, L. L. Pasinetti, & A. Roncaglia (Eds.), *The economics of Joan Robinson, op. cit.*, pp. 195–199.

Ciocca, P. (2008). Hicks versus Marx? On the theory of economic history. In R. Scazzieri, A. Sen, & S. Zamagni (Eds.), *Markets, money and capital. Hicksian economics for the twenty-first century, op. cit.*, pp. 146–156.

Cippà, R. F., & Guidi, V. (1982). Temporary equilibrium with rationing. In M. Baranzini (Ed.), *Advances in economic theory, op. cit.*, pp. 90–112.

Coffman, D'M. (2013a). Towards a New Jurusalem: The committee for regulating the excise, 1649–1653. *English Historical Review, 128*(535), 1418–1450.

Coffman, D'M. (2013b). *Excise taxation and the origins of public debt* (Palgrave studies in the history of finance). Basingstoke/New York: Palgrave Macmillan.

Coffman, D'M. (2015). The political economy of corn markets. In M. Baranzini, C. Rotondi, & R. Scazzieri (Eds.), *Resources, production and structural dynamics, op. cit.*, pp. 53–71.

Coffman, D'M., Leonard, A., & Neal, L. (Eds.). (2013). *Questioning credible commitment. Perspectives on the rise of financial capitalism.* Cambridge: Cambridge University Press.

Cohen, A. J., & Harcourt, G. C. (2003). Whatever happened to the capital theory controversies. *Journal of Economic Perspectives, 17*(1), 199–214.

Collard, D. A. (1984). The ascent of high theory. A view from the foothills. In D. A. Collard et al. (Eds.), *Economic theory and Hicksian themes* (pp. 1–10). Oxford: Clarendon Press.

Collard, D. A. (1986). Review of work and welfare in economic theory, by Ugo Pagano (Oxford: B. Blackwell, 1985). *The Economic Journal, 96*(381), 224–225.

Commendatore, P. (1999). Pasinetti and dual equilibria in a post Keynesian model of growth and institutional distribution. *Oxford Economic Papers, 51*(1), 223–236.

Commendatore, P. (2002). Inside debt, aggregate demand and the Cambridge theory of distribution: A note. *Cambridge Journal of Economics, 26*(2), 269–274.

Commendatore, P. (2003). On the post Keynesian theory of growth and "institutional" distribution. *Review of Political Economy, 15*(2), 193–209.

Commendatore, P., et al. (2003). Keynesian theories of growth. In N. Salvadori (Ed.), *The theory of economic growth: A classical perspective* (pp. 103–138). Aldershot: E. Elgar.

Commendatore, P., Panico, C., & Pinto, A. (2005). Government debt, growth and distribution in a postkeynesian approach. In R. Balducci & N. Salvadori (Eds.), *Innovation, unemployment and policy in the theories of growth and distribution*. Aldershot: E. Elgar.

Coricelli, F., Di Matteo, M., & Hahn, F. H. (1998). *New theories in growth and development*. London/New York: Macmillan/St. Martin's.

Costa, P., & Marangoni, G. D. (1995a). *Economia delle interdipendenze produttive*. Padua: Cedam.

Costa, P., & Marangoni, G. D. (1995b). Productive capital in Italy: A disaggregated estimate by sectors of origin and destination: 1985-88. *Review of Income and Wealth, 41*, 439–458.

Costabile, L. (1983a). Natural prices, market prices and effective demand in Malthus. *Australian Economic Papers, 22*, 144–170.

Costabile, L. (1983b). Note sulla relazione tra credito, accumulazione e risparmio in *Banking Policy and the Price Level* di D. H. Robertson. *Studi Economici, 21*, 115–135.

Costabile, L. (1995). Institutions, social custom, and efficiency wage models. Alternative approaches. *Cambridge Journal of Economics, 19*(5), 605–623.

Costabile, L. (1997). Robertson and the post-Keynesian approach to growth and cycles. In P. Arestis, G. Palma, & M. Sawyer (Eds.), *Essays in honour of Geoff Harcourt, op. cit.*, Vol. I, pp. 310–325.

Costabile, L. (Ed.). (2008). *Institutions for social well-being. Alternatives for Europe*. London: Palgrave-Macmillan.

Costabile, L. (2009). Current global inbalances and the Keynes plan: A Keynesian approach for reforming the international monetary system. *Structural Change and Economic Dynamics, 20*(2), 79–89.

Costabile, L. (2015). Monetary analysis, financial innovation and institutions before the industrial revolution: A paradigm case. In M. Baranzini, C. Rotondi, & R. Scazzieri (Eds.), *Resources, production and structural dynamics, op. cit.*, pp. 213–231.

Costabile, L., & Rowthorn, B. (1985). Malthus's theory of wages and growth. *Economic Journal, 95*(378), 418–437.

Costabile, L., & Scazzieri, R. (2008). Social models, growth and key currencies. In L. Costabile (Ed.), *Institutions for social well-being. Alternatives for Europe, op. cit.*, pp. 126–151.

Costabile, L., & Scazzieri, R. (2012). Il pensiero economico nei decenni successivi al secondo dopoguerra. In V. Negri Zamagni, P. L. Porta, L. Costabile, R. Faucci, C. Perrotta, R. Scazzieri, & G. Todeschini (Eds.), *Il contributo italiano alla storia del pensiero. Economia* (pp. 739–765). Rome: Enciclopedia Italiana di Scienze, Lettere ed Arti.

Cozzi, T. (1969). *Sviluppo e stabilità dell'economia.* Turin: Fondazione Luigi Einaudi.

Cozzi, T. (1972). *Teoria dello sviluppo economico.* Bologna: Il Mulino.

Cozzi, T. (Ed.). (1983). *Keynes.* Turin: Piemonte Vivo Ricerche.

Cozzi, T. (2011). La teoria della crescita e la scuola Keynesiana di Cambridge. In *Gli economisti post-keynesiani di Cambridge e l'Italia* (pp. 73–88), Atti dei Convegni Lincei. Rome: Scienze e Lettere.

Cozzi, T., & Marchionatti, R. (Eds.). (2000). *Piero Sraffa's political economy: A centenary estimate.* London: Routledge.

Cristini, A. (1995). Primary commodity prices and the OECD economic performance. *European Economic Review, 39*(1), 83–98.

Cristini, A. (1999). *Unemployment and primary commodity prices. Theory and evidence in a global perspective.* London: Macmillan.

Cristini, A. (2011). Do house prices affect consumption? A comparison exercise (Discussion paper 589). Oxford University, Department of Economics.

Cristini, A., & Pozzoli, D. (2010). Workplace practices and firm performance in manufaccturing: A comparative study of Italy and Britain. *International Journal of Manpower, 31*(7), 818–842.

Cristini, A., Eriksson, T., & Pozzoli, D. (2013). High-performance management practices and employee outcomes in Denmark. *Scottish Journal of Political Economy, 60*(3), 232–266.

D'Adda, C. (1981). La determinazione delle funzioni aggregate di offerta e di domanda: una nota di "ermeneutica" keynesiana. *Giornale degli Economisti e Annali di Economia, 40*(1/2), 19–29.

D'Adda, C. (1989). An economy of industries and its aggregate representation. *BNL Quarterly Review, 168*, 97–107. Reprinted in J. C. Wood (Ed.). (1994). *John Maynard Keynes. Critical assessments. Second series* (pp. 371–379). London/New York: Routledge.

D'Adda, C. (2011). Gli economisti post-Keynesiani e la ricerca applicata. In *Gli economisti post-keynesiani di Cambridge e l'Italia* (pp. 111–114), Atti dei Convegni Lincei. Rome: Scienze e Lettere.

D'Adda, C. (2015). Producible resources and producibility prices in a dynamic Leontief-type model. In M. Baranzini, C. Rotondi, & R. Scazzieri (Eds.), *Resources, production and structural dynamics, op. cit.*, pp. 126–135.

Dardi, M. (1993). Lord Kahn's "the economics of the short period". In L. L. Pasinetti (Ed.), *Italian economic papers* (Vol. II, pp. 189–206). Bologna/Oxford/New York: Il Mulino/Oxford University Press.

De Cecco, M. (1989). Keynes and Italian economics. In P. A. Hall (Ed.), *The political power of economic ideas: Keynesianism across nations* (pp. 195–229). Princeton: Princeton University Press.

De Cecco, M. (2008). Hick's notion and use of the concepts of fix-price and flex-price. In R. Scazzieri, A. Sen, & S. Zamagni (Eds.), *Markets, money and capital. Hicksian economics for the twenty-first century, op. cit.*, pp. 157–163.

De Fraja, G., & Delbono, F. (1989). Alternative strategies of a public enterprise in oligopoly. *Oxford Economic Papers, 41*(2), 302–311.

De Vivo, G. (1981). John Stuart Mill on value. *Cambridge Journal of Economics, 5*(1), 67–69.

De Vivo, G. (1985a). Robert Torrens and Ricardo's "Corn-Ratio" theory of profits. *Cambridge Journal of Economics, 9*(1), 89–92.

De Vivo, G. (1985b). A note on the Anglo-Italian school in the history of economics. *The History of Economics Society Bulletin, 6*(2), 37–38.

De Vivo, G. (1986). Torrens on value and distribution. *Contributions to Political Economy, 5*(1), 23–36.

De Vivo, G. (1987). David Ricardo. In *The new Palgrave: A dictionary of economics, op. cit., The new Palgrave: A dictionary of economics* (Vol. 4, pp. 183–198). London: Macmillan.

De Vivo, G. (1994). (Mis)interpreting Ricardo. *Contributions to Political Economy, 13*(1), 14–29.

De Vivo, G. (1996). Ricardo, Torrens, and Sraffa. A summing up. *Cambridge Journal of Economics, 20*(3), 387–391.

De Vivo, G. (Ed.). (2000). *Collected works of Robert Torrens,* 8 Vols. Bristol: Thoemmes Press.

De Vivo, G. (2001a). On Torrens's theory of profits. *Cambridge Journal of Economics, 25*(5), 697–703.

De Vivo, G. (2001b). Adam Smith and his books. *Contributions to Political Economy, 20*(1), 87–97.

De Vivo, G. (2003). Sraffa's path to *production of commodities by means of commodities*: An interpretation. *Contributions to Political Economy, 22*(1), 1–25.

De Vivo, G. (2004). Da Ricardo e Marx a Produzione di merci a mezzo di merci. Relazione al convegno 'Piero Sraffa' dell'Accademia Nazionale dei Lincei, febbraio 2003, Accademia Nazionale dei Lincei, *Atti dei Convegni Lincei, Convegno internazionale Piero Sraffa.* Rome: Accademia Nazionale dei Lincei.

De Vivo, G. (2007). Anglo Saxon cv continental scholarship: On critical editions of economic classics. *Contributions to Political Economy, 26*(1), 93–102.

De Vivo, G. (Ed.). (2009). *Il* Tableau Economique *di François Quesnay.* Riproduzione fotografica della copia conservata nella biblioteca della Fondazione Raffaele Mattioli. Milan: Fondazione Mattioli; and 'Introduzione', 7–12.

De Vivo, G. (2012). Malthus's theory of the "constant value of labour". *Contributions to Political Economy, 31*(1), 103–120.
De Vivo, G. (Ed.). (2014a). *Catalogue of the library of Piero Sraffa*. Milan/Turin: Mattioli/Einaudi Foundations.
De Vivo, G. (2014b). Samuel Bailey and the subversion of the classical theory of value. A note. *Contributions to Political Economy, 33*(1), 55–60.
De Vivo, G., & Gilibert, G. (2013). On Sraffa and Marx – A comment. *Cambridge Journal of Economics, 37*(6), 1443–1447.
De Vivo, G., & Sabbagh, G. (2015). The first translator in English of Turgot's reflexions *Sur la formation et la distribution des richesses*: Benjamin Vaughan. *History of Political Economy, 47*(1), 185–199.
Delbono, F. (1989). Patterns of technological leadership: A simple model with uncertainty. *Metroeconomica, 40*, 257–277.
Delbono, F., & Denicolò, V. (1991). Incentives to innovate in a Cournot Oligopoly. *Quarterly Journal of Economics, 106*(3), 951–961.
Delbono, F., & Denicolò, V. (1993). Regulating innovative activity: The role of a public firm. *International Journal of Industrial Organization, 11*(1), 35–48.
Delli Gatti, D. (1987). *Il pensiero di Keynes (1923–1936) e l'interpretazione dei post-Keynesiani "soggettivisti"*. Ph.D. Diss., Catholic University, Milan.
Delli Gatti, D., & Gallegati, M. (1990). Financial instability, income distribution and the stock market. *Journal of Post Keynesian Economics, 12*(3), 356–374.
Denicolò, V. (1993). Fixed agenda social choice theory. *Journal of Economic Theory, 59*, 324–332.
Denicolò, V. (1999). Pollution-reducing innovation under taxes or permits. *Oxford Economic Papers, 51*(1), 184–199.
Denicolò, V. (2002). Sequential innovation and the patent-antitrust conflict. *Oxford Economic Papers, 54*(4), 649–668.
Denicolò, V., & Matteuzzi, M. (1990). Public debt and the Pasinetti Paradox. *Cambridge Journal of Economics, 14*(3), 339–344.
Di Matteo, M. (1982). Two variations on a theme by Goodwin. *Economic Notes, 9*, 165–171.
Di Matteo, M. (1984). Alternative monetary policies in a classical growth cycle. In R. M. Goodwin, M. Krüger, & A. Vercelli (Eds.), *Nonlinear models of fluctuating growth, op. cit.*, pp. 14–24.
Di Matteo, M. (1988). Richard Goodwin and the evolution of a capitalistic economy. In G. Ricci, & K. V. Velupillai (Eds.), *Growth cycles and multisectoral economics: The Goodwin tradition, op. cit.*, pp. 93–101.

Di Matteo, M. (1989). Early discussions on long waves. In M. Di Matteo, R. M. Goodwin, & A. Vercelli (Eds.), *Social and technological factors in long term fluctuations, op. cit.*, pp. 403–418.

Di Matteo, M. (1990). Celebrating Richard Goodwin's 75th birthday. Quaderni del Dipartimento di Economia Politica, Università di Siena, 100, p. 89.

Di Matteo, M. (1992). Richard M. Goodwin. In P. Arestis & M. Sawyer (Eds.), *Biographical dictionary of dissenting economists*. Aldershot: E. Elgar.

Di Matteo, M. (1993). 'Foreword' of G. La Volpe. In M. Morishima (Ed.), *Studies on the theory of general dynamic economic equilibrium* (pp. xxvii–xxxiv). London: Macmillan [English translation of G. La Volpe, Studi sulla Teoria dell'Equilibrio Economico Dinamico Generale (1937)].

Di Matteo, M. (2010). On Harrod's model and instability once again. *Studi e Note di Economia, 15*(2), 285–295.

Di Matteo, M. (2011). Towards a social philosophy for the twenty first century: Critical reflections on an unpublished essay by Richard Goodwin. *Journal of Public Finance and Public Choice, 29*(1), 33–49.

Di Matteo, M. (2013). Economic dynamics as a succession of equilibria: The path travelled by Morishima. *Structural Change and Economic Dynamics, 24*(1), 123–129.

Di Matteo, M., & Vercelli, A. (2004). La Facoltà di Scienze Economiche e Bancarie di Siena: 1966–1975. In G. Garofalo, & A. Graziani (Eds.), *La formazione degli economisti in Italia (1950–1975), op. cit.*, pp. 463–480.

Di Matteo, M., Goodwin, R. M., & Vercelli, A. (Eds.). (1989). *Social and technological factors in long term fluctuations*. Berlin: Springer.

Di Matteo, M., Filippi, F., & Sordi, S. (2006). The confessions of an unrepentant model builder: Rummaging in Goodwin's archive. *Structural Change and Economic Dynamics, 17*(4), 400–414.

Dimsdale, N. H. (1973). Review of R. S. Masera's *the term structure of interest rates: An expectation model tested on post-war Italian data. Economic Journal, 83*(330), 569–571.

Dosi, G. (1988). Sources, procedures and microeconomic effects of innovation. *Journal of Economic Literature, 26*(3), 1120–1171.

Dow, S. C. (1991). Carabelli's *on Keynes's method* and O'Donnell's *Keynes: Philosophy, economics and politics. Economics and Philosophy, 7*(1), 132–139.

Eatwell, J. (1984). Piero Sraffa: Seminal economic theorist. *Science and Society, 48*(2), 535–550.

Eatwell, J., & Panico, C. (1987). Sraffa, Piero. In *The new Palgrave: A dictionary of economics, op. cit.*, London: Macmilllan, Vol. 3, pp. 445–452.

Eatwell, J., Milgate, M., & Newman, P. (Eds.). (1987). *The new Palgrave: A dictionary of economics,* 3 Vols. London: Macmillan.

Ellis, W. (1995). *The Oxbridge conspiracy: How the ancient universities kept their stranglehold on the establishment.* London: Penguin.

Eltis, W. A., Scott, M. F., & Wolfe, J. N. (Eds.). (1970). *Induction, growth and trade: Essays in honour of Sir Roy Harrod.* Oxford: Clarendon Press.

Fabel, O., Farina, F., & Punzo, L. F. (Eds.). (2000). *European economies in transition: In search of a new growth path.* Basingstoke: Macmillan.

Faria, J. R. (2000). A two-class fiscal and monetary growth model. *Structural Change and Economic Dynamics, 11*(3), 355–364.

Faria, J. R. (2001). The Pasinetti Paradox in an intertemporal dynamic model. *Political economy* (Working Paper 13/01). University of Texas, Dallas.

Fazi, E., & Salvadori, N. (1981). The existence of a two-class economy in the Kaldor model of growth and distribution. *Kyklos, 34*(4), 582–592.

Fazi, E., & Salvadori, N. (1985). The existence of a two-class economy in a general Cambridge model of growth and distribution. *Cambridge Journal of Economics, 9*(1), 155–164.

Ferri, P. (1971). *La disoccupazione in un processo di sviluppo economico.* Milan: Giuffré.

Ferri, P. (2007). The labour market and technical change in endogenous cycles. *Metroeconomica, 58*(4), 609–633.

Ferri, P. (2008). The economics of non-linear cycles. In R. Scazzieri, A. Sen, & S. Zamagni (Eds.), *Markets, money and capital. Hicksian economics for the twenty-first century, op. cit.*, pp. 309–327.

Ferrulli, S. (2012). *Economisti italiani a Cambridge (1960–1980). Processi formativi, aggiornamenti teorici e nuovi orientamenti di politica economica.* Ph. D. thesis, Rome Tre.

Fleck, F. H., & Domenghino, C.-M. (1987). Cambridge (U.K.) *versus* Cambridge (Mass.): A Keynesian solution of "Pasinetti's Paradox". *Journal of Post Keynesian Economics, 10*(1), 22–36.

Fleck, F. H., & Domenghino, C.-M. (1990). Government activity *does* invalidate the "Cambridge theorem of the rate of profit". *Journal of Post Keynesian Economics, 12*(3), 487–497.

Fodor, G. G. (1986). Why did Europe need the Marshall plan in 1947? *Political Economy Studies in the Surplus Approach, 2*(1), 73–103.

Fodor, G. G. (2007). Studiare all'estero…. In A.A.V.V. (Ed.), *Le borse di studio Bonaldo Stringher, Giorgio Mortara, Donato Menichella 1931–1985* (pp. 11–16). Rome: Banca d'Italia.

Fodor, G. G. (2011). The standard commodity and monetary theory in the first half of the twentieth century. In R. Ciccone, C. Gehrke, & G. Mongiovi (Eds.), *Sraffa and modern economics* (Vol. II, pp. 311–324). New York: Routledge.

Fontana, G. (2004). Hicks on monetary theory and history: Money as "endogenous money". *Cambridge Journal of Economics, 28*(1), 73–88.

Fontana, G. (2013). Single-period analysis and continuation analysis of endogenous money. In G. C. Harcourt, & P. Kriesler (Eds.), *The Oxford handbook of post-Keynesian economics, op. cit.*, Vol. I, pp. 188–202.

Fubini, L. (2003). Women's unemployment in Italy. In D. Del Boca & M. Repetto-Alaia (Eds.), *Women's work, the family & social policy* (pp. 109–123). Berne/Frankfurt: P. Lang.

Galavotti, M. C., Scazzieri, R., & Suppes, P. (Eds.). (2008). *Reasoning, rationality and probability*. Stanford/Chicago: CSLI Publications/Chicago University Press.

Gandolfo, G. (1981). Kaldor, Goodwin, Marrama, Palomba e la teoria non lineare del ciclo economico. In *Gli economisti post-keynesiani di Cambridge e l'Italia* (pp. 115–124), Atti dei Convegni Lincei. Rome: Scienze e Lettere.

Gandolfo, G., & Marzano, F. (Eds.). (1999). *Economic theory and social justice*. New York: St. Martin's Press.

Garbellini, N., & Wirkierman, A. L. (2013). Productivity accounting in vertically (hyper-) integrated terms: Bridging the gap between theory and empirics. *Metroeconomica, 65*(1), 154–190.

Garbellini, N., & Wirkierman, A. L. (2014a). Pasinetti's structural change and economic gorwth: A conceptual excursus. *Review of Political Economy, 26*(2), 234–257.

Garbellini, N., & Wirkierman, A. L. (2014b). Blocks and circularity in labour requirements: An interplay between clusters and subsystems in the UE. *Structural Change and Economic Dynamics, 28*, 60–74.

Garegnami, P. (1966). Switching of techniques. *Quarterly Journal of Economics, 80*(4), 554–567.

Garegnani, P. (1960). *Il capitale nelle teorie della distribuzione*. Milan: Giuffrè.

Garegnani, P. (1962). *Il problema della domanda effettiva nello sviluppo economico italiano*. Rome: SVIMET.

Garegnani, P. (1970). Heterogeneous capital, the production function and the theory of distribution. *Review of Economic Studies, 37*(3), 407–436.

Garegnani, P. (1976). On a change in the notion of equilibrium in recent work on value and distribution. In M. Brown, K. Sato, & P. Zarembka (Eds.), *Essays in modern capital theory* (pp. 25–45). Amsterdam: North Holland.

Garegnani, P. (1978–9). Notes on consumption, investment and effective demand. *Cambridge Journal of Economics, 2*(4), 335–353; *3*(1), 63–82.
Garegnani, P. (1983). On a change in the notion of equilibrium in recent work on value and distribution. In J. Eatwell & M. Millgate (Eds.), *Keynes's economics and the theory of value and distribution* (pp. 21–69). London: Duckworth.
Garegnani, P. (1984). Value and distribution in the classical economists and Marx. *Oxford Economic Papers, 36*(2), 63–82.
Garegnani, P. (1987). Surplus approach to value and distribution. *The new Palgrave: A dictionary of economics, op. cit.*, Vol. 3, pp. 560–574.
Garegnani, P. (1989). Some notes on capital, expectations and the analysis of changes. In G. R. Feiwel (Ed.), *Joan Robinson and modern economic theory* (pp. 344–367). London: Macmillan.
Garegnani, P. (1990). Sraffa: Classical *versus* Marginalist analysis. In K. Bharadwaj & B. Schefold (Eds.), *Essays on Piero Sraffa: Critical perspectives on the revival of classical theory* (pp. 112–158). London: Unwin Hyman.
Garegnani, P. (1992). Some notes for the analysis of accumulation. In E. J. Nell, D. Laibman, & J. Halevi (Eds.), *Beyond the steady-state* (pp. 47–71). London/Basingstoke: Macmillan.
Garegnani, P. (2005). On a turning point in Sraffa's theoretical and interpretive position in the late 1920s. *The European Journal of the History of Economic Thought, 12*(3), 453–492.
Garegnani, P. (2012). On the present state of the capital controversy. *Cambridge Journal of Economics, 36*(6), 1417–1432.
Garofalo, G., & Graziani, A. (Eds.). (2004). *La formazione degli economisti in Italia.* Bologna: Il Mulino.
Gilibert, G. (1991). Dr Mühlpfordt and the "transformation problem": A reassessment. *Cambridge Journal of Economics, 15*(3), 353–354.
Gilibert, G. (2003). The equations Unveiled: Sraffa's price equations in the making. *Contributions to Political Economy, 22*(1), 27–40.
Gilibert, G. (2006). The man from the moon: Sraffa's upside-down approach to the theory of value. *Contributions to Political Economy, 25*(1), 35–48.
Gilibert, G. (2013). A pictorial approach to the standard commodity with a digression. In E. S. Levrero, A. Palumbo, & A. Stirati (Eds.), *Sraffa and the reconstruction of economic theory: Volume Three. Sraffa's legacy: Interpretations and historical perspectives* (pp. 217–27). London: Palgrave Macmillan.
Goodwin, R. M. (1982a). *Essays in economic dynamics.* London/Basingstoke: Macmillan.
Goodwin, R. M. (1982b). In M. Palazzi (Ed.), *Intervista a un economista: Richard M. Goodwin.* Bologna: Clueb.

Goodwin, R. M. (1983a). A note on wages, profits and fluctuating growth rates. *Cambridge Journal of Economics, 7*(3/4), 305–309.

Goodwin, R. M. (1983b). *Essays on linear economic structures*. London: Macmillan.

Goodwin, R. M. (1989). *Essays on nonlinear economic dynamics: Collected papers 1980–1987*. Frankfurt: P. Lange.

Goodwin, R. M. (1990). *Chaotic economic dynamics*. Oxford: Clarendon Press.

Goodwin, R. M. (1993). The economy as a chaotic growth oscillator. In M. Baranzini, & G. C. Harcourt (Eds.), *The dynamics of the wealth of nations: Growth, distribution and structural change: Essays in honour of Luigi L. Pasinetti, op. cit.*, pp. 300–310.

Goodwin, R. M, & Landesmann, M. A. (2009). Structural change and macroeconomic stability in disaggregated models. In M. Landesmann, & R. Scazzieri (Eds.), *Production and economic dynamics, op. cit.*, pp. 167–187 (1st edn 1996).

Goodwin, R. M., & Punzo, L. F. (1987). *The dynamics of a capitalist economy: A multi-sectoral approach*. Oxford: Polity Press in association with B. Blackwell.

Goodwin, R. M., Krüger, M., & Vercelli, A. (Eds.). (1981). *Nonlinear models of fluctuating growth*. Berlin: Springer.

Graziani, A., & Lombardini, S. (Eds.). (1975). *Gli studi di economia in Italia*. Milan: Comunità.

Gualerzi, D. (1991). *Social environment of consumption and growth: The recovery of the 1980s in the U.S. Economy*. Ph.D. Diss., New School for Social Research, New York.

Gualerzi, D. (2002). *Consumption and growth: Recovery and structural change in the US Economy*. Cheltenham: E. Elgar.

Gualerzi, D. (2012). Growth theory, structural dynamics and the analysis of consumption. In R. Arena, & P. L. Porta (Eds.), *Structural dynamics and economic growth, op. cit.*, pp. 181–203.

Guarini, R. (2013). Il cammino di Luigi Spaventa alla Sapienza: da studente a professore emerito. *Moneta e Credito, 66*(263), 249–259.

Hagemann, H. (1990). The structural theory of economic growth. In M. Baranzini, & R. Scazzieri (Eds.), *Foundations of economics, op. cit.*, pp. 144–171.

Hagemann, H. (2012). Luigi Pasinetti's structural economic dynamics and the employment consequences of new technologies. In R. Arena, & P. L. Porta (Eds.), *Structural dynamics and economic growth, op. cit.*, pp. 204–217.

Hagemann, H., & Scazzieri, R. (2009). Capital structures and economic transitions: An introductory essay. In H. Hagemann & R. Scazzieri (Eds.), *Capital, time and transitional dynamics* (pp. 1–39). Abingdon/New York: Routledge.

Hahn, F. O. (2001). The "exogenous" in "endogenous" growth theory. In L. F. Punzo (Ed.), *Cycles, growth and structural change: Theories and empirical evidence, op. cit.*, pp. 351–365.

Halevi, J. (1975). Kalecki's conception of the economic cycle and state intervention. *Annals of Public and Cooperative Economics, 46*(3), 233–248.

Halevi, J. (1991). Proportions sectorielles, croissance et demande effective: Kaldor et Hicks vus sous l'angle de la problématique marxiste de la crise. *Economie Appliquee, 44*(4), 5–21.

Halevi, J. (1992). Accumulation and structural disequilibrium. In J. Halevi, D. Laibman, & E. Nell (Eds.), *Beyond the steady state: Revival of growth theory* (pp. 264–288). New York/London: St. Martin's Press/Macmillan.

Halevi, J. (1996). The significance of the theory of vertically integrated processes for the problem of economic development. *Structural Change and Economic Dynamics, 7*(2), 163–171.

Halevi, J. (1998). Paolo Sylos Labini. In F. Meacci (Ed.), *Italian economists of the 20th century* (pp. 228–252). Cheltenham/Northhampton: E. Elgar.

Halevi, J. (2015). Un intellettuale economista. In F. Sylos Labini (Ed.), *Paolo Sylos Labini. Economista e cittadino* (pp. 59–82). Rome: Sapienza Universitaria Editrice.

Halevi, J. (2016). Luigi Pasinetti and the political economy of growth and distribution. In J. Halevi, et al. (Eds.), *Post Keynesian essays from down under* (Vol. IV), *op. cit.*, pp. 310–326.

Halevi, J., & Kriesler, P. (1991). Kalecki, classical economics and the surplus approach. *Review of Political Economy, 3*(1), 79–92.

Halevi, J., & Kriesler, P. (2005). Stagnation and economic conflict in Europe. *International Journal of Political Economy, 34*(2), 19–45.

Halevi, J. et al. (Eds.). (2015). *Post-Keynesian essays from down under,* 4 Vols. London: Palgrave Macmillan.

Hamouda, O. F. (1993). *John R. Hicks. The economist's economist.* Oxford: B. Blackwell.

Harcourt, G. C. (1972). *Some Cambridge controversies in the theory of capital.* Cambridge: Cambridge University Press.

Harcourt, G. C. (1985). A twentieth century eclectic: Richard Goodwin. *Journal of Post Keynesian Economics, 7*, 379–387.

Harcourt, G. C. (1987). Post-Keynesian economics. In *The new Palgragve dictionary of economics, op. cit.*, vol. 3, pp. 924–928.

Harcourt, G. C. (2006). *The structure of post-Keynesian economics.* Cambridge: Cambridge University Press.

Harcourt, G. C. (2011). Foreword. In C. Sardoni (Ed.), *Unemployment, recession and effective demand: The contributions of Marx, Keynes and Kalecki, op. cit.*, pp. vii–viii.

Harcourt, G. C. (2012a). Luigi Pasinetti: The senior living heir of the Cambridge school of economics and the last of the great system-builders. In R. Arena, & P. L. Porta (Eds.), *Structural dynamics and economic growth, op. cit.*, pp. 137–144.

Harcourt, G. C. (2012b). Fusing indissolubly the cycle and the trend: Richard Goodwin's profound insight. Australian School of Business Research Paper No. 2012 ECON 30.

Harcourt, G. C., & Kerr, P. (2009). *Joan Robinson.* London: Palgrave Macmillan.

Harcourt, G. C., & Kriesler, P. (Eds). (2013). *The Oxford handbook of post-Keynesian economics*, 2 Vols. Oxford/New York: Oxford University Press.

Harcourt, G. C., & Sardoni, C. (1994). Keynes's vision: Method, analysis and "tactics". In J. B. Davis (Ed.), *The state of interpretation of Keynes* (pp. 131–152). Dordrecht/Boston: Kluwer.

Harcourt, G. C., & Sardoni, C. (1996). The general theory of employment, interest and money: Three views. In P. Arestis (Ed.), *Keynes, money and the open economy. Essays in honour of Paul Davidson* (Vol. I, pp. 1–13). Cheltenham: E. Elgar.

Hargreaves Heap, S. P., & Zizzo, D. J. (2009). The value of groups. *American Economic Review, 99*(1), 295–323.

Harré, R., & Madden, E. H. (1975). *Causal powers.* Oxford: B. Blackwell.

Hicks, J. R. (1932). *The theory of wages.* London: Macmillan.

Hicks, J. R. (1939). *Value and capital: An inquiry into some fundamental principles of economic theory.* Oxford: Oxford University Press.

Hicks, J. R. (1959). *Essays in world economics.* Oxford: Clarendon Press.

Hicks, J. R. (1965). *Capital and growth.* Oxford: Clarendon Press.

Hicks, J. R. (1969). *A theory of economic history.* Oxford: Clarendon Press.

Hicks, J. R. (1973). *Capital and time: A Neo-Austrian theory.* Oxford: Clarendon Press.

Hicks, J. R. (1974). *The crisis in Keynesian economics.* Oxford: B. Blackwell.

Hicks, J. R. (1976). "Revolutions" in economics. In S. J. Latsis (Ed.), *Method and appraisal in economics* (pp. 207–218). Cambridge: Cambridge University Press.

Hicks, J. R. (1979a). The Ricardian system: A comment. *Oxford Economic Papers, 31*(1), 133–134.

Hicks, J. R. (1979b). *Causality in economics*. Oxford: B. Blackwell.

Hicks, J. R. (1985). *Methods of dynamic economics*. Oxford: Clarendon Press.

Hicks, J. R. (1986). Is economics a science? In M. Baranzini, & R. Scazzieri (Eds.), *Foundations of economics. Structure of inquiry and economic theory, op. cit.*, pp. 91–101.

Hicks, J. R. (1990). The unification of macroeconomics. *The Economic Journal, 100*, 528–538.

Hicks, J. R., & Hollander, S. (1977). Mr. Ricardo and the moderns. *Quarterly Journal of Economics, 41*, 351–369.

Hildebrand, G. H. (1965). *Growth and structure in the economy of modern Italy*. Cambridge, MA: Harvard University Press.

Izzo, D. J. (Ed.). (2004). *Transfer of knowlegde in economic decision making*. London: Palgrave Macmillan.

Johansen, L. (1985). Richard Stone's contributions to economics. *Scandinavian Journal of Economics, 87*(1), 4–32.

Kahn, R. F. (1984). *The making of Keynes's general theory*. Cambridge: Cambridge University Press.

Kaldor, N. (1956). Alternative theories of distribution. *The Review of Economic Studies, 23*(2), 83–100.

Kerr, P., & Scazzieri, R. (2013). Structural economic dynamics and the Cambridge tradition. In G. C. Harcourt & P. Kriesler (Eds.), *Post-Keynesian handbook* (Vol. I, pp. 259–287). Oxford: Oxford University Press.

Kindleberger, C. P. (1967). *Europe's postwar growth. The Rome of labor supply*. Cambridge, MA: Harvard University Press.

King, J. E. (2002). *A history of post Keynesian economics since 1936*. Cheltenham/Northamption: E. Elgar.

King, J. E. (2003). *The Elgar companion to post-Keynesian economics*. Cheltenham/Northamption: E. Elgar.

King, J. E. (2012). *The microfoundations delusion. Metaphor and Dogma in the history of macroeconomics*. Cheltenham/Northamption: E. Elgar.

Kurz, H. D. (2002). Professor Roncaglia's Piero Sraffa. His life, thought and cultural heirtage. *History of Economic Ideas, 10*(1), 119–126.

Kurz, H. D., & Salvadori, N. (1993). The "standard commodity" and Ricardo's search for an "invariable measure of value". In M. Baranzini, & G. C. Harcourt (Eds.), *The dynamics of the wealth of nations: Growth, distribution and structural change, op. cit.*, pp. 95–123.

Kurz, H. D., & Salvadori, N. (1995). *Theory of production: A long period analysis*. Cambridge: Cambridge University Press.
Kurz, H. D., & Salvadori, N. (2003). *Classical economics and modern theory. Studies in long-period analysis*. London/New York: Routledge.
Kurz, H. D., & Salvadori, N. (2015). The classical theory of rent. In M. Baranzini, C. Rotondi, & R. Scazzieri (Eds.), *Resources, production and structural dynamics, op. cit.*, pp. 72–94.
Kurz, H. D., Pasinetti, L. L., & Salvadori, N. (Eds.). (2008). *The legacy of Piero Sraffa*. Cheltenham: E. Elgar.
La Marca, M. (2005). The public sector in a model of growth and distribution à la Pasinetti: Existence of one- or two-class economies. *Metroeconomica, 56*(2), 157–181.
Laing, N. F. (1969). Two notes on Pasinetti's theorem. *Economic Record, 45*(111), 373–385.
Lambertini, L. (Ed.). (2009). *Firm's objectives and internal organisation in a global economy: Positive and normative analysis*. Basingstoke: Palgrave Macmillan.
Landesmann, M. (1988). Where do we go from here? Technical change and dynamics. *Cambridge Journal of Economics, 12*(1), 169–177.
Landesmann, M. A., & Scazzieri, R. (1993). Commodity flows and productive subsystems: An essay in the analysis of structural change. In M. Baranzini, & G. C. Harcourt (Eds.), *The dynamics of the wealth of nations: Growth, distribution and structural change, op. cit.*, pp. 209–245.
Landesmann, M. A., & Scazzieri, R. (Eds.). (2009). *Production and economic dynamics*. Cambridge: Cambridge University Press (1st ed. 1996).
Leon, P. (1967). *Structural change and growth in capitalism*. Baltimore: Johns Hopkins University Press.
Leon, P. (2007). *Stato, mercato e collettività*. Turin: Giappichelli.
Leon, P. (2015). *Il capitalismo e lo Stato. Crisi e trasformazione delle strutture economiche*. Rome: Lit Edizioni.
Leskow, J., Puchet, M., & Punzo, L. F. (Eds.). (2005). *New tools of economic dynamics*. Berlin: Springer.
Levhari, D. (1965). A nonsubstitution theorem and switching of techniques. *Quarterly Journal of Economics, 79*(1), 98–105.
Lewis, W. A. (1954). Development with unlimited supplies of labour. *Manchester School, 22*(2), 139–191.
Lindhal, E. (1939). *Studies in the theory of money and capital*. New York: Rinehart.

Lombardini, S. (1996). Joan Robinson's contribution to economic development. In M. C. Marcuzzo, L. L. Pasinetti, & A. Roncaglia (Eds.), *The economics of Joan Robinson, op. cit.*, pp. 135–147.
Lunghini, G. (1965). Note sul concetto di struttura. *L'Industria, 4*, 581–591.
Lunghini, G. (Ed.). (1981). *Scelte politiche e teorie economiche in Italia, 1945–78*. Turin: Einaudi.
Lunghini, G. (2008). Una rivoluzione incompiuta e un programma di ricerca. Pasinetti su Keynes (e Sraffa)'. *Rivista di storia economica, 24*(1), 103–118.
Lunghini, G. (2011). La Teoria Generale e i Keynesiani: un'eredità giacente. In *Gli economisti post-keynesiani di Cambridge e l'Italia* (pp. 31–47), Atti dei Convegni Lincei. Rome: Scienze e Lettere.
Lunghini, G., & Targetti Lenti, R. (2004). Di Fenizio e l'economia politica di Keynes. In G. Garofalo, & A. Graziani (Eds.), *La formazione degli economisti in Italia (1950–1975), op. cit.*, pp. 155–181.
Lutfalla, M. (1983). Review of A. Quadrio Curzio and R. Scazzieri (Eds.), *Protagonisti del pensiero economico*, t. 3, *Rivoluzione industriale e economia politica (1817–1848)* and t. 4, *Struttura produttiva, scambio e mercati (1848–1872).* Bologna: Il Mulino (1982), *Revue d'économie politique, 93*(4), 610–611.
Lutz, V. (1962). *Italy: A study in economic development.* Oxford: Oxford University Press.
Maneschi, A. (1974). The existence of a two-class economy in the Kaldor and Pasinetti models of growth and distribution. *Review of Economic Studies, 41*(1), 149–150.
Maneschi, A. (1983). Dynamic aspects of Ricardo's international trade theory. *Oxford Economic Papers, 35*(1), 67–80.
Maneschi, A. (1992). Ricardo's international trade theory: Beyond comparative cost example. *Cambridge Journal of Economics, 16*(4), 421–437.
Maneschi, A. (1993). Ricardian comparative advantage and the perils of the stationary state. In M. Baranzini, & G. C. Harcourt (Eds.), *The dynamics of the wealth of nations: Growth, distribution and structural change. Essays in honour of Luigi L. Pasinetti, op. cit.*, pp. 124–146.
Maneschi, A. (1998). *Comparative advantage in international trade: A historical perspective*. Cheltenham/Northampton: E. Elgar.
Maneschi, A. (2001). John Stuart Mill's equilibrium terms of trade: A special case of William Whewell's 1850 formula. *History of Political Economy, 33*(3), 609–625.
Maneschi, A. (2004). The true meaning of David Ricardo's four magic numbers. *Journal of International Economics, 62*(2), 433–443.

Maneschi, A. (2006). Ricardo, machinery and comparative advantage. In G. Stathakis, & G. Vaggi (Eds.), *Economic development and social change. Historical roots and modern perspectives, op. cit.*, pp. 290–301.

Maneschi, A. (2008). How would David Ricardo have taught the principle of comparative advantage? *Southern Economic Journal, 74*(4), 1167–1176.

Mantovi, A., & Schianchi, A. (2014). *A game-theoretic traverse analysis: Price competition and strategic investment.* Mimeo/Univeristy of Parma.

Mantovi, A., & Schianchi, A. (2015). *A Neo-Austrian perspective on the value of growth prospects.* Mimeo/University of Parma.

Marangoni, G., & Fezzi, G. (2002). Input–output for management control: The case of Glaxo-SmithKline. *Economic Systems Research, 14*, 245–256.

Marcuzzo, M. C. (Ed.). (1986). *Nicholas Kaldor: Ricordi di un economista.* Milan: Garzanti.

Marcuzzo, M. C. (1994). R. F. Kahn and imperfect competition. *Cambridge Journal of Economics, 18*(1), 25–39.

Marcuzzo, M. C. (1996a). Joan Robinson and Richard Kahn: The origin of short-period analysis. In M. C. Marcuzzo, L. L. Pasinetti, & A. Roncaglia (Eds.), *The economics of Joan Robinson, op. cit.*, pp. 11–28.

Marcuzzo, M. C. (1996b). The writings of Joan Robinson. In M. C. Marcuzzo, L. L. Pasinetti, & A. Roncaglia (Eds.), *The economics of Joan Robinson, op. cit.*, pp. 330–363.

Marcuzzo, M. C. (2002). The collaboration between J. M. Keynes and R. F. Kahn from the *Treatise* to the *general theory. History of Political Economy, 34*(2), 421–447.

Marcuzzo, M. C., & Naldi, N. (2008). Cambridge as a *place* in economics. *History of Political Economy, 40*(4), 569–593.

Marcuzzo, M. C., & Rosselli, A. (1991). *Ricardo and the gold standard: The foundations of the international monetary order.* Basingstoke: Macmillan.

Marcuzzo, M. C., & Rosselli, A. (2002). Economics as history of economics: The Italian case in retrospect. In E. R. Weintraub (Ed.), *The future of the history of economics, history of political economy*, Duke University Press, Durham-London. (Vol. 34, pp. 98–109, Annual Supplement).

Marcuzzo, M. C., & Rosselli, A. (Eds.). (2005). *Economists in Cambridge. A study through their correspondence, 1907–1946.* London: Routledge.

Marcuzzo, M. C., & Rosselli, A. (2011). Sraffa and his arguments against "marginism". *Cambridge Journal of Economics, 35*(1), 219–231.

Marcuzzo, M. C., & Sanfilippo, E. (2008). Dear John, Dear Ursula (Cambridge and LSE, 1935): Eighty-Eight Letters Unearthed. In R. Scazzieri, A. Sen, & S. Zamagni (Eds.), *Markets, money and capital. Hicksian economics for the twenty-first century, op. cit.*, pp. 72–91.

Marcuzzo, M. C., Pasinetti, L. L., & Roncaglia, A. (Eds.). (1996). *The economics of Joan Robinson*. London/New York: Routledge.

Marzano, F. (1974). *Teorie del capitale e della produzione*. Padova: CEDAM.

Marzano, F. (1981). *Un confronto fra teorie keynesiane e monetariste*. Genoa: Liguori.

Marzano, F. (2004). Open and closed economic theories. *Studi Economici, 82*(1), 77–98.

Marzano, F. (2014). On Graziani's monetary theory of production. *Studi Economici, 112*(1), 90–97.

Marzano, F., & Colombi, C. (2011). A new view on economic competitiveness. *Studi Economici, 103*(1), 5–48.

Masera, R. S. (1970). Multiperiod expectations and the term structure of interest rates: Comment. *The Quarterly Journal of Economics, 84*(4), 680–687.

Masera, R. S. (1972). *The term structure of interest rates: An expectations model tested on post-war Italian data*. Oxford: Clarendon Press.

Masera, R. S. (2008). Core, mantle, and industry: A monetary perspective of banks' capital standards. In R. Scazzieri, A. Sen, & S. Zamagni (Eds.), *Markets, money and capital. Hicksian economics for the twenty-first century, op. cit.*, pp. 225–251.

Mastromatteo, G. (1989). *Government intervention, self-financing by private companies and the Pasinetti process: A few reflections*. Milan: Catholic University/Mimeo.

Mastromatteo, G. (1994). Tassazione e distribuzione del reddito in un modello post-Keynesiano. *Economia Internazionale, 47*(4), 383–391.

Mastromatteo, G. (1996). Economia monetaria post-Keynesiana e rigidità dei tassi bancari. *Rivista Internazionale di Scienze Sociali, 104*(4), 555–569.

Mastromatteo, G. (2000). Microfoundations of the post-Keynesian monetary theory. *Studi Economici, 55*(71), 47–64.

Meacci, F. (Ed.). (1998). *Italian economists of the 20th century*. Cheltenham/Northampton: E. Elgar.

Medio, A. (1979). *Harrod e il problema della dinamica economica*. Milan: Etas Libri.

Medio, A. (1992). *Chaotic dynamics. Theory and applications to economics*. Cambridge: Cambridge University Press.

Medio, A. (2001). *Nonlinear dynamics*. Cambridge: Cambridge University Press.

Menchik, P. L., & David, M. (1983). Income distribution, lifetime savings and bequests. *American Economic Review, 73*(4), 672–690.

Miconi, B. (1967). On Harrod's model of instability. *L'industria, 19*(4), 455–478.

Modigliani, F. (1975). The life-cycle hypothesis of saving twenty years later. In M. Parkin & A. R. Nobay (Eds.), *Contemporary issues in economics* (pp. 1–36). Manchester: Manchester University Press.

Moffatt, P., Sitzia, S., & Zizzo, D. J. (2015). Heterogeneity in preferences towards complexity. *Journal of Risk and Uncertainty, 51*(2), 147–170.

Mongiovi, G. (1998). Pierangelo Garegnani. In F. Meacci (Ed.), *Italian economists of the 20th century, op. cit.*, Cheltenham: E. Elgar, pp. 253–271.

Mongiovi, G., & Petri, F. (Eds.). (1999). *Value, distribution and capital. Essays in honour of Pierangelo Garegnani.* London/New York: Routledge.

Morciano, M. (1978). *La dinamica dei prezzi relativi e della distribuzione del reddito in un modello inut-output ricorrente.* Rome: M.M. e P. Editori.

Mori, P. A. (1991). Job signalling and the returns to private information. *Oxford Economic Papers, 43*(3), 351–367.

Mori, P. A. (1996). Financial information disclosure, union power and integration. *Journal of Corporate Finance, 2*(3), 283–299.

Mori, P. A. (1998). Promotion careers with multipole punitive assignements. *Economic Letters, 60*(3), 369–373.

Morroni, M. (1992). *Production process and technical change.* Cambridge: Cambridge University Press.

Morroni, M. (2006). *Knowlegde, scale and transactions in the theory of the firm.* Cambridge: Cambridge University Press.

Morroni, M. (Ed.). (2009). *Corporate governance, organization of the firm. Co-operation and outsourcing in the global economy.* Cheltenham: E. Elgar.

Morroni, M. (2014). Production of commodities by means of processes. The flow-fund model, input–output relations and the cognitive aspects of production. *Structural Change and Economic Dynamics, 29*(1), 5–18.

Mückl, W. J. (1978). On the existence of a two-class economy in the Cambridge models of growth and distribution. *Jahrbücher für National Ökonomie und Statistik, 193*(6), 508–517.

Mückl, W. J. (1984). Über den Einfluss von parametrischen Änderungen der Sparneigung auf die Gewinnquote und den Kapitalkeoffizienten. *Jahrbücher für Nationalökonomie und Statistik, 199*(1), 76–87.

Naldi, N. (2005). Robertson and the great divide: The correspondence between Kahn, Kaldor, J. Robinson and Sraffa. In M. C. Marcuzzo, & A. Rosselli (Eds.), *Economists in Cambridge: A study through their correspondence, 1907–1946, op. cit.*, pp. 371–387.

Nardozzi, G. (1996). Joan Robinson and the rate of interest these days. In M. C. Marcuzzo, L. L. Pasinetti, & A. Roncaglia (Eds.), *The economics of Joan Robinson, op. cit.*, pp. 81–87.

Nell, E. J., & Semmler, W. (Eds.). (1991). *Nicholas Kaldor and mainstream economics: Confrontation or convergence?* London: Macmillan.

Notarangelo, M. (1999). Unbalanced growth: A case of structural dynamics. *Structural Change and Economic Dynamics, 10*(2), 209–223.

Nuti, D. M. (1970). Capitalism, socialism and steady growth. *Economic Journal, 80*(318), 257–281.

Nuti, D. M. (1973). On the truncation of production flows. *Kyklos, 26*(3), 485–496.

Nuti, D. M. (Ed.). (1974a). *Economic essays on value, competition and utility*, by U.K. Dmitriev. Cambridge: Cambridge University Press.

Nuti, D. M. (1974b). On the rates of return on investment. *Kyklos*, *27*(2), 345–366.

Nuti, D. M. (1981). Socialism on earth. *Cambridge Journal of Economics, 5*(4), 391–403.

Nuti, D. M. (1986). Michal Kalecki's contributions to the theory and practice of socialist planning. *Cambridge Journal of Economics, 10*(4), 333–353.

Nuti, D. M. (2000). Domenico Mario Nuti, born 1937. In P. Arestis & M. Sawyer (Eds.), *A biographical dictionary of dissenting economists* (pp. 462–9). Cheltenham/Northhampton: E. Elgar.

O'Donnell, R. M. (1989). *Philosophy, economics and politics: The philosophical foundations of Keynes's thought and their influence on his economics and politics*. London: Macmillan.

O'Sullivan, E. et al. (2013). What is new in the new industrial policy? A manufacturing system perspective. *Oxford Review of Economic Policy, 29*(2), 432–462.

Onofri, P., & Stagni, A. (2008). On the Hicksian definition of income in applied economic analysis. In R. Scazzieri, A. K. Sen, & S. Zamagni (Eds.), *Markets, money and capital. Hicksian economics for the twenty-first century, op. cit.*, pp. 164–181.

Pabst, A., & Scazzieri, R. (2012). The political economy of civil society. *Constitutional Political Economy, 23*(4), 337–356.

Pabst, A., & Scazzieri, R. (2016). The political economy of constitution. *Constitutional Political Economy*, forthcoming.

Pagano, U. (1985). *Work and welfare in economic theory*. Oxford/New York: B. Blackwell.

Pagano, U. (1991). Property rights, asset specificity, and the division of labour under alternative capitalist relations. *Cambridge Journal of Economics, 15*(3), 315–342.

Pagano, U. (1992a). Organizational equilibria and production efficiency. *Metroeconomica, 43*(1/2), 227–246.

Pagano, U. (1992b). Authority, co-ordination and disequilibrium: An explanation of the co-existence of markets and firms. *Structural Change and Economic Dynamics, 3*(1), 53–77.

Pagano, U. (2000). Public markets, private orderings and corporate governance. *International Review of Law and Economics, 20*(4), 453–477.

Pagano, U. (2003). Nationalism, development and integration: The political economy of Ernest Gellner. *Cambridge Journal of Economics, 27*(5), 623–646.

Pagano, U. (2007). Cultural globalisation, institutional diversity and the unequal accumulation of intellectual capital. *Cambridge Journal of Economics, 31*(5), 649–667.

Pagano, U. (2014). The crisis of intellectual monopoly capitalism. *Cambridge Journal of Economics, 38*(6), 1409–1429.

Pagano, U., & Rossi, M. A. (2004). Incomplete contracts, intellectual property and institutional complementaries. *European Journal of Law and Economics, 18*(1), 55–76.

Pagano, U., & Rowthorn, R. (1994). Ownership, technology and institutional stability. *Structural Change and Economic Dynamics, 5*(2), 221–242.

Panico, C. (1985). Market forces and the relationship between the rate of interest and the rate of profits. *Contributions to Political Economy, 4*(1), 37–60.

Panico, C. (1987). Interest and profit. In *The new Palgrave: A dictionary of economics, op. cit.*, Vol. 2, London: Macmillan, pp. 877–879.

Panico, C. (1988). *Interest and profit in the theories of value and distribution.* Basingstoke/New York: Macmillan/St. Martin's Press.

Panico, C. (1992). Un confronto tra i modelli macroeconomici finanziari di Tobin e quelli di derivazione Kaldoriana. In B. Jossa & A. Nardi (Eds.), *Lezioni di Macroeconomia* (pp. 329–380). Bologna: Il Mulino.

Panico, C. (1997). Government deficits in post Keynesian theories of growth and distribution. *Contribution to Political Economy, 16*(1), 61–86.

Panico, C. (1998). Interest and profit. In H. D. Kurz & N. Salvadori (Eds.), *The Elgar companion to classical economics* (Vol. I, pp. 425–430). Cheltenham/Northampton: E. Elgar.

Panico, C. (1999). The government sector in the post-Keynesian theory of growth and personal distribution. In G. Mongiovi, & F. Petri (Eds.), *Value, distribution and capital, essays in honour of P. Garegnani, op. cit.*, pp. 339–353.

Panico, C., & Salvadori, N. (Eds.). (1993). *Post Keynesian theory of growth and distribution*. Aldershot/Brookfield: E. Elgar.

Parrinello, S. (2011). Un'infondata portata attribuita alla teoria Ricardiana dei vantaggi comparati: un punto di vista post-Keynesiano. In *Gli economisti post-keynesiani di Cambridge e l'Italia* (pp. 103–110), Atti dei Convegni Lincei. Rome: Scienze e Lettere.

Pasinetti, L. L. (1959). On concepts and measures of changes in productivity. *The Review of Economics and Statistics, 41*(3), 270–282.

Pasinetti, L. L. (1960a). A mathematical formulation of the Ricardian system. *Review of Economic Studies, 27*(2), 78–98.

Pasinetti, L. L. (1960b). Cyclical fluctuations and economic growth. *Oxford Economic Papers, 12*(2), 215–241.

Pasinetti, L. L. (1962). Rate of profit and income distribution in relation to the rate of economic growth. *Review of Economic Studies, 29*(4), 267–279.

Pasinetti, L. L. (1963). A multi-sector model of economic growth. Revised Ph.D. Diss., King's College, Cambridge.

Pasinetti, L. L. (1965a). Causalità e interdipendenza nell'analisi econometrica e nella teoria economica. In *Annuario dell'Università Cattolica del Sacro Cuore 1964–65* (pp. 233–250). Milan: Vita e Pensiero.

Pasinetti, L. L. (1965b). A new theoretical approach to the problems of economic growth. *Pontificiae Academiae Scientiarum Scripta Varia, 28*, 572–696.

Pasinetti, L. L. (1966). Changes in the rate of profit and switches of techniques. *Quarterly Journal of Economics, 80*(4), 503–517.

Pasinetti, L. L. (1969). Switches of techniques and the "rate of return" in capital theory. *Economic Journal, 79*(315), 508–531.

Pasinetti, L. L. (1973). The notion of vertical integration in economic analysis. *Metroeconomica, 25*, 1–29; Reprinted in L. L. Pasinetti (Ed.), *Essays on the theory of joint production, op. cit.*, pp. 16–43.

Pasinetti, L. L. (1974). *Growth and income distribution: Essays in economic theory*. Cambridge: Cambridge University Press.

Pasinetti, L. L. (1975). Determinatezza del saggio di profitto nella teoria Post-Keynesiana: Risposta al Professor Campa. *Giornale degli Economisti e Annali di Economia, 34*, 639–647.

Pasinetti, L. L. (1977). *Lectures on the theory of production*. London: Macmillan (Italian original 1975, Bologna: Il Mulino).

Pasinetti, L. L. (1979). Kaldor, Nicholas. In *International encyclopaedia of the social sciences, biographical supplement* (Vol. 18, pp. 366–369). London/New York: Collier Macmillan/The Free Press.

Pasinetti, L. L. (Ed.). (1980). *Essays in the theory of joint production*. London: Macmillan (Italian original, 1977, Bologna: Il Mulino).

Pasinetti, L. L. (1981). *Structural change and economic growth: A theoretical essay on the dynamics of the wealth of nations*. Cambridge: Cambridge University Press.

Pasinetti, L. L. (1982). A comment on the "new view" of the Ricardian theory. In M. Baranzini (Ed.), *Advances in economic theory, op. cit.*, pp. 240–242.

Pasinetti, L. L. (1983). Conditions of existence of a two class economy in the Kaldor and more general models of growth and income distribution. *Kyklos, 36*(1), 91–102.

Pasinetti, L. L. (1985). 'Nicholas Kaldor', introduction to N. Kaldor. *Economia senza equillibrio* (pp. 9–21, Italian version of Kaldor's Yale Lectures). Bologna: Il Mulino.

Pasinetti, L. L. (1986). Theory of value – A source of alternative paradigms in economic analysis. In M. Baranzini, & R. Scazzieri (Eds.), *Foundations of economics., op. cit.*, pp. 409–431.

Pasinetti, L. L. (1988). Growing subsystems, vertically hyper-integrated sectors and the labour theory of value. *Cambridge Journal of Economics, 12*(2), 125–134.

Pasinetti, L. L. (1989a). Ricardian debt/taxation equivalence in the Kaldor theory of profits and income distribution. *Cambridge Journal of Economics, 13*(1), 25–36.

Pasinetti, L. L. (1989b). Government deficit spending is not incompatible with the Cambridge theorem of the rate of profit: A reply to Fleck and Domenghino. *Journal of Post Keynesian Economics, 11*(4), 641–647.

Pasinetti, L. L. (1989c). *'Address', at the King's College Chapel R. F. Kahn Memorial Service* (pp. 6–11). Cambridge: King's College.

Pasinetti, L. L. (1991). Richard Ferdinand Kahn: 1905–1989. *Proceedings of the British Academy, 76*, 423–443.

Pasinetti, L. L. (1993). *Structural economic dynamics: A theory of the economic consequences of human learning*. Cambridge: Cambridge University Press.

Pasinetti, L. L. (1996). Richard Murphey Goodwin (1913–1996): A pupil's tribute to a great teacher. *Cambridge Journal of Economics, 20*(6), 645–649.

Pasinetti, L. L. (2003). 'Letter to the editor', in 'Comments – Cambridge Capital Controversies'. *Journal of Economic Perspectives, 17*(4), 227–228. (A Comment on A. J. Cohen and G. C. Harcourt's 'Cambridge Capital Theory Controversies') same *Journal, 17*(1), 199–214.

Pasinetti, L. L. (2007). *Keynes and the Cambridge Keynesians: A 'revolution in economics' to be accomplished*. Cambridge: Cambridge University Press.

Pasinetti, L. L. (2014). Piero Sraffa and his books. A foreword to the catalogue of his inimitable library. In G. De Vivo (Ed.), *Catalogue of the library of Piero Sraffa, op. cit.*, pp. XI–XXIX.

Pasinetti, L. L. (2015). On the origin of the theory of rent in economics. In M. Baranzini, C. Rotondi, & R. Scazzieri (Eds.), *Resources, production and structural dynamics, op. cit.*, pp. 35–52.

Pasinetti, L. L. (2017). *A theory of value.* London: Routledge forthcoming.

Pasinetti, L. L., & Mariutti, G. (2008). Hick's "conversion" – From J. R. to John. In R. Scazzieri, A. Sen, & S. Zamagni (Eds.), *Markets, money and capital. Hicksian economics for the twenty-first century, op. cit.*, pp. 52–71.

Pasinetti, L. L., & Roncaglia, A. (2006). Le scienze umane in Italia: il caso dell'economia politica. *Rivista Italiana degli Economisti, 11*(3), 463–501.

Pasinetti, L. L., & Scazzieri, R. (1987a). Capital theory: Paradoxes. In *The new Palgrave: A dictionary of economics, op. cit.*, Vol. 1, pp. 363–368.

Pasinetti, L. L., & Scazzieri, R. (1987b). Structural economic dynamics. In *The new Palgrave: A dictionary of economics, op. cit.*, Vol. 4, pp. 525–528.

Pasinetti, L. L., & Scazzieri, R. (2008). Capital theory: Paradoxes. In S. N. Durlauf, & L. E. Blume (Eds.), *The new Palgrave dictionary of economics* (2nd ed., Vol. 1, pp. 675–684), London: Palgrave Macmillan (1st edn 1987).

Pasinetti, L. L., & Spaventa, L. (1960). Verso il superamento della modellistica aggregata nella teoria dello sviluppo economico'. *Rivista di Politica Economica, 50.9*(10), 1–35.

Petri, F. (1978). The difference between long-period and short period general equilibrium and the capital theory controversy. *Australian Economic Papers, 17*(31), 246–260.

Petri, F. (1980). Positive profits without exploitation: A note on the generalized fundamental Marxian theorem. *Econometrica, 48*(2), 531–533.

Petri, F. (1987). Rate of exploitation. In *The new Palgrave: A dictionary of economics, op. cit.*, Vol. 4, pp. 66–68.

Petri, F. (1992). Pierangelo Garegnani. In P. Arestis, & M. Sawyer (Eds.), *A biographical dictionary of dissenting economists, op. cit.*, pp. 170–178.

Petri, F. (1998). Labour theory of value. In H. D. Kurz & N. Salvadori (Eds.), *The Elgar companion to classical economics* (Vol. II, pp. 12–22). Cheltenham: E. Elgar.

Petri, F. (1999). Professor Hahn on the Neo-Ricardians criticisms of neoclassical economics. In G. Mongiovi, & F. Petri (Eds.), *Value, distribution and capital: Essays in honour of Pierangelo Garegnani, op. cit.*, pp. 19–68.

Petri, F. (2003a). 'Introduction' and 'A "Sraffian" critique of general equilibrium theory, and the classical-Keynesian alternative. In F. Petri, & F. Hahn (Eds.), *General equilibrium: Problems and prospects, op. cit.*, pp. 1–26 and pp. 387–421.

Petri, F. (2003b). Should the theory of endogenous growth be based on say's law and the full employment of resources? In N. Salvadori (Ed.), *The theory of economic growth: A 'classical' perspective* (pp. 139–160). Cheltenham: E. Elgar.

Petri, F. (2004). *General equilibrium, capital and macroeconomics: A key to recent controversies in equilibrium theory*. Cheltenham: E. Elgar.

Petri, F. (2011). On the recent debate on capital theory and general equilibrium. In V. Caspari (Ed.), *The evolution of economic theory. Essays in honour of Bertram Schefold* (pp. 55–99). London: Routledge.

Petri, F., & Hahn, F. O. (Eds.). (2003). *General equilibrium: Problems and prospects*. London/New York: Routlegde.

Pettenati, P. (1967). Il teorema di Pasinetti in un diverso quadro di riferimento. *Studi economici, 22*(6), 581–588.

Pettenati, P. (1993). Pasinetti's theorem in a modern institutional framework. In C. Panico, & N. Salvadori (Eds.), *Post Keynesian theory of growth and distribution, op. cit.*, pp. 229–237.

Picchio del Mercato, A. (1975). Il modello di Lewis e la teoria classica della distribuzione. *Rivista Internazionale di Scienze Economiche e Commerciali, 22*(11), 1048–1084.

Picchio del Mercato, A. (1981). Social reproduction and the basic structure of labour markets. In F. Wilkinson (Ed.), *The dynamics of labour market segmentation* (pp. 193–209). London: Academic Press.

Picchio del Mercato, A. (1992). *Social reproduction and the basic structure of the labour market*. Cambridge: Cambridge University Press.

Picchio del Mercato, A. (1998). Subsistence. In H. Kurz & N. Salvadori (Eds.), *The Elgar companion of classical economics*. Aldershot: E. Elgar.

Picchio del Mercato, A. (2003a). Needs and passions of human subsistence in the moral economy in the early 18th century. *History of Economic Ideas: Defoe and Mandeville, 11*(2), 7–29.

Picchio del Mercato, A. (Ed.). (2003b). *Unpaid work and the economy: Standards of living in a gender perspective*. London: Routledge.

Picchio del Mercato, A. (2011). Hay, carrots, bread and roses: Subsistence and surplus wages in Sraffa's papers. In R. Ciccone, C. Gehrke, & G. Mongiovi (Eds.), *Sraffa and modern economics* (Vol. I, pp. 385–404). London: Routledge.

Picchio del Mercato, A. (2015). A macro–micro classical political-economy approach to well-being gender budgets. *Journal of Economic Policy, 31*(2), 155–174.

Pivetti, M. (Ed.). (1975). *Edwin Cannan. Storia delle teorie della produzione e della distribuzione*. Turin: Isedi.

Pivetti, M. (1987a). Distribution theories: Classical. In *The new Palgrave: A dictionary of economics, op. cit.*, Vol. I, pp. 872–876.
Pivetti, M. (1987b). Interest and profit in Smith, Ricardo and Marx. *Political Economy, 3*(1), 63–74.
Pivetti, M. (1991). *An essay on money and distribution*. Basingstoke: Macmillan.
Pivetti, M. (1996). Joan Robinson and the rate of interest: An important change of view on a topical issue. In M. C. Marcuzzo, L. L. Pasinetti, & A. Roncaglia (Eds.), *The economics of Joan Robinson, op. cit.*, pp. 75–80.
Pivetti, M. (1999). On Sraffa's "cost & surplus" concept of wages and its policy implications. *Rivista italiana degli economisti, 4*(2), 279–300.
Pivetti, M. (2003). The rate of interest. In J. E. King (Ed.), *The Elgar companion to post Keynesian economics* (pp. 299–303). Cheltenham: E. Elgar.
Pivetti, M. (2006). The "principle of scarcity", pension policy and growth. *Review of Political Economy, 18*(3), 379–390.
Poni, C., & Scazzieri, R. (Eds.). (1994). *Production networks: Market rules and social norms.* Eleventh international economic history congress, Milan: Bocconi University, 12th–16th September 1994, Session C.11.
Poni, C., & Scazzieri, R. (2007). Environmental crisis and property rights: Historical contexts and theoretical frameworks. In A. Prinz, A. E. Steenge, & J. Schmidt (Eds.), *The rules of the game: Institutions, law and economics* (pp. 81–101). Berlin: LIT Verlag.
Porta, P. L. (Ed.). (1983a). *Opere di David Ricardo, Vol. I Princìpi di economia politica e dell'imposta*. Turin: Utet.
Porta, P. L. (1983b). Introduzione. In P. L. Porta (Ed.) *Opere di David Ricardo,* Vol. I *Princìpi di economia politica e dell'imposta, op. cit.*, pp. 9–102.
Porta, P. L. (1984a). *Scuola classica e teoria economica*. Milan: Giuffrè.
Porta, P. L. (1984b). Piero Sraffa. *Rivista Internazionale di Scienze Economiche e Commerciali, 31*(1), 14–20.
Porta, P. L. (1990). David Ricardo. La sistemazione teorica della concorrenza e del mercato. In G. Becattini (Ed.), *Il pensiero economico: temi, problemi, correnti, scuole* (pp. 101–147). Turin: UTET.
Porta, P. L. (Ed.). (1992). *David Ricardo: Notes on Malthus's 'measure of value'.* Cambridge: Cambridge University Press.
Porta, P. L. (2015). Conquering scarcity: Institutions, learning and creativity in the history of economic ideas. In M. Baranzini, C. Rotondi, & R. Scazzieri (Eds.), *Resources, production and structural dynamics, op. cit.*, pp. 299–319.
Porta, P. L. (2016). *The classical school in economic theory: A new interpretation.* Cheltenham: E. Elgar, forthcoming.

Potier, J.-P. (1987). *Piero Sraffa, Unorthodox Economist (1898–1983). A biographical essay*. London: Routledge.
Pugno, M. (1992). *Roy F. Harrod: dall'equilibriodinamico all'instabilità ciclica*. Bologna: Il Mulino.
Punzo, L. F., Feijo, A., & Anyul, M. P. (Eds.). (2012). *Beyond the global crisis: Structural adjustments and regional integration in Europe and Latin America*. Abingdon/New York: Routledge.
Quadrio Curzio, A. (1967). *Rendita e distribuzione in un modello economico plurisettoriale* (Rent and distribution in a multi-sectoral economic model). Milan: Giuffrè.
Quadrio Curzio, A. (1975). *Accumulazione del capitale e rendita* (Accumulation of Capital and Rent). Bologna: Il Mulino.
Quadrio Curzio, A. (1977). Rendita, distribuzione del reddito, ordine di efficienza e di redditività. In L. L. Pasinetti (Ed.), *Contributi alla teoria della produzione congiunta* (pp. 301–327). Bologna: Il Mulino.
Quadrio Curzio, A. (1980). Rent, income distribution and orders of efficiency and rentability. In L. L. Pasinetti (Ed.), *Essays on the theory of joint production, op. cit.*, pp. 219–40. Reprinted in H. D. Kurz, & N. Salvadori (Eds.). (2003). *The legacy of Piero Sraffa* (Vol. II, pp. 311–41). Cheltenham: E. Elgar.
Quadrio Curzio, A. (1986). Technological scarcity: An essay on production and structural change. In M. Baranzini, & R. Scazzieri (Eds.), *Foundations of economics – Structure of inquiry and economic theory, op. cit.*, pp. 311–338.
Quadrio Curzio, A. (1987). Land rent. In *The new Palgrave: A dictionary of economics, op. cit.*, London: Macmillan, Vol. 3, pp. 118–121.
Quadrio Curzio, A. (1988). Le «scarsità relative» nella storia della teoria economica e rilevanza attuale. In C. M. Guerci & G. Zanetti (Eds.), *Sviluppo economico e vincolo energetico* (pp. 39–53). Bologna: Il Mulino.
Quadrio Curzio, A. (1990). *Rent, distribution and economic structure: A collection of essays* (Quaderni IDSE, 1). Milan: CNR.
Quadrio Curzio, A. (1993a). On economic science, its tools and economic reality. In M. Baranzini, & G. C. Harcourt (Eds.), *The dynamics of the wealth of nations: Growth, distribution and structural change. Essays in honour of Luigi L. Pasinetti, op. cit.*, pp. 246–271.
Quadrio Curzio, A. (1993b). Distribuzione della ricchezza e del reddito. In *Enciclopedia delle Scienze Sociali* (pp. 194–207). Rome: Istituto della Enciclopedia italiana Treccani.
Quadrio Curzio, A. (1996a). Production and efficiency with global technologies. In M. A. Landesmann, & R. Scazzieri (Eds.), *Production and economic dynamics, op. cit.*, pp. 105–126.

Quadrio Curzio, A. (1996b). Distribuzione dinamica del reddito e risorse scarse. In T. Cozzi, et al. (Eds.), *Benessere, equilibrio e sviluppo. Studi in onore di Siro Lombardini* (Vol. III, pp. 203–254). Milan: Vita e Pensiero.

Quadrio Curzio, A. (1998). Rent. In H. D. Kurz & N. Salvadori (Eds.), *The Elgar Companion to Classical Economics (ECCE)* (pp. 189–193). Cheltenham: E. Elgar.

Quadrio Curzio, A. (2000). *La Società Italiana degli Economisti. 50 anni di attività.* Bologna: Il Mulino.

Quadrio Curzio, A. (2007) *Economisti ed economia. Per un'Italia europea: paradigmi tra il XVIII e il XX secolo.* Bologna: Il Mulino.

Quadrio Curzio, A. (2011). *Resources and economic dynamics, technology and rents.* Milan: Working Papers Cranec/Vita e Pensiero.

Quadrio Curzio, A. (2014). Economia politica. *Journal of Analytical and Institutional Economics, 31*(3), 265–276.

Quadrio Curzio, A., & Fortis, M. (Eds.). (2012). *L'industria nei 150 anni dell'Unità d'Italia. Paradigmi e protagonisti* (Collana della Fondazine Edison). Bologna: Il Mulino.

Quadrio Curzio, A., & Miceli, V. (2010). *Sovereign wealth funds. A complete guide to state-owned investment funds.* Petersfield: Harriman House.

Quadrio Curzio, A., & Pellizzari, F. (1996). *Risorse, tecnologie, rendita.* Bologna: Il Mulino.

Quadrio Curzio, A., & Pellizzari, F. (1999). *Rent, resources, tecnologies.* Berlin: Springer.

Quadrio Curzio, A., & Pellizzari, F. (2004a). Rent, technology, and the environment. In R. Arena, & N. Salvadori (Eds.), *Money, credit and the role of the state. Essays in honour of Augusto Graziani* (pp. 335–348), Burlington: Ashgate.

Quadrio Curzio, A., & Rotondi, C. (2004b). Sulle ricerche di economia politica in Cattolica: proiezioni specialistiche ed internazionali. In G. Garofalo, & A. Graziani (Eds.), *La formazione degli economisti in Italia (1950–1975), op. cit.*, pp. 361–422.

Quadrio Curzio, A, & Rotondi, C. (Eds.). (2013a). *Un economista eclettico. Distribuzione, tecnologie e sviluppo nel pensiero di Nino Andreatta.* Bologna: Il Mulino.

Quadrio Curzio, A., & Rotondi, C. (2013b). Premessa. In A. Q. Curzio, & C. Rotondi (Eds.), *Un economista eclettico. Distribuzione, tecnologie e sviluppo nel pensiero di Nino Andreatta, op. cit.*, pp. 15–108.

Quadrio Curzio, A., & Scazzieri, R. (Eds.), (1977–1982). *Protagonisti del pensiero economico*, 4 Vols. Bologna: Il Mulino.

Quadrio Curzio, A., & Scazzieri, R. (1983). *Sui momenti costitutivi dell'economia politica*, vol. II of *Protagonisti del Pensiero Economico*. Bologna: Il Mulino.

Quadrio Curzio, A., & Scazzieri, R. (1986). The exchange-production duality and the dynamics of economic knowledge. In M. Baranzini, & R. Scazzieri (Eds.), *Foundations of economics, op. cit.*, pp. 377–407.

Quadrio Curzio, A., & Scazzieri, R. (1990). Profili di dinamica economica strutturale: introduzione. In A. Quadrio Curzio & R. Scazzieri (Eds.), *Dinamica economica strutturale* (pp. 11–51). Bologna: Il Mulino.

Quadrio-Curzio, A., & Scazzieri, R. (2008). Historical stylizations and monetary theory. In R. Scazzieri, A. Sen, & S. Zamagni (Eds.), *Markets, money and capital: Hicksian economics for the twenty-first century, op. cit.*, pp. 185–203.

Quadrio Curzio, A., Manara, C. F., & Faliva, M. (1987). Produzione ed efficienza con tecnologie globali. *Economia Politica, 4*(1), 11–47.

Quadrio Curzio, A., Nicola, P. C., & Rotondi, C. (2010). *Distribution and growth, technology and development: Reflections on Nino Andreatta's theoretical analysis*. Milan: Vita e Pensiero.

Raffaelli, T., Becattini, G., & Dardi, M. (Eds.). (2006). *The Elgar companion to Alfred Marshall*. Cheltenham/Northampton: E. Elgar.

Raffaelli, T., et al. (Eds.). (2010). *The impact of Alfred Marshall's ideas. The global diffusion of his works*. Cheltenham/Northampton: E. Elgar.

Rampa, G., Stella, L., & Thirlwall, A. (Eds.). (1988). *Economic dynamics, trade and growth: Essays on Harrodian themes*. London/New York: Macmillan/St. Martin's Press.

Ranchetti, F. (1998). Choice without utility? In M. Bianchi (Ed.), *The active consumer* (pp. 28–30). London: Routledge.

Ranchetti, F. (2001). On the relationship between Sraffa and Keynes. In T. Cozzi, & R. Marchionatti (Eds.), *Piero Sraffa's political economy: A centenary estimate, op. cit.*, pp. 311–332.

Ranchetti, F. (2005). Communications and intellectual integrity. The correspondence between Keynes and Sraffa. In M. C. Marcuzzo, & A. Rosselli (Eds.), *Economists in Cambridge: A study through their correspondence 1907–1946, op. cit.*, pp. 119–148.

Reati, A. (1998a). Technological revolutions in Pasinetti's model of structural change. *Structural Change and Economic Dynamics, 9*(3), 245–262.

Reati, A. (1998b). A long-wave pattern for output and employment in Pasinetti's model of structural change. *Economie Appliquee, 51*(2), 29–77.

Reati, A. (2012). *The economic policy of structural change: An outline and missed opportunities*. Paper presented at the conference 'the economics of structural change: Theory, institutions and policies, in honour of Luigi L. Pasinetti'. Gonville and Caius College.

Reati, A. (2014). Economic policy for structural change. *Review of Political Economy, 26*(1), 1–22.

Reati, A., & Raganelli, V. (1993). Introducing long waves into Pasinetti's model of structural change: The price movements. *Economie Appliquee, 46*(1), 5–29.

Ricci, G., & Velupillai, K. V. (Eds.). (1988). *Growth cycles and multisectoral economics: The Goodwin tradition*. Berlin: Springer.

Ricottilli, M. (1976). Autonomous expenditure, output, growth: A sub-sector approach. *Economic Notes, 5*(3), 59–80.

Ricottilli, M. (1984). The investment performance of three industrialized economies: The USA, West Germany and France. *Economic Notes, 13*(2), 90–120.

Ricottilli, M. (1988). Le decisioni di investimento per la sostituzione di impianti superati dal progresso tecnico. *Economia Politica, 5*(3), 387–408.

Ricottilli, M. (1994). Technical progress, innovative activity and development policies. *The International Journal of Technology Management, 9*(3–4), 297–313.

Ricottilli, M. (2009). Traverse, division of labour and emerging structures. In H. Hagemann, & R. Scazzieri (Eds.), *Capital, time and transitional dynamics, op. cit.*, pp. 190–219.

Ricottilli, M. (2013). Development theory and transition. In Y. Ma & H. M. Trautwein (Eds.), *Thoughts on economic development in China* (pp. 195–216). London: Routledge.

Ricottilli, M. (2015). Innovation through local interaction, imitation and investment waves. *Structural Change and Economic Dynamics, 33*(2), 58–70.

Roncaglia, A. (1974). Labour-power, subsistence wage and the rate of wages. *Australian Economic Papers, 13*(22), 133–143.

Roncaglia, A. (1975). *Sraffa e la teoria dei prezzi*. Rome/Bari: Laterza.

Roncaglia, A. (1976). The Sraffian revolution. In S. Weintraub (Ed.), *Modern economic thought* (pp. 163–177). Philadelphia: University of Pennsylvania Press.

Roncaglia, A. (1978). *Sraffa and the theory of prices*. New York: Wiley.

Roncaglia, A. (1980). Production prices and the theory of the firm: A comment. *Journal of Post Keynesian Economics, 3*(1), 100–104.

Roncaglia, A. (1981). Piero Sraffa's contribution to political economy. In J. Shackleton & G. Locksley (Eds.), *Twelve contemporary economists* (pp. 240–256). London: Macmillan.

Roncaglia, A. (1982). Hollander's Ricardo. *Journal of Post Keynesian Economics, 4*(4), 339–359. Reprinted in G. Caravale (Ed.). (1985). *The legacy of Ricardo* (pp. 105–123). Oxford: B. Blackwell.

Roncaglia, A. (1988). The Neo-Ricardian approach and the distribution of income. In A. Asimakopulos (Ed.), *Theories of income distribution* (pp. 158–180). Boston: Kluwer Academic.

Roncaglia, A. (1993). Toward a post-Sraffian theory of income distribution. *Journal of Income Distribution, 3*(1), 3–27.

Roncaglia, A. (2001). *Piero Sraffa: His life, thought and cultural heritage.* London/New York: Routledge.

Roncaglia, A. (2005). *The wealth of ideas: A history of economic thought.* Cambridge/New York: Cambridge University Press.

Roncaglia, A. (2006). Paolo Sylos Labini, 1920-2005. *Moneta e Credito, 59*(233), 196–229.

Roncaglia, A. (2009). *Piero Sraffa.* London: Palgrave Macmillan.

Roncaglia, A. (2011). Cambridge e Italia: teorie post-Keynesiane della distribuzione. Una nota. In *Gli economisti post-keynesiani di Cambridge e l'Italia* (Atti dei Convegni Lincei, pp. 125–138). Rome: Scienze e Lettere.

Roncaglia, A. (2013). Luigi Spaventa. *PSL Quarterly Review, 66*(266), 171–199.

Roncaglia, A., & Hollander, S. (1982). Hollander's Ricardo. *Journal of Post Keynesian Economics, 4*(3), 339–375.

Roncaglia, A., & Tonveronachi, M. (1974). Appunti per una teoria della distribuzione. Un quadro di riferimento per il breve periodo. *Note Economiche, 3*, 114–139.

Roncaglia, A., & Tonveronachi, M. (1978). Commenti a un recente studio di Modigliani e Padoa Schioppa. *Moneta e Credito, 31*(121), 3–21.

Roncaglia, A., & Tonveronachi, M. (1985). Pre-Keynesian roots of the neoclassical synthesis. *Cahiers d'Economie Politique, 10*(1), 51–65.

Roncaglia, A., & Tonveronachi, M. (2014). Post-Keynesian, post-Sraffian economics: An outline. In D. B. Papadimitriou (Ed.), *Contributions to economic theory, policy, development and finance, essays in honor of Jan A. Kregel* (pp. 40–64). New York/London: Palgrave Macmillan.

Rossi, A. A. (1966). *La dinamica Ricardiana.* Lugano: Buona Stampa.

Rossi, A. A., & Leighton T. L. (1971). Inflation in the post-war Swiss economy. An econometric study of the interaction between immigration and the labour market. *Schweizerische Zeitschrift für Volkswirtschaft und Statistik, 107*(4), 761–790.

Rossi, A. A., & Schiltknecht, K. (1972). Uebernachfrage und Lohnentwicklung in der Schweiz – Eine neue Hypothese. *Kyklos, 25*(2), 239–254.

Rossini Favretti, R., Sandri, G., & Scazzieri, R. (Eds.). (1999). *Incommensurability and transmission. Kuhnian perspectives on scientific communication and theory change.* Cheltenham/Northampton: E. Elgar.

Rotondi, C. (2014). Un giovane economista tra crescita e sviluppo. In A. Quadrio Curzio, & C. Rotondi (Eds.), *Gli allievi ricordano Andreatta, op. cit.*, pp. 27–35.

Rotondi, Z., & Vaciago, G. (2003). The reputation of a newborn central bank. *BNL Quarterly Review, 56*(224), 3–22.

Russo, M., & Natali, A. (2008). *Sebastiano Brusco e la scuola Italiana di sviluppo locale, 605.* Modena: Dipartimento di Economia Politica.

Salter, W. E. (1961). *Productivity and technical change.* Cambridge: Cambridge University Press.

Salvadori, N. (1991). Post-Keynesian theory of distribution in the long-run. In E. J. Nell, & W. Semmler (Eds.), *Nicholas Kaldor and mainstream economics: Confrontation or convergence?, op. cit.*, pp. 164–189.

Salvadori, N. (1996). "Productivity curves" in the accumulation of capital. In M. C. Marcuzzo, L. L. Pasinetti, & A. Roncaglia (Eds.), *The economics of Joan Robinson, op. cit.*, pp. 232–248.

Salvadori, N., & Panico, C. (Eds.). (1993). *Post Keynesian theory of growth and distribution.* Aldershot: E. Elgar, and 'Introduction', pp. xiii–xxxi.

Salvati, M. (1981). May 1968 and the hot autumn of 1969: The responses of two ruling classes. In S. Berger (Ed.), *Organizing interests in Western Europe* (pp. 329–363). Cambridge: Cambridge University Press.

Salvati, M. (1984). Political business cycles and long waves in industrial relations. Notes on Kalecki and Phelps Brown. In C. Freeman (Ed.), *Long waves in the world economy* (pp. 202–224). London: F. Pinter.

Salvati, M. (1985). The Italian inflation. In L. Lindberg & C. Maier (Eds.), *The politics of inflation and economic stagnation* (pp. 509–563). Washington, DC: The Brookings Institution.

Samuelson, P. A. (1959). A modern treatment of the Ricardian theory. *Quarterly Journal of Economics*, 1–35 and 217–31.

Samuelson, P. A. (1962). Parable and realism in capital theory. The surrogate production function. *Review of Economic Studies, 29*(3), 193–206.

Samuelson, P. A. (1966). A summing up. *Quarterly Journal of Economics, 80*(4), 568–583.

Samuelson, P. A. (1978). The Canonical classical model of political economy. *Journal of Economic Literature, 16*(4), 1415–1434.

Samuelson, P. A. (1987). Foreword. In R. M. Goodwin, & L. F. Punzo (Eds.), *The dynamics of a capitalist economy: A multi-sectoral approach, op. cit.*, p. ix.

Samuelson, P. A. (1991). Extirpating error contamination concerning the post-Keynesian anti-Pasinetti equilibrium. *Oxford Economic Papers, 43*(2), 177–186.

Samuelson, P. A., & Modigliani, F. (1966). The Pasinetti paradox in neoclassical and more general models. *Review of Economic Studies, 33*(4), 269–301.

Sarcinelli, M. (2013). Per ricordare Luigi Spaventa. *Moneta e Credito, 66*(263), 279–297.

Sardoni, C. (1981). Multisectoral models of balanced growth and the Marxian schemes of expanded reproduction. *Australian Economic Papers, 20*(37), 383–397.

Sardoni, C. (1984). Some ties of Kalecki to the 1926 "Sraffian Manifesto". *Journal of Post Keynesian Economics, 6*(3), 458–465.

Sardoni, C. (1986). Marx and Keynes on effective demand and unemployment. *History of Political Economy, 18*(3), 419–441.

Sardoni, C. (1987). *Marx and Keynes on economic recession*. New York: New York University Press.

Sardoni, C. (1989–90). Chapter 18 of the general theory. Methodological issues. *Journal of Post Keynesian Economics, 12*(2), 293–307.

Sardoni, C. (Ed.). (1992a). *On political economists and modern political economy. Selected essays of G. C. Harcourt*. London/New York: Routledge.

Sardoni, C. (1992b). Market forms and effective demand: Keynesian results with perfect competition. *Review of Political Economy, 4*(4), 377–395.

Sardoni, C. (1994). *The general theory* and the critique of decreasing returns. *Journal of the History of Economic Thought, 16*(1), 61–85.

Sardoni, C. (1997). Wages and employment: A Keynesian model. In R. Rotheim (Ed.), *New Keynesian economics. Post Keynesian alternative* (pp. 107–117). London/New York: Routledge.

Sardoni, C. (1999). The debate on excess capacity in the 1930s. In C. Sardoni, & P. Kriesler (Eds.), *Keynes, post-Keynesianism and political economy. Essays in honour of Geoff Harcourt* (pp. 259–283). London/New York: Routledge.

Sardoni, C. (2002). On the microeconomic foundations of macroeconomics: A Keynesian perspective. In P. Arestis, M. Desai, & S. Dow (Eds.), *Methodology, microeconomics and Keynes. Essays in honour ro victoria chick* (pp. 4–14). London/New York: Routledge.

Sardoni, C. (2011). *Unemployment, recession and effective demand: The contributions of Marx, Keynes and Kalecki*. Cheltemham/Northampton: E. Elgar.

Sardoni, C. (2013). Marx and the-Postkeynesians. In G. C. Harcourt, & P. Kriesler (Eds.), *The Oxford handbook of Post-Keynesian economics, op. cit.*, Vol. I, pp. 231–244.

Sardoni, C., & Kriesler, P. (Eds.). (1999). *Keynes, post-Keynesianism and political economy: Essays in honour of Geoff Harcourt* (Vol. III). London: Routledge.

Scazzieri, R. (1981). *Efficienza produttiva e livelli di attività. Un contributo di teoria economica.* Bologna: Il Mulino.

Scazzieri, R. (1982). Scale and efficiency in model of production. In M. Baranzini (Ed.), *Advances in economic theory, op. cit.*, pp. 19–42.

Scazzieri, R. (1983). Economic dynamics and structural change: A comment on Pasinetti. *Rivista Internazionale di Scienze Economiche e Commerciali, 30*(1), 73–90.

Scazzieri, R. (1990). Vertical integration in economic theory. *Journal of Post Keynesian Economics, 13*(1), 20–46.

Scazzieri, R. (1993a). *A theory of production: Tasks, processes and technical practices.* Oxford: Clarendon Press.

Scazzieri, R. (1993b). Action, processes and economic theory. In A. Heertje (Ed.), *The makers of modern economics* (Vol. I, pp. 84–114). Aldershot/ Brookfield: E. Elgar.

Scazzieri, R. (1996a). Introduction to Pasinetti's structural economic dynamics: A symposium. *Structural Change and Economic Dynamics, 7*(2), 123–125.

Scazzieri, R. (1996b). The accumulation of capital and structural economic dynamics. In M. C. Marcuzzo, L. L. Pasinetti, & A. Roncaglia (Eds.), *The economics of Joan Robinson, op. cit.*, pp. 174–187.

Scazzieri, R. (1999). Modelli di società civile. *Filosofia politica, 13*(3), 363–378.

Scazzieri, R. (2001). Analogy, causal patterns and economic choice. In M. C. Galavotti, P. Suppes, & D. Costantini (Eds.), *Stochastic causality* (pp. 123–139). Stanford: CSLI Publications/Chicago University Press.

Scazzieri, R. (2004). Economisti a Bologna: 1950-1975. In G. Garofalo, & A. Graziani (Eds.), *La formazione degli economisti in Italia (1950–1975), op. cit.*, pp. 423–462.

Scazzieri, R. (2006). A Smithian theory of choice. *Adam Smith Review, 2*, 1–54.

Scazzieri, R. (2008a). Context, conguence and coordination. In M. C. Galavotti, R. Scazzieri, & P. Suppes (Eds.), *Reasoning, rationality and probability* (pp. 187–207). Stanford: CSLI Publications/Chicago University Press.

Scazzieri, R. (2008b). The diffusion of economic ideas and the formation of the market tradition. In R. Scazzieri & R. Simili (Eds.), *The migration of ideas* (pp. 73–97). Sagamore Beach: Science History Publications.

Scazzieri, R. (2009a). Traverse analysis and methods of economic dynamics. In H. Hagemann, & R. Scazzieri (Eds.), *Capital, time and transitional dynamics, op. cit.*, pp. 96–132.

Scazzieri, R. (2009b). The feasibility of normative structures. In M. C. Galavotti (Ed.), *Bruno de Finetti. Radical Probabilist* (pp. 129–152). London: College Publications.

Scazzieri, R. (2011a). A theory of similarity and uncertainty. In S. Marzetti & R. Scazzieri (Eds.), *Fundamental uncertainty, rationality and plausible reasoning* (pp. 73–103). London: Palgrave Macmillan.

Scazzieri, R. (2011b). Structural economic dynamics: Looking back and forging ahead. In *Gli economisti post-keynesiani di Cambridge e l'Italia* (Atti dei Convegni Lincei, pp. 205–233). Rome: Scienze e Lettere.

Scazzieri, R. (2011c). Patterns of rationality and the varieties of inference. *Journal of Economic Methodology, 8*(1), 105–110.

Scazzieri, R. (2012a). The concept of "natural economic system": A tool for structural analysis and an instrument for policy design. In R. Arena, & P. L. Porta (Eds.), *Structural dynamics and economic growth, op. cit.*, pp. 218–240.

Scazzieri, R. (2012b). The political economy of *production of commodities by means of commodities. Cambridge Journal of Economics, 36*(6), 1315–1322.

Scazzieri, R. (2014a). A structural theory of increasing returns. *Structural Change and Economic Dynamics, 29*, 75–88.

Scazzieri, R. (2014b). L'illuminismo delle riforme civili: divisione del lavoro, commercio, produzione della ricchezza. In P. L. Porta & R. Scazzieri (Eds.), *L'illuminismo delle riforme civili: il contributo degli illuministi lombardi* (Vol. 64, pp. 13–38). Milan: Istituto Lombardo, Accademia di Scienze e Lettere, Incontro di studio.

Scazzieri, R., & Zamagni, S. (2008). Between theory and history: On the identity of hicks's economics. In R. Scazzieri, A. Sen, & S. Zamagni (Eds.), *Markets, money and capital. Hicksian economics for the twenty-first century, op. cit.*, pp. 1–37.

Scazzieri, R., Sen, A. K., & Zamagni, S. (Eds.). (2008). *Markets, money and capital. Hicksian economics for the twenty-first century*. Cambridge: Cambridge University Press.

Schefold, B. (1998). Piero Sraffa. In F. Meacci (Ed.), *Italian economists of the 20th century* (pp. 179–205). Cheltenham: E. Elgar.

Schianchi, A. (1978). Crescita e distribuzione in un modello a tre classi. *Ricerche Economiche, 1*, 103–106.

Schianchi, A. (1982). A comment of the economics of natural resources. In M. Baranzini (Ed.), *Advances in economic theory, op. cit.*, pp. 302–310.

Schianchi, A. (2011). Multiple optimal solutions in the portfolio selection model with short-selling. *International Journal of Theoretical and Applied Finance, 6*(7), 703–720.

Screpanti, E., & Zamagni, S. (1993). *An outline of the history of economic thought*. Oxford: Clarendon Press.

Seccareccia, M. (1996). Post Keynesian fundism and monetary circulation. In G. Delaplace & E. J. Nell (Eds.), *Money in motion: The post Keynesian and circulation approaches* (pp. 400–416). London: Macmillan.

Simonazzi, A. (2003). Innovation and growth: Supply and demand factors in the US expansion. *Cambridge Journal of Economics, 27*(5), 647–669.

Simonazzi, A. (2009). Care regimes and national employment models. *Cambridge Journal of Economics, 33*(2), 211–232.

Simonazzi, A. (2015). Italy: Continuity and change in welfare state retrenchment. In D. Vaughan-Whitehead (Ed.), *The European social model in crisis – Is Europe losing its soul?* (pp. 255–290). Geneva: ILO.

Simonazzi, A., & Picchi, S. (2013). Affordability of care and quality of work: New trends in elderly care. In F. Bettio, J. Plantenga, & M. Smith (Eds.), *Gender and the European labour market* (pp. 108–132). London: Routledge.

Simonazzi, A., & Vianello, F. (2007). Price and prejudice. The statics and dynamics of money-wage flexibility. In M. C. Marcuzzo & A. Giacomin (Eds.), *Money and markets* (pp. 115–132). London: Routledge.

Simonazzi, A., & Villa, P. (2000). Employment, growth and income inequality: Some open questions. In M. A. Landesmann & K. Pichelmann (Eds.), *Unemployment in Europe* (pp. 50–96). London: Palgrave Macmillan.

Simonazzi, A. et al. (2009). Continuity and change in the Italian model. In J. Rubery, G. Bosch, & S. Lehndorff (Eds.), *European employment models in flux. A comparison of institutional change in nine European countries* (pp. 201–222). London: Palgrave Macmillan.

Simonazzi, A., Ginzburg, A., & Nocella, G. (2013). Economic relations between Germany and Southern Europe. *Cambridge Journal of Economics, 37*(3), 653–675.

Solari, L. L. (1968). Fonction de consommation semi-agrégée pour la Suisse, 1948-1966. *Revue Suisse d'Economie Politique et Statistique, 104*(2), 11–54.

Solari, L. L. (1971). *Théorie des choix et fonctions de consommation semi-agrégées: modèles statistiques*. Geneva: Droz.

Solari, L. L., & du Pasquier, J.-N. (Eds.). (1976). *Private and enlarged Consumption*. Amsterdam: North Holland.

Solari, L. L., & Rossier, E. (1977). *De l'économie qualitative à l'économie quantitative. Pour une méthodologie de l'approche formalisée en sciences économiques*. Paris: Masson.

Solow, R. M. (1957). Technical change and the aggregate production function. *Review of Economics and Statistics, 39*(3), 312–320.

Solow, R. M. (1959). Comment on Pasinetti. *Review of Economics and Statistics, 41*(3), 282–285.

Solow, R. M. (2012). 'On Pasinetti and the unfinished Keynesian revolution', and 'first afterword: Pasinetti on structural dynamics. In R. Arena, & P. L. Porta (Eds.), *Structural dynamics and economic growth, op. cit.*, pp. 267–273, and pp. 274–275.

Soro, B. (2012). Harrod, Kaldor, and the idea of the "foreign trade *multiplier*". *Economia Internazionale, 65*(1), 173–187.

Spaventa, L. (1959). Dualism in economic growth. *BNL Quarterly Review, 12*(51), 386–434.

Spaventa, L. (1960). Problems of intermediate stages of growth. *The Economic Weekly, 12*(27), 1077–1082.

Spaventa, L. (1966). The use of econometric models for long-term policies. A critical view. *BNL Quarterly Review, 19*(77), 99–120.

Spaventa, L. (1968a). *Appunti di economia politica*. Roma: Bulzoni Editore.

Spaventa, L. (1968b). Realism without parables in capital theory. In *Recherches récentes sur la fonction de production* (Vol. 2, pp. 13–45). Namur: Centre d'études et de recherches universitaires.

Spaventa, L. (1970a). Rate of profit, rate of growth, and capital intensity in a simple production model. *Oxford Economic Papers, 22*(2), 129–147.

Spaventa, L. (1970b). Significato e portata della critica alla teoria marginalista della distribuzione. *Giornale degli economisti e Annali di Economia, 9*(10), 677–703.

Spaventa, L. (1973). Notes on problems of transition between techniques. In J. A. Mirrlees & N. H. Stern (Eds.), *Models of economic growth* (pp. 168–202). London: Macmillan.

Spaventa. L. (1982). Una svolta ad U della teoria economica. In AA. VV. *Scritti in onore di Innocenzo Gasparini* (pp. 1037–1058). Milan: Giuffré.

Spaventa, L. (1987). The growth of pubklic debt: Sustainability, fiscal rules and monetary rules. *IMF Staff Papers, 34*(2), 374–399.

Spaventa, L. (2002). Economics and institutions: Some reflections on Pasinetti and Caravale. In D. Tosato (Ed.), *Essays in memory of Giovanni Caravale* (pp. 354–356). London/New York: Routledge.
Spaventa, L., & Giavazzi, F. (Eds.). (1987). *High public debt: The Italian experience*. Cambridge: Cambridge University Press.
Sraffa, P. (1922a). The bank crises in Italy. *Economic Journal, 32*(1), 178–197.
Sraffa, P. (1922b). Italian banking today. *Manchester Guardian Commercial: Reconstruction in Europe, 7*, 675–676. Section XI, December.
Sraffa, P. (1926). The laws of returns under competitive conditions. *Economic Journal, 34*(144), 535–550.
Sraffa, P. (jointly with J. M. Keynes) (1938). 'Introduction' to David Hume. *An Abstract of a Treatise on Human Nature* (1740). Cambridge: Cambridge University Press.
Sraffa, P. (1951). Introduction. In P. Sraffa with the collaboration of M. H. Dobb (Eds.), *The works and correspondence of David Ricardo* (Vol. I, pp. xiii–lxii), Cambridge: Cambridge University Press.
Sraffa, P. (1960). *Production of commodities by means of commodities: Prelude to a critique of economic theory*. Cambridge: Cambridge University Press.
Sraffa, P. (1962). Production of commodities – A comment. *Economic Journal, 72*(286), 477–479.
Stathakis, G., & Vaggi, G. (Eds.), (2006). *Economic development and social change. Historical roots and modern perspectives*. London/New York: Routledge.
Steedman, I. (1972). The state and the outcome of the Pasinetti process. *Economic Journal, 82*(328), 1387–1395.
Stiglitz, J. E. (1975). Review of *growth and income distribution: Essays in economic theory*, by L. L. Pasinetti. *Journal of Economic Literature, 13*(4), 1327–1328.
Stone, J. R. N. (1951). The use and development and national income and expenditure estimates. In D. N. Chester (Ed.), *Lessons of the British war economy* (pp. 83–87). Cambridge: Cambridge University Press.
Stone, J. R. N. (1973). Process, capacity and control in an input–output system. *L'Industria, 14*(1–2), 3–17.
Stone, J. R. N. (1978). *Tribute to Luigi Solari*. Paper presented at the European Meeting of the Econometric Society, Geneva.
Stone, J. R. N., & Stone, G. (1977). *National income and expenditure* (1st ed.). London: Bowes & Bowes (1971).
Stone, J. R. N., et al. (1962). *A social accounting Matrix for 1960*. London: Chapman and Hall.

Sylos-Labini, P. (1962). *Oligopoly and technical progress.* Cambridge, MA: Harvard University Press.
Sylos-Labini, P. (1984). *The forces of economic growth and decline.* Cambridge, MA: MIT Press.
Sylos-Labini, P. (1993). Long-run changes in the wage and price mechanisms and the process of growth. In M. Baranzini, & G. C. Harcourt (Eds.), *The dynamics of the wealth of nations: Growth, distribution and structural change: Essays in honour of Luigi L. Pasinetti, op. cit.*, pp. 311–347.
Taniguchi, K. (1987). *The existence of traverse in Pasinetti's model of growth and distribution* (Discussion Paper No. 11). University of Osaka Prefecture.
Taniguchi, K. (2009). Simulation of the full employment traverse of capital and time. In H. Hagemann, & R. Scazzieri (Eds.), *Capital, time and transitional dynamics, op. cit.*, pp. 168–189.
Targetti, F. (1985). Growth and the terms of trade: A Kaldorian two sector model. *Metroeconomica, 37*(1), 79–96.
Targetti, F. (1986). Kaldor. *Studi Economici, 41*, 3–70.
Targetti, F. (1991). Change and continuity in Kaldor's thought on growth and distribution. In E. J. Nell, & W. Semmler (Eds.), *Nicholas Kaldor and mainstream economics. Confrontation or convergence?, op. cit.*, pp. 411–420.
Targetti, F. (1992). *Nicholas Kaldor.* Oxford/New York: Oxford University Press.
Targetti, F. (1993). Vecchie e nuove teorie della crescita: una rassegna. *Economia Politica, 10*(2), 261–349.
Targetti, F., & Thirlwall, A. P. (Eds.). (1983). *Further essays on economic theory and policy.* London: Duckworth.
Teixeira, J. R. (1998). Luigi L. Pasinetti. In F. Meacci (Ed.), *Italian economists of the 20th century, op. cit.*, pp. 272–294.
Tonveronachi, M. (1983). *J. M. Keynes. Dall'instabilità ciclica all'equilibrio di sottooccupazione.* Rome: NIS.
Tonveronachi, M. (1992). Keynes and equilibrium. A note. In M. Sebastiani (Ed.), *The notion of equilibrium in Keynesian theory* (pp. 18–31). London: Macmillan.
Tonveronachi, M. (1994). Old and new-old theories of income distribution. *Journal of Income Distribution, 3*(1), 28–47.
Tonveronachi, M. (2006). Foreign debt and financial fragility in the perspective of emerging countries. *BNL Quarterly Review, 59*(236), 23–48.
Tonveronachi, M. (2010). Empowering supervisors with more principles and discretion to implement them will not reduce the dangers of the prudential approach to financial regulation. *PSL Quarterly Review, 63*(255), 363–378.

Tonveronachi, M. (2015). Making the ECB the central bank of a non coalition of states. *PSL Quarterly Review, 68*(273), 91–114.
Vaciago, G. (1975). Increasing returns and growth in advanced economies: A re-evaluation. *Oxford Economic Papers, 27*(2), 232–239.
Vaciago, G. (1985). Monetary policy with credit targets: The Italian experience. *Greek Economic Review, 7*(1), 1–33.
Vaciago, G., & Giarda, P. (Eds.). (1965). *The econometric approach to development planning.* Amsterdam: North-Holland.
Vaggi, G. (1985). A physiocratic model of relative prices and income distribution. *Economic Journal, 95*(380), 928–947.
Vaggi, G. (1987). *The economics of François Quesnay.* London/Durham: Macmillan/Duke University Press.
Vaggi, G. (2002). Quesnay and the road to modernity: Technology, markets, and polity. *Journal of the History of Economic Thought, 24*(1), 73–89.
Vaggi, G. & Groenewegen, P. D. (2003). *A concise history of economic thought: From Mercantilism to Monetarism.* London: Palgrave Macmillan.
Varri, P. (1996). Harrod's dynamic economics and Joan Robinson's generalization of the general theory. In M. C. Marcuzzo, L. L. Pasinetti, & A. Roncaglia (Eds.), *The economics of Joan Robinson, op. cit.*, pp. 188–194.
Velupillai, K. V. (Ed.). (1989). *Nonlinear and multisectoral macrodynamics. Essays in honour of Richard Goodwin.* London: Macmillan.
Velupillai, K. V. (1998a). Richard Goodwin: 1913-1996. *Economic Journal, 108*(448), 1436–1449.
Velupillai, K. V. (1998b). The vintage economist. *Journal of Economic Behaviour and Organisation, 37*(1), 1–31.
Velupillai, K. V. (2008). A perspective on a Hicksian non-linear theory of the trade cycle. In R. Scazzieri, A. Sen, & S. Zamagni (Eds.), *Markets, money and capital. Hicksian economics for the twenty-first century, op. cit.*, pp. 328–345.
Vercelli, A. (1991). *Methodological foundations of macroeconomics: Keynes and Lucas.* Cambridge: Cambridge University Press.
Vercelli, A. (1999). Coherence, meaning and responsibility in the language of economics. In R. Rossini-Favretti, G. Sandri, & R. Scazzieri (Eds.), *Incommensurability and translation, op. cit.*, pp. 351–367.
Vercelli, A. (2012). 'Sustainability', entry in G. Ritzer (Ed.), *The Wiley-Blackwell encyclopedia of globalization.* Oxford/New York: Blackwell Publishing Ltd.
Vianello, F. (1985). The pace of accumulation. *Political Economy. Studies in the Surplus Approach, 1*(1), 69–87.

Vianello, F. (1987). Labour theory of value. In *The new Palgrave: A dictionary of economics, op. cit.*., Vol. 3, pp. 107–113.
Vianello, F. (1996). Joan Robinson on normal prices (and the normal rate of profits). In M. C. Marcuzzo, L. L. Pasinetti, & A. Roncaglia (Eds.), *The economics of Joan Robinson, op. cit.*, pp. 112–120.
Vianello, F. (1999). Social accounting in Adam Smith. In G. Mongiovi, & F. Petri (Eds.), *Value, distribution and capital. Essays in honour of Pierangelo Garegnani, op. cit.*, pp. 165–180.
Vianello, F. (2004). La Facoltà di Economia e Commercio di Modena. In G. Garofalo, & A. Graziani (Eds.), *La formazione degli economisti in Italia (1950–1975), op. cit.*, pp. 481–534.
Vicarelli, F. (1984). *Keynes: The instability of capitalism*. New York/London: Macmillan.
Villa, P. (1981). Labour market segmentation and the construction industry in Italy. In F. Wilkinson (Ed.), *The dynamics of labour market segmentation* (pp. 133–149). London/New York: Academic.
Villa, P. (2015). The meaning of gender equality in the European employment strategy. In E. Bellè, B. Poggio, & G. Selmi (Eds.), *Districare il nodo genere-potere* (pp. 268–289). Trento: Dipartimento di Sociologia e Ricerca Sociale CSG – Università degli Studi di Trent0.
Visco, I. (2005). Dalla teoria alla pratica nei modelli macroeconomici l'eclettismo post-Keynesiano. *Moneta e Credito, 58*, 71–96.
Visco, I. (2011). Sul ruolo delle aspettative nell'economia di Keynes e in quella d'oggi. In *Gli economisti post-keynesiani di Cambridge e l'Italia* (Atti dei Convegni Lincei, pp. 91–102). Rome: Scienze e Lettere.
Vivenza, G. (1999a). The division of land and the division of labour. Analogies and differences between ancient and modern times in Adam Smith's thought. In P. L. Porta, R. Scazzieri, & A. Skinner (Eds.), *Knowledge, social institutions and the division of labour, op. cit.*, pp. 331–350.
Vivenza, G. (1999b). Translating aristotle: At the origin of the terminology and ontent of economic value. In R. Rossini Favretti, G. Sandri, & R. Scazzieri (Eds.), *Incommensurability and translation, op. cit.*, pp. 131–156.
Vivenza, G. (2001). *Adam Smith and the classics. The classical heritage of Adam Smith's thought*. Oxford: Oxford University Press.
Zamagni, S. (1973). Struttura del capitale e crescita non uniforme, Appendix to J. R. Hicks. *Capitale e tempo. Una teoria neo-austriaca* (pp. 247–286). Milan: Etas Libri.

Zamagni, S. (1983). Strumentalismo causale *versus* realismo causale in economia. In M. C. Galavotti & G. Gambetta (Eds.), *Causalità e modelli probabilistici* (pp. 111–146). Bologna: CLUEB.

Zamagni, S. (1984). On Ricardo and Hayek effects in a Fixwage model of traverse. In D. A. Collard et al. (Eds.), *Economic theory and Hicksian themes* (pp. 135–151). Oxford: Clarendon Press.

Zamagni, V. (1993). *The economic history of Italy, 1860–1990*. Oxford: Clarendon Press.

Zamagni, S. (1996). Joan Robinson and reswitching. An interpretative note. In M. C. Marcuzzo, L. L. Pasinetti, & A. Roncaglia (Eds.), *The economics of Joan Robinson, op. cit.*, pp. 218–222.

Zamagni, S. (2015). Development, capabilities and institutions. In M. Baranzini, C. Rotondi, & R. Scazzieri (Eds.), *Resources, production and structural dynamics, op. cit.*, pp. 279–298.

Zamagni, V., & Zamagni, S. (2002). Italian economists and Linacre College. *The Linacre Journal, 6*, 25–38.

Zambelli, S. (Ed.). (2010). *Computable, constructive and behavioural economic dynamics. Essays in honour of Kumaraswamy (Vela) Velupillai*. London: Routledge.

Name Index

M. Baranzini, A. Mirante, *A Compendium of Italian Economists at Oxbridge*, DOI 10.1007/978-3-319-32219-3

C

N

T

Subject Index[1]

[1] Note: Page numbers with "n" denote notes.

M. Baranzini, A. Mirante, *A Compendium of Italian Economists at Oxbridge*, DOI 10.1007/978-3-319-32219-3

The manufacturer's authorised representative in the EU is Springer Nature Customer Service Centre GmbH, Europaplatz 3, 69115 Heidelberg, Germany. If you have any concerns regarding our products, please contact ProductSafety@springernature.com

Printed and bound by CPI Group (UK) Ltd, Croydon, CR0 4YY
30/09/2026
02225216-0008